Archibald Forbes

Camps, Quarters and Casual Places

Archibald Forbes

Camps, Quarters and Casual Places

ISBN/EAN: 9783337423940

Printed in Europe, USA, Canada, Australia, Japan

Cover: Foto ©Lupo / pixelio.de

More available books at **www.hansebooks.com**

CAMPS, QUARTERS

AND

CASUAL PLACES

BY

ARCHIBALD FORBES, LL.D.

London
MACMILLAN AND CO., Ltd.
NEW YORK: THE MACMILLAN CO.
1896

All rights reserved

NOTE

MY obligations for permission to incorporate some of the articles in this volume are due to Messrs. George Routledge and Sons, Mr. James Knowles of the *Nineteenth Century*, Mr. Percy Bunting of the *Contemporary Review*, and the Proprietor of *M'Clure's Magazine*.

LONDON, *June* 1896.

CONTENTS

		PAGE
1.	MATRIMONY UNDER FIRE	1
2.	REVERENCING THE GOLDEN FEET	13
3.	GERMAN WAR PRAYERS	39
4.	MISS PRIEST'S BRIDECAKE	55
5.	A VERSION OF BALACLAVA	67
6.	HOW I "SAVED FRANCE"	89
7.	CHRISTMAS IN A CAVALRY REGIMENT	104
8.	THE MYSTERY OF MONSIEUR REGNIER	120
9.	RAILWAY LIZZ	141
10.	MY NATIVE SALMON RIVER	153
11.	THE CAWNPORE OF TO-DAY	179
12.	BISMARCK BEFORE AND DURING THE FRANCO-GERMAN WAR	196
13.	THE INVERNESS "CHARACTER" FAIR	217
14.	THE WARFARE OF THE FUTURE	233
15.	GEORGE MARTELL'S BANDOBAST	259
16.	THE LUCKNOW OF TO-DAY	271
17.	THE MILITARY COURAGE OF ROYALTY	298
18.	PARADE OF THE COMMISSIONAIRES	310
19.	THE INNER HISTORY OF THE WATERLOO CAMPAIGN	321

MATRIMONY UNDER FIRE

THE interval between the declaration of the Franco-German war of 1870-71, and the "military promenade," at which the poor Prince Imperial received his "baptism of fire," was a pleasant, lazy time at Saarbrücken; to which pretty frontier town I had early betaken myself, in the anticipation, which proved well founded, that the tide of war would flow that way first. What a pity it is that all war cannot be like this early phase of it, of which I speak! It was playing at warfare, with just enough of the grim reality cropping up occasionally, to give the zest which the reckless Frenchwoman declared was added to a pleasure by its being also a sin. The officers of the Hohenzollerns—our only infantry regiment in garrison—drank their beer placidly under the lime-tree in the market-place, as their men smoked drowsily, lying among the straw behind the stacked arms ready for use at a moment's notice. The infantry patrol skirted the frontier line every morning in the gray dawn, occasionally exchanging with little result a few shots with the French outposts on the Spicheren or down in the valley bounded by the Schönecken wood. The Uhlans, their piebald lance-pennants fluttering in the wind, cantered leisurely round the crests of the little knolls which formed the vedette posts, despising mightily the straggling chassepot bullets which were pitched at them from time to time in a desultory way; but which, desultory as they were, now and then brought lance-pennant and its bearer to the ground—an occurrence invariably followed by a little spurt of lively hostility.

I had my quarters at the Rheinischer Hof, a right comfortable hotel on the St. Johann side of the Saar, where most of the Hohenzollern officers frequented the *table d'hôte* and where quaint little Max, the drollest imp of a waiter imaginable, and pretty Fraülein Sophie the landlord's niece, did all that in them lay to contribute to the pleasantness and comfort of the house. Not a few pleasant evenings did I spend at the table of the long dining-room, with the close-cropped red head of silent and genial Hauptmann von Krehl looming large over the great ice-pail, with its *chevaux de frise* of long-necked Niersteiner bottles—the worthy Hauptmann supported by blithe Lieutenant von Klipphausen, ever ready with the *Wacht am Rhein;* quaint Dr. Diestelkamp, brimful of recollections of "six-and-sixty" and as ready to amputate your leg as to crack a joke or clink a glass; gay young Adjutant von Zülow—he who one day brought in a prisoner from the foreposts a red-legged Frenchman across the pommel of his saddle; and many other good fellows, over most of whom the turf of the Spicheren, or the brown earth of the Gravelotte plain, now lies lightly.

But although the Rheinischer Hof associates itself in my mind with many memories, half-pleasant, half-sad, it was not the most accustomed haunt of the casuals in Saarbrücken, including myself. Of the waifs and strays which the war had drifted down to the pretty frontier town the great rendezvous was the Hôtel Hagen, at the bend of the turn leading from the bridge up to the railway station. The Hagen was a free-and-easy place compared with the Rheinischer, and among its inmates there was no one who could sing a better song than manly George—type of the Briton at whom foreigners stare—who, ignorant of a word of their language, wholly unprovided with any authorisation save the passport signed "Salisbury," and having not quite so much business at the seat of war as he might have at the bottom of a coal-mine, gravitates into danger with inevitable certainty, and stumbles through all manner of difficulties and bothers by reason of a serene good-humour that nothing can ruffle and a cool resolution before which every obstacle fades away. Was there ever a more compositely polyglot cosmopolitan than poor young de Liefde — half Dutchman, half German by birth, an Englishman by adoption, a Frenchman in temperament, speaking with equal fluency the language of all four countries, and an unconsidered trifle of some half-dozen European languages besides? Then there was the English student from Bonn, who had come down to the front accompanied by a terrible brute of a dog, vast, shaggy, self-willed, and dirty; an animal which, so to speak, owned his owner, and was so much the horror and disgust of everybody that on account of him the company of his master—one of the pleasantest fellows alive—was the source of general apprehension.

There was young Silberer the many-sided and eccentric, an Austrian nobleman, a Vienna feuilletonist and correspondent, a rowing man, a gourmet, ever thinking of his stomach and yet prepared for all the roughness of the campaign—warm-hearted, passionate, narrow-minded, capable of sleeping for twenty-three out of the twenty-four hours, and the wearer of a Scotch cap. There was Küster, a German journalist with an address somewhere in the Downham Road; and Duff, a Fellow of ——— College, the strangest mixture of nervousness and cool courage I ever met.

We were a kind of happy family at the Hagen; the tone of the coterie was that of the easiest intimacy into which every newcomer slid quite naturally. Thus when on the 31st July there was a somewhat sensational arrival, the stolid landlord had not turned the gas on in the empty saal before everybody knew and sympathised with the errand of the strangers. The party consisted of a plump little girl of about eighteen with a bonny round face and fine frank eyes; her sister who was some years older; and a brother, the eldest of the three. They had come from Silesia on rather a strange tryst. Little Minna Vogt had for her *Bräutigam* a young Feldwebel of the second battalion of the Hohenzollerns, a native of Saarlouis. The battalion quartered there was under orders to join its first battalion at Saarbrücken, and young Eckenstein had written to his betrothed to come and meet him there, that the marriage-knot might be tied before he should go on a campaign from which he might not return. The arrangement was certainly a charming one; we should have a wedding in the

Hagen! There was no nonsense about our young *Braut*. She told me the little story at supper on the night of her arrival in the most matter-of-fact way possible, drank her two glasses of red wine, and went off serenely to bed with a dainty lisping *Schlafen Sie wohl!*

While Minna was between the sheets in the pleasant chamber in the Hagen her lover was lying in bivouac some fifteen miles away. In the afternoon of the next day his battalion approached Saarbrücken and bivouacked about two miles from the town. Of course we all went out to welcome it; some bearing peace-offerings of cigars, others the drink-offering of potent Schnapps. The Vogt family were left the sole inmates of the Hagen, delicacy preventing their accompanying us. The German journalist, however, had a commission to find out young Eckenstein and tell him of the bliss that awaited him two short miles away. Right hearty fellows were the officers of the second battalion—from the grizzled Oberst down to the smooth-faced junior lieutenant; and the men who had been marching and bivouacking for a fortnight looked as fresh as if they had not travelled five miles. Küster soon found the young Feldwebel; and the Hauptmann of his company when he heard the state of the case, smiled a grim but kindly smile, and gave him leave for two days with the proviso, that if any hostile action should be taken in the interval he should rejoin the colours immediately and without notice. "No fear of that!" was Eckenstein's reply with a significant down glance at his sword; and then, after a cheery "good-night" to the hardy bivouackers, we visitors started in triumph on our return to the Hagen, the young Feldwebel in our midst. It was good to see the unrestraint with which Minna—she of the apple face and frank eyes—threw herself round the neck of her betrothed as she met him on the steps of the Hagen, and his modest manly blush as he returned the embrace. Ye gods! did not we make a night of it! Stolid Hagen came out of his shell for once, and swore, *Donner Wetter* that he would give us a supper we should remember; and he kept his word. The good old pastor of the snow-white hair and withered cheeks—he had been engaged to perform the ceremony of the morrow—we voted into the chair whether he would or not; and on his right sat Minna and Eckenstein, their arms interlacing and whispering soft speeches which were not for our ears. The table was covered with bottles of Blume de Saar, the champagne peculiar of the Hagen; and the speed with which the full bottles were converted into "dead marines" was a caution to teetotallers. Then de Liefde the polyglot gave the health of the happy couple in a felicitous but composite speech, in which half a dozen languages were impartially intermixed so that all might understand at least a portion. George the jolly insisted in leading off the honours with a truly British "three times three;" and that horrible dog of Hyndman's gave the time, like a beast as he was, with stentorian barkings. Then Minna and her sister retired, followed by Herr Pastor; and after a considerable number of more bottles of Blume de Saar had met their fate we formed a procession and escorted the happy Eckenstein to the Rheinischer Hof where he was to sleep.

Next morning by eleven, we had all reassembled

in the second saal of the Hagen. In the great room the marriage-breakfast was laid out, and in the kitchen Hagen and his Frau were up to their eyes in mystic culinary operations. Minna looked like a rosebud in her pretty low-necked blue dress, and the pastor in his cassock helped to the diversity of colour. We had done shaking hands with the bride and bridegroom after the ceremony, and were sitting down to the marriage feast, when young Eckenstein started and made three strides to the open window. His accustomed ear had caught a sound which none of us had heard. It was the sharp peremptory note of the drum beating the alarm. As it came nearer and could no longer be mistaken, the bright colour went out from poor Minna's cheek and she clung with a brave touching silence to her sister. In two minutes more Eckenstein had his helmet on his head and his sword buckled on, and then he turned to say farewell to his girl ere he left her for the battle. The parting was silent and brief; but the faces of the two were more eloquent than words. Poor Minna sat down by the window straining her eyes as Eckenstein, running at speed, went his way to the rendezvous.

When I got up to the Bellevue the French were streaming in overwhelming force down the slope of the Spicheren into the intervening valley. It was a beautiful sight; but I am not going to describe it here. Ere an hour was over the shells and chassepôt bullets were sweeping across the Exercise Platz, and it was no longer a safe spot for a non-combatant like myself. Before I got back into the Hagen after paying my bill at the Rheinischer and fetching away my knapsack, the French guns were on the Exercise Platz. I heard for the first time the angry screech of the mitrailleuse and saw the hailstorm of its bullets spattering on the pavement of the bridge. Somehow or other the whole of our little coterie had found their way into the Hagen; by a sort of common impulse, I imagine. The landlady was already in hysterics; the Vogt girls were pale but plucky. Presently the shells began to fly. The Prussians had a gun or two on the railway esplanade above us, the fire of which the French began to return fiercely. Every shell that fell short tumbled in or about the Hagen; and a company of the Hohenzollerns was drawn up in the street in front of it, in trying to dislodge which the French fire could not well miss the Hagen and the houses opposite. A shell burst in the back-yard and the landlady fainted. Another came crashing in through a first-floor window, and, bursting, knocked several bedrooms into one. Then we thought it time to get the women down into the cellar—rather a risky undertaking since the door of it was in the back-yard. However, we got them all down in safety and came up into the second saal to watch the course of events. Hagen gave a fearful groan as a shell broke into the kitchen behind us, and, bursting in the centre of the stove, sent his *chefs-d'œuvre* of cookery sputtering in all directions. He gave a still deeper groan as another shell crashed into the principal dining-room and knocked the long table, laid out as it was for the marriage-feast, into a chaos of splinters, tablecloth, and knives and forks. The

Restauration Küche on the other side was in flames, so was the stable of the hotel to the left rear. In this pleasing situation of affairs George produced a pack of cards and coolly proposed a game of whist. Küster, de Liefde, and Hyndman joined him; and the game proceeded amidst the crashing of the projectiles. Silberer and myself took counsel together and agreed that the occupation of the town by the French was only a question of a few hours at latest. We were both correspondents; and although the French would do us no harm our communications with our journals would inevitably be stopped—a serious contingency to contemplate at the beginning of a campaign. We both agreed that evacuation of the Hagen was imperative; but then, how to get out? The only way was up the esplanade to the railway station, and upon it the French shells were falling and bursting in numbers very trying to the nerves. However, there was nothing for it but to make a rush through the fire; and saying good-bye to the whist-players we sallied forth. To my disgust I found that Silberer positively refused to make a rush of it. Although an Austrian all his sympathies were Prussian, and he had the utmost contempt for the French. In his broken language his invariable appellation for them was "God-damned Hundsöhne!" and he would not run before them at any price. I would have run right gladly at top-speed; but I did not like to run when another man walked, and so he made me saunter at the rate of two miles an hour till we got under shelter. After a hot walk of several miles, we reached the Hôtel Till in the village of Duttweiler.

After all the French, although they might have done so, did not occupy Saarbrücken; and towards evening our friends came dropping into the Hôtel Till, singly or in pairs. Küster and George brought the Vogt sisters out in a waggon—it was surprising to see the coolness and composure of the girls. By nightfall we were all reunited, except one unfortunate fellow who had been slightly wounded and whom a Saarbrücken doctor had kindly received into his house.

On the 6th August came the Prussian repossession of Saarbrücken and the desperate storm of the Spicheren. The 40th was the regiment to which was assigned the place of honour in the preliminary recapture of the Exercise Platz height. Kameke rode up the winding road to the Bellevue; then came the march across the broad valley and after much bloodshed the final storm of the Spicheren, in which the 40th occupied about the left centre of the Prussian advance. Three times did the blue wave surge up the green steep, to be beaten back three times by the terrible blast of fire that crashed down upon it from above. Yet a fourth time it clambered up again, and this time it lipped the brink and poured over the intrenchment at the top. But I am not describing the battle.

When it was over or at least when it had drifted away across the farther plateau, I followed on in the broad wake of dying and dead which the advance had left. The familiar faces of the Hohenzollerns were all around me; but either still in death or writhing in the torture of wounds. About the centre of the valley lay the genial Hauptmann von

Krehl, more silent than ever now, for a bullet had gone right through that red head of his and he would never more quaff of the Niersteiner; neither would Lieutenant von Klipphausen ever again stir the blood of the sons of the Fatherland with the *Wacht am Rhein;* he lay dead close by the first spur of the slope—what of him at least a bursting shell had left. On a little flat half up sat quaint Dr. Diestelkamp, like Mark Tapley jolly under difficulties; by his side lay a man who had just bled to death as the good doctor explained to me. While he had been applying the tourniquet under a hot fire his right arm had been broken; and before he could pull himself up and go to the rear another bullet had found its billet in his thigh. There the little man sat, contentedly smoking till somebody would be good enough to come and take him away. Von Zülow too—he of the gay laugh and sprightly countenance—was on his back a little higher up, with a bullet through the chest. I heard the ominous sound of the escaping air as I raised him to give him a drink from my flask. What needs it to become diffuse as to the terrible sights which that steep and the plateau above it presented on this beautiful summer evening? It was farther to the right, in ground more broken with gullies and ravines, that the second battalion of the Hohenzollerns had gone up; and I wandered along there among the carnage eking out the contents of my flask as far as I could, and when the wounded had exhausted the brandy in it filling it up with water and still toiling on in a task that seemed endless. At last, in a sitting posture, his back against a hawthorn tree in one of the grassy ravines, I saw one whom I thought I recognised. "Eckenstein!" I cried as I ran forward; for the posture was so natural that I could not but think he was alive. Alas! no answer came; the gallant young Feldwebel was dead, shot through the throat. He had not been killed outright by the fatal bullet; the track was apparent by the blood on the grass along which he had crawled to the hawthorn tree against which I found him. His head had fallen forward on his chest and his right hand was pressed against his left breast. I saw something white in the hollow of the hand and easily moved the arm for he was yet warm; it was the photograph of the little girl he had married but three short days before. The frank eyes looked up at me with a merry unconsciousness; and the face of the photograph was spotted with the life-blood of the young soldier.

I sent the death-token to Saarlouis by post to the young widow. I never knew whether she received it, for all the address I had was Saarlouis. Eckenstein I saw buried with two officers in a soldier's grave under the hawthorn. Any one taking the ascent up the fourth ravine Forbach-ward from the bluff of the Spicheren, may easily find it about half-way up. It may be recognised by the wooden cross bearing the rude inscription: "Hier ruhen in Gott 2 Officiere, 1 Feldwebel, 40ste Hohenzol. Fus. Regt."

REVERENCING THE GOLDEN FEET

1879

By Christmas 1878 the winter had brought to a temporary standstill the operations of the British troops engaged in the first Afghan campaign, and I took the opportunity of this inaction to make a journey into Native Burmah, the condition of which seemed thus early to portend the interest which almost immediately after converged upon it, because of King Thebau's wholesale slaughter of his relatives. Reaching Mandalay, the capital of Native Burmah, in the beginning of February 1879, I immediately set about compassing an interview with the young king. Both Mr. Shaw, who was our Resident at Mandalay at the time of my visit, and Dr. Clement Williams whose kindly services I found so useful, are now dead, and many changes have occurred since the episode described below; but no description, so far as I am aware, has appeared of any visit of courtesy and curiosity to the Court of King Thebau of a later date than that made by myself at the date specified.

One of my principal objects in visiting Mandalay, or, in Burmese phrase, of "coming to the Golden Feet," was to see the King of Burmah in his royal state in the Presence Chamber of the Palace. Certain difficulties stood in the way of the accomplishment of this object. I had but a few days to spend in Mandalay. With the approval of Mr. Shaw, the British Resident, I determined to pursue an informal course of action, and with this intent I enlisted the good offices of an English gentleman resident in Mandalay, who had intimate relations with the Ministers and the Court.

This gentleman, Dr. Williams, was good enough to help me with zeal and address. The line of strategy to adopt was to interest in my cause one of the principal Ministers. Of these there were four, who constituted the *Hlwot-dau*, or High Court and Council of the Monarchy. These "Woonghys" or "Menghyis," as they were more commonly called— "Menghyi," meaning "Great Prince"—were of equal rank; but the senior Minister, the Yenangyoung Menghyi, who had precedence, was then in confinement, and, indeed, a decree of degradation had gone forth against him. Obviously he was of no use; but a more influential man than he ever was, and having the additional advantages of being at liberty, in power and in favour, was the "Kingwoon Menghyi." He was in effect the Prime Minister of the King of Burmah. His position was roughly equivalent to that of Bismarck in Germany, or of Gortschakoff in Russia, since, in addition to his internal influence, he had the chief direction of foreign affairs. Now this "Kingwoon Menghyi" had for a day or two been relaxing from the cares of State. Partly for his own pleasure, partly by way of example, he had laid out a beautiful garden on the low ground near the river. Within this garden he had the intention to build himself a suburban residence, which meanwhile was represented by a summer pavilion of teak and bamboo. He was a liberal-minded man, and it was a satisfaction to him that the shady walks and pleasant rose-groves of this garden should be enjoyed by the people of Mandalay. He was a reformer, this "Kingwoon Menghyi," and believed in the humanising effect of free access to the charms of nature. His garden laid out and his pavilion finished, he was celebrating the event by a series of *fêtes*. He was "at home" in his pavilion to everybody; bands of music played all day long and day after day, in the kiosks, among the young palm trees and the rose-bushes. Mandalay, high and low, made holiday in the mazy walks of his garden and in an improvised theatre, wherein an interminable *pooey*, or Burmese drama, was being enacted before ever-varying and constantly appreciative audiences. Dr. Williams opined that it would conduce to the success of my object that we should call upon the Minister at his garden-house and request him to use his good offices in my behalf.

It was near noon when we reached the entrance to the garden. Merry but orderly sightseers thronged its alleys, and stared with wondering admiration at a rather attenuated jet of water which rose into the clear air some thirty feet above a rockwork fountain in the centre. Dignitaries strolled about under the stemless umbrellas like huge shields, with which assiduous attendants protected them from the sun; and were followed by posses of retainers, who prostrated themselves whenever their masters halted or looked round. Ladies in white jackets and trailing silk skirts of vivid hue were taking a leisurely airing, each with her demure maid behind her carrying the lacquer-ware box of betel-nut. As often as not the fair ones were blowing copious clouds from huge reed-like cheroots. Sounds of shrill music were heard in the distance. Walking up the central alley between the rows of palms and the hedges of roses, we found in the veranda a mixed crowd of laymen and priests, the latter distinguishable by their shaved heads and yellow robes. The Minister was just finishing his morning's work of distributing offerings to the latter, in commemoration of the opening of his gardens. In response to a message, he at once sent to desire that we should come to him. The great "shoe-question," the *quæstio vexata* between British officialism and Burmah officialism, did not trouble me. I had no official position; I wanted to gain an object. I have a respect for the honour of my country, but I could not bring myself to realise that the national honour centres in my shoes. So I parted with them at the top of the steps leading up into the Minister's pavilion, and walking on what is known as my "stocking-feet," and feeling rather shuffling and shabby accordingly, was ushered through a throng of prostrate dependents into the presence of the Menghyi. He came forward frankly and cordially, shook hands with a hearty smile with Dr. Williams and myself, and beckoned us into an inner alcove, carpeted with rich rugs and panelled with mirrors. Placing himself in a half-sitting, half-kneeling attitude which did not expose his feet, he beckoned to us to get down also. I own to having experienced extreme difficulty in keeping my feet out of sight, which was a point *de rigueur;* but his Excellency was not censorious. There was with him a secretary who had resided several years in Europe, and who spoke fluently English, French, and Italian. This gentleman knew London thoroughly, and was perfectly familiar both with the name of the *Daily News* and of myself. He introduced me formally to his Excellency, who, I ought to have mentioned, was the head of the Burmese Embassy which had visited Europe a few years previously. That his Excellency had some sort of knowledge of the political character of the *Daily News* was obvious from the circumstance that when its name was mentioned he nodded and exclaimed, "Ah! ah! Gladstone, Bright!" in tones of manifest approval, which was no doubt accounted for by the fact that he himself was a pronounced Liberal. I explained that I had come to Mandalay to learn as much about Burmese manners, customs, and institutions as was possible in four days, with intent to embody my impressions in letters to England; and that as the King was the chief institution of the country, I had a keen anxiety to see him and begged of his Excellency to lend me his aid toward doing so. He gave no direct reply, but certainly did not frown on the request. We were served with tea (without cream or sugar) in pretty china cups, and then the Menghyi, observing that we were looking at some quaint-shaped musical instruments at the foot of the dais, explained that they belonged to a band of rural performers from the Pegu district, and proposed that we should first hear them play and afterwards visit the theatre and witness the *pooey*. We assenting, he led the way from his pavilion through the garden to a pretty kiosk half-embosomed in foliage, and chairs having been brought the party sat down. We had put on our shoes as we quitted the dais. The Menghyi explained that it was pleasanter for him, as it must be for us, that we should change the manner of our reception from the Burmese to the European custom ; and we were quite free to confess that we would sooner sit in chairs than squat on the floor. More tea was brought, and a plateful of cheroots. After we had sat a little while in the kiosk we were joined by the chief Under-Secretary for Foreign Affairs, the Baron de Giers of Burmah, a jovial, corpulent, elderly gentleman who had the most wonderful likeness to the late Pio Nono, and who clasped his brown hands over his fat paunch and kicked about his plump bare brown feet in high enjoyment when anything that struck him as humorous was uttered. He wholly differed in appearance from his superior, who was a lean-faced and lean-figured man, grave, and indeed somewhat sad both of eye and of visage when his face was in repose. As we talked, our conversation being through the interpreting secretary, there came to the curtained entrance to the kiosk a very dainty little lady. I had noticed her previously sauntering around the garden under one of the great shield-like shades, with a following of serving-men and serving-women behind her. She greeted the Menghyi very prettily, with the most perfect composure, although strangers were present. She was clearly a great pet with the Menghyi; he took her on his knee and played with her long black hair, as he told her about the visitors. The little lady was in her twelfth year, and was the daughter of a colleague and a relative of the Menghyi. She had an olive oval face, with lovely dark eyes, like the eyes of a deer. She wore a tiara of feathery white blossoms. In her ears were rosettes of chased red gold. Round her throat was a necklace of a double row of large pearls. Her fingers—I regret to say her nails were not very clean—were loaded with rings set with great diamonds of exceptional sparkle and water; one stone in particular must have been worth many thousands of pounds. She wore a jacket of white silk, and round her loins was girt a gay silken robe that trailed about her bare feet as she walked. She shook hands with us with a pretty shyness and immediately helped herself to a cheroot, affably accepting a light from mine. The Menghyi told us she was a great scholar—could read and write with facility, and had accomplishments to boot.

By this time the provincial band had taken its place under one of the windows of the kiosk, and it presently struck up. Its music was not pretty. There were in the strange weird strain suggestions of gongs, bagpipes, penny whistles, and the humble tom-tom of Bengal. The gentleman who performed on an instrument which seemed a hybrid between a flute and a French horn, occasionally arrested his instrumental music to favour us with vocal strains, but he failed to compete successfully with the cymbals. I do not think the Menghyi was enraptured by the music of the strollers from Pegu, for he presently asked us whether we were ready to go to the *pooey*. He again led the way through a garden, passing in one corner of it a temporary house of which a company of Burmese nuns, short-haired, pallid-faced, unhappy-looking women, were in possession; and passing through a gate in the wicker-work fence ushered us into the "state-box" of the improvised theatre. There is very little labour required to construct a theatre in Burmah. Over a framework of bamboo poles stretch a number of squares of matting as a protection from the sun. Lay some more down in the centre as a flooring for the performers. Tie a few branches round the central bamboo to represent a forest, the perpetual set-scene of a Burmese drama; and the house is ready. The performers act and dance in the central square laid with matting. A little space on one side is reserved as a dressing and green room for the actresses; a similar space on the other side serves the turn of the actors; and then come the spectators crowding in on all four sides of the square. It is an orderly and easily managed audience; it may be added an easily amused audience. The youngsters are put or put themselves in front and squat down; the grown people kneel or stand behind. Our "state-box" was merely a raised platform laid with carpets and cushions, from which as we sat we looked over the heads of the throng squatting under and in front of us. Of the drama I cannot say that I carried away with me particularly clear impressions. True, I only saw a part of it—it was to last till the following morning; but long before I left the plot to me had become bewilderingly involved. The opening was a ballet; of that at least I am certain. There were six lady dancers and six gentlemen ditto. The ladies were arrayed in splendour, with tinsel tiaras, necklaces, and bracelets, gauzy jackets and waving scarfs; and with long, light clinging silken robes, of which there was at least a couple of yards on the "boards" about their feet. They were old, they were ugly, they leered fiendishly; their faces were plastered with powder in a ghastly fashion, and their coquetry behind their fans was the acme of caricature. But my pen halts when I would describe the gentlemen dancers. I believe that in reality they were not meant to represent fallen humanity at all; but were intended to personify *nats*, the spirits or princes of the air of Burmese mythology. They carried on their heads pagodas of tinsel and coloured glass that towered imposingly aloft. They were arrayed in tight-bodiced coats with aprons before and behind of fantastic outline, resembling the wings of dragons and griffins, and these coats were an incrusted mass of spangles and pieces of coloured glass. Underneath a skirt of tartan silk was fitfully visible. Their brown legs and feet were bare. The expression of their faces was solemn, not to say lugubrious —one performer had a most whimsical resemblance to Mr. Toole when he is sunk in an abyss of dramatic woe. They realised the responsibilities of their position, and there were moments when these seemed too many for them. The orchestra, taken as a whole, was rather noisy; but it comprised one instrument, the "bamboo harmonicon," which deserves to be known out of Burmah because of its sweetness and range of tone. There were lots of "go" in the music, and every now and then one detected a kind of echo of a tune not unfamiliar in other climes. One's ear seemed to assure one that *Madame Angot* had been laid under contribution to tickle the ears of a Mandalay audience, yet how could this be? The explanation was that the instrumentalists, occasionally visiting Thayet-myo or Rangoon, had listened there to the strains of our military bands, and had adapted these to the Burmese orchestra in some deft inscrutable manner, written music being unknown in the musical world of Burmah.

Next day the Kingwoon Menghyi took the wholly unprecedented step of inviting to dinner the British Resident, his suite, and his visitor— myself. Mr. Shaw accepted the invitation, and I considered myself specially fortunate in being a participator in a species of intercourse at once so novel, and to all seeming so auspicious.

About sundown the Residency party, joined *en route* by Dr. Williams, rode down to the entrance to the gardens. Here we were warmly received by the English-speaking secretary, and by the jovial bow-windowed minister who so much resembled the late Pio Nono. We were escorted to the verandah of the pavilion, where the Menghyi himself stood waiting to greet us, and were ushered up to the broad, raised, carpeted platform which may be styled the drawing-room. Here was a semicircle of chairs. On our way to these, a long row of squatting Burmans was passed. As the Resident approached, the Menghyi gave the word, and they promptly stood erect in line. He explained that they were the superior officers of the army quartered in the capital—generals, he called them—whom he had asked to meet us. Of these officers one commanded the eastern guard of the Palace, the other the western; two others were aides-de-camp after a fashion. Just as the Menghyi and his subordinate colleagues represented the Ministry, so these military people represented the Court. The former was the moderate constitutional element of the gathering; the latter the "jingo" or personal government element, for the Burmese Court was reactionary, and those military sprigs were of the personal suite of the King and were understood to abet him in his falling away from the constitutional promise with which his reign began. Their presence rendered the occasion all the more significant. That they were deputed from the Palace to attend and watch events was pretty certain, and indeed the two aides went away immediately after dinner, their excuse being that his Majesty was expecting their personal attendance. After a little while of waiting, the *mauvais quart d'heure* having the edge of its awkwardness taken off by a series of introductions, dinner was announced, and the Menghyi, followed by the Resident, led the way into an adjoining dining-room. Good old Pio Nono, who, I ought to have said, had been with the Menghyi a member of the Burmese Embassy to Europe, jauntily offered me his arm, and gave me to understand that he did so in compliance with English fashion. The Resident sat on the right of the Menghyi, I was on his left; the rest of the party, to the number of about fifteen, took their places indiscriminately; Mr. Andrino, an Italian in Burmese employ, being at the head of the table, Dr. Williams at the foot. Our meal was a perfectly English dinner, served and eaten in the English fashion. The Burmese had taken lessons in the nice conduct of a knife and fork, and fed themselves in the most irreproachably conventional manner, carefully avoiding the use of a knife with their fish. Pio Nono, who sat opposite the Menghyi, tucked his napkin over his ample paunch and went in with a will. He was in a most hilarious mood, and taxed his memory for reminiscences of his visit to England. These were not expressed with useless expenditure of verbiage, nor did they flow in unbroken sequence. It was as if he dug in his memory with a spade, and found every now and then a gem in the shape of a name, which he brandished aloft in triumph. He kept up an intermittent and disconnected fire all through dinner, with an interval between each discharge, "White-bait!" "Lord Mayor!" "Fishmongers!" "Cremorne!" "Crystal Palace!" "Edinburgh!" "Dunrobin!" "Newcastle!" "Windsor!"—each name followed by a chuckle and a succession of nods. The Menghyi divided his talk between the Resident and myself. He told me that of all the men he had met in England his favourite was the late Duke of Sutherland; adding that the Duke was a nobleman of great and striking eloquence, a trait which I had not been in the habit of regarding as markedly characteristic of his Grace. He spoke with much warmth of a pleasant visit he had paid to Dunrobin, and said he should be heartily glad if the Duke would come to Burmah and give him an opportunity of returning his hospitality. Here Pio Nono broke in with one of his periodical exclamations. This time it was "Lady Dudley." Of her, and of her late husband, the Menghyi then recalled his recollections, and if more courtly tributes have been paid to her ladyship's charms and grace, I question if any have been heartier and more enthusiastic than was the appreciation of this Burmese dignitary. The soldier element was at first somewhat stiff, but as the dinner proceeded the generals warmed in conversation with the Resident. But the aides were obstinately supercilious, and only partially thawed in acknowledgment of compliments on the splendour of their jewelry. Functionaries attached to the personal suite of his Majesty wore huge ear-gems as a distinguishing mark. The aides had these in blazing diamonds, and were good enough to take out the ornaments and hand them round. The civil ministers wore no ornaments and their dress was studiously plain. We were during dinner entertained by music, instrumental and vocal, sedulously modulated to prevent conversation from being drowned. The meal lasted quite two hours, and when it was finished the Menghyi led the way to coffee in one of the kiosks of the garden. I should have said that no wine was on the table at dinner. The Burmese by religion are total abstainers, and their guests were willing to follow their example for the time and to fall in with their prejudices.

After coffee we were ushered into the drawing-room, and listened to a concert. The only solo-vocalist was the prima donna *par excellence*, Mdlle. Yeendun Male. The burden of her songs was love, but I could not succeed in having the specific terms translated. Then she sang an ode in praise of the Resident, and gracefully accepted his pecuniary appreciation of her performance. Pio Nono then beckoned to her to flatter me at close quarters; but, mistaking the index, she addressed herself to the Residency chaplain in strains of hyperbolical encomium. The mistake having been set right, much to the reverend gentleman's relief, the songstress overpowered my sensitive modesty by impassioned requests in verse that I should delay my departure; that, if I could not do so, I should take her away with me; and that, if this were beyond my power, I should at least remember her when I was far away. The which was an allegory and cost me twenty rupees.

When the good-nights were being said, the Menghyi gratified me by the information that the King had given his consent to my presentation, and that I was to have the opportunity next morning of "Reverencing the Golden Feet."

The Royal Palace occupied the central space of the city of Mandalay. It was almost entirely of woodwork, and was not only the counterpart of the palace which Major Phayre saw at Amarapoora, but the identical palace itself, conveyed piecemeal from its previous site and re-erected here. Its outermost enclosure consisted of a massive teak palisading, beyond which all round was a wide clear space laid out as an esplanade, the farther margin of which was edged by the houses of ministers and court officials. The Palace enclosure was a perfect square, each face about 370 yards. The main entrance, the only one in general use, was in the centre of the eastern face, almost opposite to which, across the esplanade, was the *Yoom-daù*, or High Court. This gate was called the *Yive-daù-yoo-Taga*, or the Royal Gate of the Chosen, because the charge of it was entrusted to chosen troops. As I passed through it on my way to be presented to his Majesty, the aspect of the "chosen" troops was not imposing. They wore no uniform, and differed in no perceptible item from the common coolies of the outside streets. They were lying about on charpoys and on the ground, chewing betel or smoking cheroots, and there was not even the pretence of there being sentries under arms. Some rows of old flintlock guns stood in racks in the gateway, rusty, dusty, and untended; they might have been untouched since the last insurrection. Crossing an intermediate space overgrown with shrubbery, we passed through a high gateway cut in the inner brick wall of the enclosure; and there confronted us the great Myenan of Mandalay—the Palace of the "Sun-descended Monarch." The first impression was disappointing, for the whole front was covered with gold-leaf and tawdry tinselwork which had become weather-worn and dingy. But there was no time now to halt, inspect details, and rectify perchance first impressions. A message came that the Kingwoon Menghyi, my host of the previous evening—substantially the Prime Minister of Burmah, desired that we—that was to say, Dr.

Williams, my guide, philosopher, and friend, and myself—should wait upon him in the *Hlwot-daù*, or Hall of the Supreme Council, before entering the Palace itself. The *Hlwot-daù* was a detached structure on the right front of the Palace as one entered by the eastern gate. It was the Downing Street of Mandalay. Its sides were quite open, and its fantastic roof of grotesquely carved teak plastered with gilding, painting, and tinsel, was supported on massive teak pillars painted a deep red. Taking off our shoes we ascended to the platform of the *Hlwot-daù*, where we found the Menghyi surrounded by a crowd of minor officials and suitors squatting on their stomachs and elbows, with their legs under them and their hands clasped in front of their bent heads. The Menghyi came forward several paces to meet us, conducted us to his mat, and sitting down himself and bidding us do the same, explained that as it was with him a busy day, he would not be able personally to present me to the King as he had hoped to have done, but that he had made all arrangements and had delegated the charge of us to our old friend whom I have ventured to call "Pio Nono." That corpulent and jovial worthy made his appearance at this moment along with his English-speaking subordinate, and with cordial acknowledgments and farewells to the Menghyi we left the *Hlwot-daù* under their guidance. They led us along the front of the Palace, passing the huge gilded cannon that flanked on either side the central steps leading up into the throne-room; and turning round the northern angle of the Palace front, conducted us to the Hall of the *Bya-dyt*, or Household Council.

We had to leave our shoes at the foot of the steps leading up to it. The *Bya-dyt* was a mere open shed; its lofty roof borne up by massive teak timbers. What splendour had once been its in the matter of gilding and tinsel was greatly faded. The gold-leaf had been worn off the pillars by constant friction, and the place appeared to be used as a lumber-room as well as a council-chamber. On the front of one of a pile of empty cases was visible, in big black letters, the legend, " Peek, Frean, and Co., London." State documents reposed in the receptacle once occupied by biscuits. Clerks lay all around on the rough dusty boards, writing with agate stylets on tablets of black papier-mâché; and there was a constant flux and reflux of people of all sorts, who appeared to have nothing to do and who were doing it with a sedulously lounging deliberation that seemed to imply a gratifying absence of arrears of official work. We sat down here for a while along with Pio Nono and his assistant, who busied himself in dictating to a secretary a description of myself and a catalogue of my presents to be read by the herald to his Majesty when I should be presented. Then Pio Nono went away and presently came back, saying that it was intended to bestow upon me some souvenirs of Mandalay, and that to admit of the preparation of these the audience would not take place for an hour or so. He invited us in the meantime to inspect the public apartments of the Palace itself and the objects of interest in the Palace enclosure. So we got up, and still without our shoes walked through the suite leading to the principal throne-room or great hall of audience.

These were simply a series of minor throne-rooms. The first one in order from the private apartments was close to the *Bya-dyt*. It must be borne in mind that the whole suite, including the great audience hall, were not rooms at all in our sense of the word. They were simply open-roofed spaces, the roofs gabled, spiked, and carved into fantastic shapes, laden with dingy gold-leaf garishly picked out with glaring colours and studded with bits of stained glass; the roofs, or rather I should say, the one continuous roof, supported on massive deep red pillars of teak-wood. The whole palace was raised from the ground on a brick platform some 10 feet high. The partitions between the several walls were simply skirtings of planking covered with gold-leaf. The whole palace seemed an armoury. Some ten or twelve thousand stand of obsolete muskets were ranged along these partitions and crammed into the anteroom of the throne-room proper. The whole suite was dingy, dirty, and uncared-for; but on a great day, with the gilding renewed, carpets spread on the rugged boards, banners waving, and the courtiers in full dress, no doubt the effect would have been materially improved. The vista from the throne of the great hall of audience looked right through the columned arcade to the "Gate of the Chosen"; and that we might imagine the scene more vividly, we considered ourselves as on our way to Court on one of the great days, and going back to the gate again began our pilgrimage anew. The pillared front of the Palace stretched before us raised on the terrace, its total length 260 feet. Looking between the two gilded cannon, we saw at the foot of the central steps a low gate of carved and gilded wood. That gate, it seemed, was never opened except to the King—none save he might use those central steps. Raising our eyes we looked right up the vista of the hall to the lofty throne raised against the gilded partition that closed at once the vista and the hall. We had been looking down the great central nave, as it were, toward the west gate, in the place of which was the throne. But along the eastern front of the terrace ran a long colonnade, whose wings formed transepts at right angles to the nave. The throne-room was shaped like the letter T, the throne being at the base of the letter and the cross-bar representing the colonnade. Entering at the extremity of one of these, we traversed it to the centre and then faced the nave. The throne was exactly before us, at the end of the pillared vista. Five steps led up to the dais. Its form was peculiar, contracting by a gradation of steps from the base upwards to mid-height, and again expanding to the top, on which was a cushioned ledge such as is seen in the box of a theatre. On the platform, which now was bare planks, the King and Queen on a great reception day would sit on gorgeous carpets. The entrance was through gilded doors from a staircase in the ante-room beyond. There was a rack of muskets round the foot of the throne, and just outside the rails a half-naked soldier lay snoring. Our Burman companion assured us that seeing the throne-room now in its condition of dismantled tawdriness, I could form no idea of the fine effect when King and Court in all their splendour were gathered in it on a ceremonial day. I tried to accept his assurances, but it was not easy to imagine such forlorn dinginess changed into dazzling splendour. Just over the throne, and in the centre of the Palace and of the city, rose in gracefully diminishing stages of fantastic woodcarving a tapering *phya-sath* or spire similar to those surmounting sacred buildings, and crowned with the gilded *Htee*, an honour which royalty alone shared with ecclesiastical sanctity. The spire, like everything else, had been gilt, but it was now sadly tarnished and had lost much of its brilliancy of effect.

Having looked at the hall of audience we strolled through the Palace esplanade. A wall parted this off from the private apartments and the pleasure grounds occupying the western section of the Palace enclosure. A series of carved and gilded gables roofed with glittering zinc plates was visible over the wall. The grounds were said to be well planted with flowering shrubs and fruit trees and to contain lakelets and rockeries. Built against the outer wall and facing the enclosed space were barracks for soldiers and gun sheds. The accommodation was as primitive as are the weapons, and that was saying a good deal. Pio Nono led us across to a big wooden house, scarcely at all ornamented, which was the everyday abode of the "Lord White Elephant." His "Palace," or state apartment, was not pointed out to us. His lordship, in so far as his literal claim to be styled a white elephant, was an impostor of the deepest dye and a very grim and ugly impostor to boot. He was a great, lean, brown, flat-sided brute, his ears, forehead, and trunk mottled with a dingy cream colour. But he belonged all the same to the lordly race. "White elephants" were a science which had a literature of its own. According to this science, it was not the whiteness that was the criterion of a " white elephant." So much, indeed, was the reverse, that a " white elephant" according to the science may be a brown elephant in actual colour. The points were the mottling of the face, the shape and colour of the eyes, the position of the ears, and the length of the tail. Certainly the " Lord White Elephant" had, to the most cursory observation, a peculiar and abnormal eye. The iris was yellow, with a reddish outer annulus and a small, clear, black pupil. It was essentially a shifty, treacherous eye, and I noticed that everybody took particularly good care to keep out of range of his lordship's trunk and tusks. The latter were superb—long, massive, and smooth, their tips quite meeting far in front of his trunk. His tail was much longer than in the Indian elephants, and was tipped with a bunch of long, straight, black hair. Altogether he was an unwholesome, disagreeable-looking brute, who munched his grass morosely and had no elephantine geniality. He was but a youngster—the great, old, really white elephant which Yule describes had died some time back, after an incumbency dating from 1806. The " White Elephant" was never ridden now, but the last King but one used frequently to ride its predecessor, acting as his own mahout. We did not see his trappings, as our visit was paid unawares when he was quite in undress; but Yule says that when arrayed in all his splendour his head-stall was of fine red cloth, studded with great rubies, interspersed with valuable diamonds. When caparisoned he wore on his forehead, like other Burmese digni-

D

taries including the King himself, a golden plate inscribed with his titles and a gold crescent set with circles of large gems between the eyes. Large silver tassels hung in front of his ears, and he was harnessed with bands of gold and crimson set freely with large bosses of pure gold. He was a regular " estate of the realm," having a *woon* or minister of his own, four gold umbrellas, the white umbrellas which were peculiar to royalty, with a large suite of attendants and an appanage to furnish him with maintenance wherewithal. When in state his attendants had to leave their shoes behind them when they enter his Palace. In a shed adjacent to that occupied by the "Lord White Elephant" stood his lady wife, a browner, plumper, and generally more amiable-looking animal. Contrary to universal experience elsewhere, elephants in Burmah breed in captivity, but this union was unfertile and the race of " Lord White Elephants" had to be maintained *ab extra*. The so-called white elephants are sports of nature, and are of no special breed. They are called Albinoes, and are more plentiful in the Siam region than in Burmah.

By this time the hour was approaching that had been fixed for the presentation, and we returned to the *Bya-dyt*. The summons came almost immediately. Ushered by Pio Nono and accompanied by several courtiers, we traversed some open passages and finally reached a kind of pagoda or kiosk within the private gardens of the Palace. The King was not to appear in state, and this place had been selected by reason of its absolute informality. There was no ornament anywhere, not so much as a speck of gilding or an atom of tinsel. We solemnly squatted down on a low platform covered with grass matting, through which pierced the teak columns supporting the lofty roof. A space had been reserved for us in the centre, on either side of which, their front describing a semicircle, a number of courtiers lay crouching on their stomachs but placidly puffing cheroots. On our left were two or three superior military officers of the Palace guard, distinguishable only by their diamond ear-jewels. My presents—they were trivial: an opera-glass, a few boxes of chocolate, and a work-box—were placed before me as I sat down. There were other offerings to right and to left of them—a huge bunch of cabbages, a basket of *Kohl-rabi*, and three baskets of orchids. In the clear space in front I observed also a satin robe lined with fur, a couple of silver boxes, and a ruby ring. These, I imagined, were also for presentation, but it presently appeared they were his Majesty's return gifts for myself. Before us, at a higher elevation, there was a plain wooden railing with a gap in the centre, and the railing enclosed a sort of recess that looked like a garden-house. Over a ledge where the gap was, had been thrown a rich crimson and gold trapping that hung low in front, and on the ledge were a crimson cushion, a betel box, and a tall oval spittoon in gold set with pearls. A few minutes passed, beguiled by conversation in a low tone, when six guards armed with double-barrelled firearms of very diverse patterns, mounted the platform from the left side and took their places on either side, squatting down. The guards wore black silk jackets lined with fur and with scarlet kerchiefs bound round their heads. Then a door opened in the left side of the garden-house, and there entered first an old gaunt beardless man—the chief eunuch—closely followed by the King, otherwise unattended. His Majesty came on with a quick step, and sat down, resting his right arm on the crimson cushion on the ledge in the centre of the railing. He wore a white silk jacket, and a *loonghi* or petticoat robe of rich yellow and green silk. His only ornaments were his diamond ear-jewels. As he entered all bent low, and when he had seated himself a herald lying on his stomach read aloud my credentials. The literal translation was as follows:—" So-and-so, a great newspaper teacher of the *Daily News* of London, tenders to his Most Glorious Excellent Majesty, Lord of the Ishaddan, King of Elephants, master of many white elephants, lord of the mines of gold, silver, rubies, amber, and the noble serpentine, Sovereign of the empires of Thunaparanta and Tampadipa, and other great empires and countries, and of all the umbrella-wearing chiefs, the supporter of religion, the Sun-descended Monarch, arbiter of life, and great, righteous King, King of kings, and possessor of boundless dominions, and supreme wisdom, the following presents." The reading was intoned in a uniform high recitative, strongly resembling that used when our Church Service is intoned; and the long-drawn "Phya-a-a-a-a" (my lord) which concluded it, added to the resemblance, as it came in exactly like the "Amen" of the Liturgy.

The reading over, the return presents were picked up by an official and bundled over to me without any ceremony, the King meanwhile looking on in silence, chewing betel and smoking a cheroot.

Several of the courtiers were following his example in the latter respect. Presently the King spoke in a distinct, deliberate voice—

"Who is he?"

Dr. Williams acting as my introducer, replied in Burmese—

"A writer of the *Daily News* of London, your Majesty."

"Why does he come?"

"To see your Majesty's country, and in the hope of being permitted to reverence the Golden Feet."

"Whence does he come?"

"From the British army in Afghanistan, engaged in war against the Prince of Cabul."

"And does the war prosper for my friends the English?"

"He reports that it has done so greatly and that the Prince of Cabul is a fugitive."

"Where does Cabul lie in relation to Kashmir?"

"Between Kashmir and Persia, in a very mountainous and cold region."

There had been pauses more or less long between each of these questions; the King obviously reflecting what he should ask next; then there was a longer, and, indeed, a wearisome pause. Then the King spoke again.

"Where is the Kingwoon Menghyi?"

"In Court, your Majesty," replied Pio Nono. "It is a Court day."

"It is well. I wish the Ministers to make every day a Court day, and to labour hard to give prompt justice to suitors, so that there be no complaint of arrears."

With this laudable injunction, his Majesty rose and walked away, and the audience was over.

The King of Burmah, when I saw him, was little over twenty, and he had been barely four months on the throne. He was a tall, well-built, personable young man, very fair in complexion, with a good forehead, clear, steady eyes, and a firm but pleasant mouth. His chin was full and somewhat sensual-looking, but withal he was a manly, frank-faced young fellow, and was said to have gained self-possession and lost the early nervous awkwardness of his new position with great rapidity. Circumstances had even then occurred to prove that he was very far from destitute of a will of his own, and that he had no favour for any diminution of the Royal Prerogative. As we passed out of the Palace after the interview a house in the Palace grounds was pointed out to me, within which had been imprisoned in squalid misery ever since the mortal illness of the previous King, a number of the members of the Burmese blood royal.

P.S.—A few days after my visit, all these unfortunately were massacred with fiendish refinements of cruelty.

GERMAN WAR PRAYERS

1870-71

IN the multifarious ramifications of their military organisation the Germans by no means neglect religion. Each army corps is partitioned into two divisions and each division has its field chaplain. In those corps in which there is a large admixture of the Catholic element, there is a cleric of that denomination to each division as well as a Protestant chaplain. The former is known as a *Feldgeistliger*, a word which in itself means nothing more distinctive than a "field ecclesiastic," while the Protestant chaplain has usually the title of *Feldpastor*. Of the priest I can say but little. The pastors, for the most part, are young and energetic men. They may be divided into two classes: those who have at home no stated charges, and those who have temporarily left their charge for the duration of the war. The former generally are regularly posted to a division; the latter, equally recognised but not perhaps quite so official, are chiefly to be found in the lazarettoes, in the battlefield villages whither the wounded are borne to have their fresh wounds roughly seen to, and on the battlefield itself. Not that the regular divisional chaplains do not face the dangers of the battlefield with devoted courage; but their duties, in the nature of their special avocation, lie more among the hale and sound who yet stand up before an enemy, than with the poor fellows who have been stricken down. Earnestness and devotion are the chief characteristics of those pastors. It struck me that their education was not of a very high order—certainly not on a par with that of the average regimental officer.

The *Feldpastor* wears an armlet of white and light purple to denote his calling; but indeed it is not easy to mistake him for anything else than he is. He has his quarters with the Divisional General, and preaches whenever and wherever it is convenient to get a congregation. A church is passed on the wayside, a regiment halts and defiles into it, and the pastor mounts the steps of the altar and holds forth therefrom for half an hour. There is a quiet meadow near a village, in which a brigade is lying. Looking over the hedge, you may see in the meadow a hollow square of helmeted men with the general and the pastor in the centre, the latter speaking simple, fervent words to the fighting men. When, as during the siege of Paris, a division occupies a certain district for a long time, you may chance—let me say on a New Year's night —on the village church all ablaze with light. The garrison have decorated the gaunt old Norman arches with laurels and evergreens; they have cleared out the market-vendor's stock of tallow-dips to illuminate the church wherewithal. The band has been practising the glorious *Nun Danket alle Gott* for a week; the vocalists of the regiments have been combining to perfect themselves in part-singing. The gorgeous trumpery of Roman Catholic church paraphernalia, unheeded as it is, looks strangely out of place and contrasts curiously with the simple Protestant forms.

The church is crowded with a denser congregation than ever its walls contained before. The *Oberst* sits down with the under-officer; the general gropes for half a chair between two stalwart *Kerle* of the line. Hymn-cards are distributed as at the Brighton volunteer service in the Pavilion on Easter Sunday. As the pastor enters and takes his way up the altar steps—he goes not to the pulpit—there bursts out a volume of vocal devotional harmony, which is so pent in the aisles and under the arches that the sound seems almost to become a substance. Then the pastor delivers a prayer and there is another hymn. He enunciates no text when he next begins to speak; he chops not a subject up into heads, as the grizzled major who listens to him would partition out his battalion into companies. There is no "thirteenthly and lastly" in his simple address. But he gets nearer the hearts of his hearers than if he assailed them with a battery of logic with multitudinous texts for ammunition. For he speaks of the people at home, in the quiet corners of the Fatherland; he tells the soldier in language that is of his profession, how the fear of the Lord is a better arm than the truest-shooting *Zündnadelgewehr;* how preparedness for death and for what follows after death, is a part of his accoutrement that the good soldier must ever bear about with him.

Herr Pastor has other functions than to preach

to the living. The day after a battle, his horse must be very tired before the stable-door is reached. The burial parties are excavating great pits all over the field, while others pick up the dead in the vicinity and bear them unto the brink of the common grave. Herr Pastor cannot be ubiquitous. If he is not near when the hole is full, the *Feldwebel* who commands the party bares his head, and mutters, " In the name of God, Amen," as he strews the first handful of mould on the dead—it may be on friends as well as on foes. If the pastor can reach the brink of the pit, it is his to say the few words that mark the recognition of the fact that those lying stark and grim below him are not as the beasts that perish. The Germans have no set funeral service, and if they had, there would be no time for it here. " Earth to earth, ashes to ashes, dust to dust, in sure and certain hope of the resurrection to eternal life, *durch unsern Herr Jesu Christe.* Amen ; " words so familiar, yet never heard without a new thrill.

They are slightly uncouth in several matters, these *Feldpastoren*, and would not quite suit sundry metropolitan charges one wots of. They do not wear gloves, nor are they addicted to scent on their pocket-handkerchiefs. Their boots are too often like boats, and when they are mounted there is frequently visible an interval of more or less dusky stocking between the boot-top and the trouser-leg. They slobber stertorously in the consumption of soup, and cut their meat with a square-elbowed energy of determination that might make one think that they had vanquished the Evil One and had him down there under their knife and fork. But they are simple-hearted and valiant servants of their Master. Who was it, in the bullet-storm that swept the slope of Wörth, from facing which the stout hearts of the fighting men blenched and quailed, that there walked quietly into it, to speak words of peace and consolation to the dying men whom that terrible storm had beaten down? A smooth-faced stripling with the *Feldpastor's* badge on his arm, the gallant Christian son of an eminent Prussian divine, Dr. Krummacher of Berlin. At one of the battles (I forget which) a pastor came to fill a grave, not to consecrate it. Shall I ever forget the unswerving hurry to the front of Kummer's divisional chaplain when the *Landwehrleute*, his flock, were going down in their ranks as they held with stubbornness unto death the villages in front of Maizières les Metz? Let the *Feldpastoren* slobber and welcome, say I, while they gild their slobbering with such devotion as this! But there must be times and seasons when Herr Pastor is not at hand; nor can the ministration of any pastor stand in the stead of private prayer. The German soldier's simple needs in this matter are not disregarded. Each man is served out when he gets his kit with a tiny gray volume less than quarter the size of this page, the title of which is *Gebetbuch für Soldaten*—the Soldier's Prayer-Book. It is supplied from the Berlin depôt of the Head Society for the Promotion of Christian Knowledge in Germany, and it is a compendium of simple war prayers for almost every conceivable situation, with one significant exception — there is no prayer in defeat. The word is blotted out of the German war vocabulary. It has been said that the belief in the divinity of our Saviour is rapidly on the wane in Germany. If this war prayer-book avails aught, the taint of the heresy may not enter into the army.

Germany is at war. While Paris is frantically shouting *À Berlin!*, while all Germany is singing and meaning *Die Wacht am Rhein*, Moltke's order goes forth into the towns and villages of the Fatherland for the mobilisation of the Reserves. Hans was singing *Die Wacht am Rhein* last night over his beer; but there is little heart for song left in him as he looks from that paper on the deal table into Gretchen's face. She is weeping bitterly as her children cling around her, too young to realise the cause of their parents' sorrow. Hans rises moodily, and pulling down what military belongings he has not given into the arsenal after the last drill, falls a turning over of them abstractedly. By chance his hand rests upon the little gray volume, the *Gebetbuch für Soldaten*. It opens in his hand, and he comes and sits down by Gretchen and reads in a voice that chokes sometimes, the

Prayer in Strait and Sorrow

O Lord Jesus Christ! let the crying and sighing of the poor come before Thee. Withhold not Thy countenance from the tears and beseechings of the woebegone. Help by Thine outstretched arm, and avert our sorrow from us. Awake us who are lying dead in sin and in great danger, and whose thoughts often wander from Thee. Let us trust with all our hearts that nothing can be so broad, so deep, so high, nor so arduous that Thy grace and favour cannot overcome it; that we so can and must be holpen out of every difficulty and discomfiture when Thou takest compassion upon us. Help us, then, through grace, and so I will praise Thee from now to all eternity.

Hans has bidden good-bye to Gretchen, and has kissed the children he may never see more. He has marched with his fellows to the depôt, and got his uniform and arms. The *Militärzug* has carried him to Kreuznach, and thence he has marched sturdily up the Nahe Valley and over the ridge into the Kollerthaler Wald. His last halt was at Puttingen, but Kameke has sent an aide back at the gallop to summon up all supports. The regiment stacks arms for ten minutes' breathing-time while the cannon-thunder is borne backward on the wind to the ears of the soldiers. In two hours more they will be across the French frontier, storming furiously up the Spicheren Berg. As Hans gropes in his tunic pocket for his tinder-box, the little war prayer-book somehow gets between his fingers. He takes it out with the pipe-light, and finds in its pages a prayer surely suited to the situation—the prayer

For the Outmarching

O gracious God! I defile from out my Fatherland and from the society of my friends,[1] and out of the house of my father into a strange land, to campaign against the enemies of our king. Therefore I would cast myself with life and soul upon Thy divine bosom and guardianship; and I pray Thee, with prostrate humility, that Thou willst guide me with Thine eye, and overshadow me with Thy wings. Let Thine angels camp round about me, and Thy

---

[1] Every now and then one comes across a German word untranslatable in its compact volume of expressiveness. How weakly am I forced to render *Freundschaft* here! "Outmarching," though a literal, is a poor equivalent for *Ausmarsch*. In the old Scottish language we find an exact correspondent for *aus;* the "Furthmarch" gives the idea to a hair's-breadth.

grace protect me in all the difficulties of the marches, in all camps and dangers. Give me wisdom and understanding for my ways and works. Give success and blessing to our ingoings and outcomings, so that we may do everything well, and conquer on the field of battle; and after victory won, turn our steps homeward as the heralds who announce peace. So shall we praise Thee with gladsomeness, O most gracious Father, for Thy dear Son's sake, Jesus Christ!

It is the morning of Gravelotte. King Wilhelm has issued his laconic order for the day, and all know how bloody and arduous is the task before his host. The French tents are visible away in the distance yonder by the auberge of St. Hubert, and already the explosion of an occasional shell gives earnest of the wrath to come. The regiment in which Hans is a private has marched to Caulre Farm, and is halted for breakfast there before beginning the real battle by attacking the French outpost stronghold in Verneville. The tough ration beef sticks in poor Hans' throat. He is no coward, but he thinks of Gretchen and the children, and the Reserve-man draws aside into the thicket to commune with his own thoughts. He has already found comfort in the little gray volume, and so he pulls it out again to search for consolation in this hour of gloom. He finds what he wants in the prayer

For the Battle

Lord of Sabaoth, with Thee is no distinction in helping in great things or in small. We are going now, at the orders of our commanders, to do battle in the field with our enemies. Let us give proof of Thy might and honour. Help us, Lord our God, for we trust in Thee, and in Thy name we go forth against the enemy. Lord Christ, Thou hast said, "I am with thee in the hour of need; I will pull thee out, and place thee in an honourable place." Bethink Thee, Lord, of Thy word, and remember Thy promise. Come to our aid when we are sore pressed, when the close grapple is imminent, when the enemy overmatches us, and we have been surrounded by them. Stand by us in need, for the aid of man is of no avail. Through Thee we will vanquish our enemies, and in Thy name we will tread under the foot those who have set themselves in array against us. They trust in their own might, and are puffed up with pride; but we put our trust in the Almighty God, who, without one stroke of the sword, canst smite into the dust not only those who are now formed up against us, but also the whole world. God, we await on Thy goodness. Blessed are those who put their trust in Thee. Help us, that our enemies may not get the better of us, and wax triumphant in their might; but strike disorder into their ranks, and smite them before our eyes, so that we may overwhelm them. Show us Thy goodness, Thou Saviour, of those who trust in Thee. Art Thou not God the Lord unto us who are called after Thy name? So be gracious unto us, and take us—life and soul—under the protection of Thy grace. And since Thou only knowest what is good for us, so we commend ourselves unto Thee without reserve, be it for life or for death. Let us live comforted; let us fight and endure comforted; let us die comforted, for Jesus Christ, Thy dear Son's sake. Amen.

Alvensleben is sitting on his horse on the little hillock behind the hamlet of Flavigny, pulling his gray moustache, and praying that he might see the *Spitze* of Barneckow's division show itself on the edge of the plain up from out the glen of Gorze. Rheinbaben's cavalry are half of them down, the other half of them are rallying for another charge to save the German centre. Hans is in the wood to the north of Tronville, helping to keep back

Lebœuf from swamping the left flank. The shells from the French artillery on the Roman Road are crashing into the wood. The bark is jagged by the slashes of venomous chassepot bullets. Twice has Ladmirault come raging down from the heights of Bruville, twice has he been sent staggering back. Now, with strong reinforcements, he is preparing for a third assault. Meanwhile there is a lull in the battle. Hans, grimed and powder-blackened, may let the breech of his *Zündnadelgewehr* cool and may wipe his blood-stained bayonet on the forest moss. He has a moment for a glance into the little gray volume, and it opens in his blackened fingers at the prayer

In the Agony of the Battle

O Thou Lord and Ruler of Thine own people, awake and look now in grace upon Thy folk. Lord Jesus Christ, be now our Jesus, our Helper and Deliverer, our rock and fortress, our fiery wall, for Thy great name's sake. Be now our Emmanuel, God with us, God in us, God for us, God by the side of us. Thou mighty arm of Thy Father, let us now see Thy great power, so that men shall hail Thee their God, and the people may bend their knees unto Thee. Strengthen and guide the fighting arm of Thy believing soldiers, and help them, Thou invincible King of Battles. Gird Thyself up, Thou mighty fighting Hero; gird Thy sword on Thy loins, and smite our enemy hip and thigh. Art Thou not the Lord who directest the wars of the whole world, who breakest the bow, who splinterest the spear, and burnest the chariots with fire? Arouse Thyself, help us for Thy good will, and cast us not from Thee, God of our Saviour; cease Thy wrath against us, and think not for ever of our sins. Consider that we are all Thine handiwork; give us Thy countenance again, and be gracious unto us. Return unto us, O Lord, and go forth with our army.

Restore happiness to us with Thy help and counsel, Thou staunch and only King of Peace, who with Thy suffering and death hast procured for us eternal peace. Give us the victory and an honourable peace, and remain with us in life and in death. Amen.

Hans has marched from before Metz towards the valley of the Meuse, and the regimental camp for the night is on the slopes of the Ardennes, over against Chemery. The setting sun is glinting on the windows of the Château of Vendresse, where the German King is quartered for the night. The birds are chirruping in the bosky dales of the Bar. The morrow is fraught with the hot struggle of Sedan, but honest Hans, a simple private man, knows nought of strategic moves and takes his ease on the sward while he may. He has oiled the needle-gun and done his cooking; a stone is under his head and his mantle is about him. As he ponders in the dying rays of the setting sun there comes over him the impulse to have a look into the pages of the *Gebetbuch*, and he finds there this prayer

In the Bivouac

Heavenly Father, here I am, according to Thy divine will, in the service of my king and war-master, as is my duty as a soldier; and I thank Thee for Thy grace and mercy that Thou hast called me to the performance of this duty, because I am certain that it is not a sin, but is an obedience to Thy wish and will. But as I know and have learnt through Thy gracious Word that none of our good works can avail us, and that nobody can be saved merely as a soldier, but only as a Christian, I will not rely on my obedience and upon my labours, but will perform my duties for Thy sake, and to Thy service. I believe with all my heart that the innocent blood of Thy dear Son Jesus Christ, which He has shed for me, delivers and saves me, for He was obedient to Thee even unto death. On this I rely, on this I live and die, on this I fight, and on this I do all things. Retain and increase, O God, my Father, this belief by Thy Holy Ghost. I commend body and soul to Thy hands. Amen.

It is the evening of Sedan, the most momentous victory of the century. The bivouac fires light up the sluggish waters of the Meuse, not yet run clear from blood. The burning villages still blaze on the lower slopes of the Ardennes, and the tired victors, as they point to the beleaguered town, exclaim in a kind of maze of sober triumph, "*Der Kaiser ist da!*" Hans is joyous with his fellows, chaunts with them Luther's glorious hymn, *Nun Danket alle Gott;* and as the watch-fire burns up he rummages in the *Gebetbuch* for something that will chime with the current of his thoughts. He finds it in the prayer

After the Victory

God of armies! Thou hast given us success and victory against our enemies, and hast put them to flight before us. Not unto us, O Lord, not unto us, but to Thy holy name alone be all the honour! Thou hast done great things for us, therefore our hearts are glad. Without Thy aid we should have been worsted; only with God could we have done mighty deeds and subdued the power of the enemy. The eye of our general Thou hast quickened and guided; Thou hast strengthened the courage of our army, and lent it stubborn valour. Yet not the strategy of our leader, nor our courage, but Thy great mercy has given us the victory. Lord, who are we, that we dare to stand before Thee as soldiers, and that our enemies yield and fly before us? We are sinners, even as they are, and have deserved Thy fierce wrath and punishment; but for the sake of Thy name Thou hast been merciful to us, and hast so marked the sore peril of our threatened Fatherland, and hast heard the prayer of our king, our people, and our army, because we called upon Thy name, and held out our buckler in the name of the Lord of Sabaoth. Blessed be Thy holy name for ever and ever. Amen.

The surrender of the French army of Sedan has been consummated, and Napoleon has departed into captivity; while Hans, marching down by Rethel, and through grand old Rheims, and along the smiling vinebergs of the Marne Valley, is now *vor Paris*. He is on the *Feldwache* in the forest of Bondy before Raincy, and his turn comes to go on the uttermost sentry post. As the snow-drift blows to one side he can see the French watch-fires close by him in Bondy; nearer still he sees the three stones and the few spadefuls of earth behind which, as he knows, is the French outpost sentry confronting him. The straggling rays of the watery moon now obscured by snow-scud, now falling on him faintly, could not aid him in reading even if he dared avert his eyes from his front. But Hans had come to know the value of the little gray volume; and while he lay in the *Feldwache* waiting for his spell of sentry go, he had learnt by heart the following prayer

For Outpost Sentry Duty

Lord Jesus Christ, I stand here on the foremost fringe of the camp, and am holding watch against the enemy; but wert Thou, Lord, not to guard us, then the watcher watcheth in vain. Therefore, I pray Thee, cover us with Thy grace as with a shield, and let Thy holy angels be round about us to guard and preserve us that we be not fallen upon at unawares by the enemy. Let the darkness of the night not terrify me; open mine eyes and ears that I may observe the oncoming of the enemy from afar, and that I may study well the care of myself and of the whole army. Keep me in my duty from sleeping on my post and from false security. Let me continually call to Thee with my heart, and bend Thyself unto me with Thine almighty presence. Be Thou with me and strengthen me, life and soul, that in frost, in heat, in rain, in snow, in all storms, I may retain my strength and return in health to the *Feldwache*. So I will praise Thy name and laud Thy protection. Amen.

It is the evening of the 2nd of December. Duerot has tried his hardest to sup in Lagny, and has been balked by German valour. But not without terrible loss. On the plateau and by the party wall before Villiers, dead and wounded Germans lie very thick. In one of the little corries in the vineberg poor Hans has gone down. The shells from Fort Nogent are bursting all around, endangering the *Krankenträger* while prosecuting their duties of mercy and devotion. Hans has somehow bound up his shattered limb; and as he pulled his handkerchief from his pocket the little *Gebetbuch* has dropped out with it. There is none on earth to comfort poor Hans; let him open the book and find consolation there in the prayer

For the Sick and Wounded

Dear and trusty Deliverer, Jesus Christ, I know in my necessity and pains no whither to flee to but to Thee, my Saviour, who hast suffered for me, and hast called unto all aliing and miserable ones, "Come unto Me, all ye who are weary and heavy laden, and I will give you rest." Oh, relieve me, also, of Thy love and kindness, stretch out Thy healing and almighty hand, and restore me to health. Free me with Thy aid from my wounds and my pains, and console me with Thy grace who art vouchsafed to heal the broken heart, and to console all the sorrowful ones. Dost Thou take pleasure in our destruction? Our groaning touches Thee to the heart, and those whom Thou hast cast down Thou wilt lift up again. In Thee, Lord Jesus, I put my trust; I will not cease to importune Thee that Thou bringest me not to shame. Help me, save me, so I will praise Thee for ever. Amen.

Alas for Gretchen and her brood! The 4th of December has dawned, and still Hans lies unfound in the corrie of the vineberg. He has no pain now, for his shattered limb has been numbed by the cruel frost. His eyes are waxing dim and he feels the end near at hand. The foul raven of the battlefield croaks above him in his enfeebled loneliness, impatient for its meal. The grim king of terrors is very close to thee, poor honest soldier of the Fatherland; but thou canst face him as boldly as thou hast faced the foe, with the help of the little book of which thy frost-chilled fingers have never lost the grip. The gruesome bird falls back as thou murmurest the prayer

AT THE NEAR APPROACH OF DEATH

Merciful heavenly Father, Thou God of all consolation, I thank Thee that Thou hast sent Thy dear Son Jesus Christ to die for me. He has through His death taken from death his sting, so that I have no cause to fear him more. In that I thank Thee, dear Father, and pray Thee receive my spirit in grace, as it now parts from life. Stand by me and hold me with Thine almighty hand, that

I may conquer all the terrors of death. When my ears can hear no more, let Thy Spirit commune with my spirit, that I, as Thy child and co-heir with Christ, may speedily be with Jesus by Thee in heaven. When my eyes can see no more, so open my eyes of faith that I may then see Thy heaven open before me and the Lord Jesus on Thy right hand; that I may also be where He is. When my tongue shall refuse its utterance, then let Thy Spirit be my spokesman with indescribable breathings, and teach me to say with my heart, "Father, into Thy hands I commit my spirit." Hear me, for Jesus Christ's sake. Amen.

Would it harm the British soldier, think you, if in his kit there was a *Gebetbuch für Soldaten?*

MISS PRIEST'S BRIDECAKE

1879

IN broad essentials the marryings and givings in marriage of India nowadays do not greatly differ from these natural phenomena at home; but to use a florist's phrase, they are more inclined to "sport." The old days are over when consignments of damsels were made to the Indian marriage-market, in the assured certainty that the young ladies would be brides-elect before reaching the landing ghât. The increased facilities which improved means of transit now offer to bachelors for running home on short leave have resulted in making the Anglo-Indian "spin" rather a drug in the market; and operating in the same untoward direction is the growing predilection on the part of the Anglo-Indian bachelor for other men's wives, in preference to hampering himself with the encumbrance of a wife of his own. Among other social products of India old maids are now occasionally found; and the fair creature who on her first arrival would smile only on commissioners or colonels has been fain, after a few—yet too many —hot seasons have impaired her bloom and lowered her pretensions, to put up with a lieutenant or even with a dissenting *padre*. Slips between the cup and the lip are more frequent in India than in England. Loving and riding away is not wholly unknown in the Anglo-Indian community; and indeed, by both parties to the contract, engagements are frequently regarded in the mistaken light of ninepins. Hearts are seldom broken. At Simla during a late season a gallant captain persistently wore the willow till the war broke out, because he had been jilted in favour of a colonel; but his appetite rapidly recovered its tone on campaign, and he was reported to have reopened relations by correspondence from the tented field with a former object of his affections. Not long ago there arrived in an up-country station a box containing a wedding trousseau, which a lady had ordered out from home as the result of an engagement between her and a gallant warrior. But in the interval the warrior had departed elsewhere and had addressed to the lady a pleasant and affable communication, setting forth that there was insanity in his family and that he must have been labouring under an access of the family disorder when he had proposed to her. It was hard to get such a letter, and it must have been harder still for her to gaze on the abortive wedding-dress. But the lady did not abandon herself to despair; she took a practical view of the situation. She determined to keep the trousseau by her for six months, in case she might within that time achieve a fresh conquest, when it would come in happily. Should fortune not favour her thus far she meant to advertise the wedding-gear for sale.

Miss Priest was no "spin" lingering on in spinsterhood against her will. It is true that when I saw her first she had already been "out" three years, but she might have been married a dozen times over had she chosen. I have seen many pretty faces in the fair Anglo-Indian sisterhood, but Miss Priest had a brightness and a sparkle that were all her own. At flirting, at riding, at walking, at dancing, at performing in amateur theatricals, at making fools of men in an airy, ruthless, good-hearted fashion, Miss Priest, as an old soldier might say, "took the right of the line." There was a fresh vitality about the girl that drew men and women alike to her. You met her at dawn cantering round Jakko on her pony. Before breakfast she had been rinking for an hour, with as likely as not a waltz or two thrown in. She never missed a picnic to Annandale, the Waterfalls, or Mashobra. Another turn at the Benmore rink before dinner, and for sure a dance after, rounded off this young lady's normal day during the Simla season. But if pleasure-loving, capricious, and reckless, she scraped through the ordeal of Simla gossip without incurring scandal. She was such a frank, honest girl, that malign tongues might assail her indeed, but ineffectually. And she had given proof that she knew how to take care of herself, although her only protectress was a perfectly inoffensive mother. On the occasion of the Prince of Wales's visit to Lahore, had she not boxed the ears of a burly and somewhat boorish swain, who had chosen the outside of an elephant as an eligible *locale* for a proposal, the uncouth abruptness of which did not accord with her notion of the fitness of things?

Miss Priest may be said to have lived in a chronic state of engagements. The engagements never seemed to come to anything, but that was on account mostly of the young lady's wilfulness. It bothered her to be engaged to the same man for more than from a week to ten days on end. No bones were broken; the gentleman resigned the position at her behest, and she would genially dance with him the same night. Malice and heartburning were out of the question with a lissom, winsome, witching fairy like this, who played with her life as a child does with soap-bubbles, and who was as elusory and irresponsible as a summer-day rainbow. But one season at Mussoorie Miss Priest contracted an engagement somewhat less evanescent. Mussoorie of all Himalayan hill-stations is the most demure and proper. Simla occasionally is convulsed by scandals, although dispassionate inquiry invariably proves that there is nothing in them. The hot blood of the quick and fervid Punjaub—casual observers have called the Punjaub stupid, but the remark applies only to its officials—is apt to stir the current of life at Murree. The chiefs of the North-West are invariably so intolerably proper that occasional revolt from their austerity is all but forced on Nynee Tal, the sanatorium of that province. But Mussoorie, undisturbed by the presence of frolicsome viceroys or austere lieutenant-governors, is a limpid pool of pleasant propriety. It is not so much that it is decorous as that it is genuinely good; it is a favourite resort of clergymen and of clergymen's wives. It was at Mussoorie that Miss Priest met Captain Hambleton, a gallant gunner. They danced together at the Assembly Rooms; they rode in company round the Camel's Back; they went to the same picnics at "The Glen." The captain proposed and was accepted. For about the nineteenth time Miss Priest was an engaged young lady. And Captain Hambleton was a lover of rather a different stamp from the men with whom her name previously had been nominally coupled. He was in love and he was a gentleman; he had proposed to the girl, not that he and she should be merely engaged but that they should be married also. This view of the subject was novel to Miss Priest and at first she thought it rather a bore; but the captain pegged away and gradually the lady came rather to relish the situation. Men and women concurred that the wayward pinions of the fair Bella were at last trimmed, if not clipped; and to do her justice the general opinion was that, once married, she would make an excellent wife. As the close of the Mussoorie season approached the invitations went out for Bella Priest's wedding, and for "cake and wine afterwards at the house." The wedding-breakfast is a comparatively rare *tamasha* in India; the above is the formula of the usual invitation at the hill-stations.

It happened that just two days before the day fixed for the marriage of Miss Priest and Captain Hambleton, there was a fancy-dress ball in the Assembly Rooms at Mussoorie. I think that as a rule fancy-dress balls are greater successes in India than at home. People in India give their minds more to the selection and to the elaboration of costumes; and there is less of that *mauvaise honte* when masquerading in fancy costume, which makes a ball of this description at home so wooden and wanting in go. At a fancy ball in India "the devil" acts accordingly, and manages his tail with adroitness and grace. It is a fact that at a recent fancy-dress ball in Lahore a game was played on the lap of a lady who appeared as "chess," with the chess-men which had formed her head-dress. This Mussoorie ball, being the last of the season, was to excel all its predecessors in inventive variety. A *padre's* wife conceived the bright idea of appearing as Eve; and only abandoned the notion on finding that, no matter what species of thread she used, it tore the fig-leaves—a result which, besides causing her a disappointment, imperilled her immortal soul by engendering doubts as to the truth of the Scriptural narrative of the creation. Miss Priest determined to go to this ball, although doing so under the circumstances was scarcely in accordance with the *convenances;* but she was a girl very much addicted to having her own way. Captain Hambleton did not wish her to go, and there was a temporary coolness between the two on the subject; but he yielded and they made it up. The principle as to her going once established, Miss Priest's next task was to set about the invention of a costume. It was to be her last effort as a "spin"; and she determined it should be worthy of her reputation for brilliant inventiveness. She had shone as a *Vivandière*, as the Daughter of the Regiment, as a Greek Slave, Grace Darling, and so forth, times out of number; but those characters were stale. Miss Priest had a form of supple rounded grace, nor had Diana shapelier limbs. A great inspiration came to her as she sauntered pondering on the Mall. Let her go as Ariel, all gauze, flesh-tints, and natural curves. She hailed the happy thought and invested in countless yards of gauze. She had the tights already by her.

Now Miss Priest, knowing the idiosyncrasy of Captain Hambleton, had little doubt that he would put his foot down upon Ariel. But she knew he loved her, and with characteristic recklessness determined to trust to that and to luck. She too loved him, even better, perhaps, than Ariel; but she hoped to keep both the captain and the character. She did not, however, tell him of her design, waiting perhaps for a favourable opportunity. But even in Arcadian Mussoorie there are the "d——d good-natured friends" of whom Byron wrote; and one of those—of course it was a woman—told Captain Hambleton of the character in which Miss Priest intended to appear at the fancy ball. The captain was a headstrong sort of man — what in India is called *zubburdustee*. Instead of calling on the girl and talking to her as a wise man would have done, he sat down and wrote her a terse letter forbidding her to appear as Ariel, and adding that if she should persist in doing so their engagement must be considered at an end. Miss Priest naturally fired up. Strangely enough, being a woman, she did not reply to the captain's letter; but when the evening of the ball came, she duly appeared as Ariel with rather less gauze about her shapely limbs than had been her original intention. She created an immense sensation. Some of the ladies frowned, others turned up their noses, yet others tucked in their skirts when she approached; and all vowed that they would decline to touch Miss Priest's hand in the quadrille. Miss Priest did not care a jot for these demonstrations, and she never danced square dances. Among the gentlemen she created a perfect furore.

Captain Hambleton was present at the ball. For the greater part of the evening he stood near the door with his eye fixed on Miss Priest, apparently rather in sorrow than in anger. His gaze seemed but to stimulate her to more vivacious flirtation; and she "carried on above a bit," as a cynical subaltern remarked, with the gallant major to whom she had been penultimately engaged. Toward the close of the evening Captain Hambleton relinquished his post of observation, seemed to accept the situation, and was observed at supper-time paying marked attention to a married lady with whom his name had been to some extent coupled not long before his engagement to Miss Priest.

Next morning Miss Priest took time by the forelock. She waited for no further communication from Captain Hambleton; he had already sent his ultimatum and she had dared her fate. The morrow was the day fixed for the marriage. Many people had been bidden. Mussoorie, including Landour, is a large station, and the postal delivery of letters is not particularly punctual. So she adopted a plan for warning off the wedding-guests identical with that employed in Indian stations for circulating notifications as to lawn-tennis gatherings and unimportant intimations generally. At the head of the paper is written the notification, underneath are the names of the persons concerned. The document is intrusted to a messenger known as a *chuprassee*, who goes away on his circuit; and each person writes " Seen " opposite his or her name in testimony of being posted in the intelligence conveyed in the notification. Miss Priest divided the invited guests into four rounds and despatched four *chuprassees*, each bearing a document curtly announcing that " Miss Priest's marriage will not come off as arranged, and the invitations therefore are to be regarded as cancelled."

Miss Priest had no fortune, and her mother was by no means wealthy. It may seem strange to English readers—not nearly so much so, however, as to Anglo-Indian ones—that Captain Hambleton had thought it a graceful and kindly attention to provide the wedding-cake. It had reached him across the hills from Peliti's the night of the ball, and now here it was on his hands—a great white elephant. Whether in the hope that it might be regarded as an olive-branch, whether that he burned to be rid of it somehow, or whether, knowing that Miss Priest was bound to get married some day and thinking that it would be a convenience if she had a bridecake by her handy for the occasion, there is no evidence. Anyhow, he sent it to Mrs. Priest with his compliments. That very sensible woman did not send it back with a cutting message, as some people would have done. Having considerable Indian experience, she had learned practical wisdom and the short-sighted folly of cutting messages. She kept the bridecake, and enclosed to the gallant captain Gosslett's bill for the dozen of simkin that excellent firm had sent in to wash it down wherewithal.

Bridecakes are bores to carry about from place to place, and Miss Priest and her mother were rather birds of passage. Peliti declined to take this particular bridecake back, for all Simla had seen it in his window and he saw no possibility of "working it in." So the Priests, mother and daughter, determined to realise on it in a somewhat original and indeed cynical fashion. The cake was put up to be raffled for.

All the station took tickets for the fun of the thing. Captain Hambleton was anxious to show that there was no ill-feeling, and did not find himself so unhappy as he had expected—perhaps from the *redintegratio amoris* in another quarter; so he took his ticket in the raffle like other people. It is needless to say that he won; and the cake duly came back to him.

Had Captain Hambleton been a superstitious man, he might have regarded this strange occurrence as indicating that the Fates willed it that he should compass somehow a union with Miss Priest. But the captain had no superstition in his nature; and, indeed, had begun to think that he was well out of it; besides which it was currently reported that Miss Priest had already re-engaged herself to another man. But the bridecake was upon him as the Philistines upon Samson; and the question was, what the devil to do with it? He could not raffle it over again; nobody would take tickets. He had half a mind to trundle it over the *khud* (*Anglice*, precipice) and be done with it; but then, again, he reflected that this would be sheer waste and might seem to indicate soreness on his part. It cost him a good many pegs before he thought the matter out in all its bearings, for, as has been said, he was a gunner, but as he sauntered away from the club in the small hours a happy thought came to him.

He would give a picnic at which the bogey bridecake should figure conspicuously, and then be laid finally by the process of demolition. His leave was nearly up; he had experienced much hospitality and a picnic would be a graceful and genial acknowledgment thereof. And he would ask the Priests just like other people, and no doubt they would enter into the spirit of the thing and not send a "decline." Bella, he knew, liked picnics nearly as well as balls, and it must be a powerful reason indeed that would keep her away from either.

Captain Hambleton's picnic was the last of the season, and everybody called it the brightest. "The Glen" resounded to the laughter at tiffin, and the shades of night were falling ere stray couples turned up from its more sequestered recesses. Amid loud cheers Miss Priest, although still Miss Priest, cut up her own bridecake with a serene equanimity that proved the charming sweetness of her disposition. There was no marriage-bell yet all went merry as a marriage-bell, which is occasionally rather a sombre tintinnabulation; and the *débris* of the bridecake finally fell to the sweeper.

I would fain that it were possible, having a regard to truth, to round off this little story prettily by telling how in a glade of "The Glen" after the demolition of the bridecake, Miss Priest and the captain "squared matters," were duly married and lived happily ever after, as the story-books say. But this consummation was not attained. Miss Priest indeed was in the glade, but it was not with the captain, or at least this particular captain; and as for him, he spent the afternoon placidly smoking cigarettes as he lay at the feet of his married consoler. To the best of my knowledge Miss Priest is Miss Priest still.

A VERSION OF BALACLAVA

REFERRING to a particular phase of this memorable combat, Mr. Kinglake wrote: "The question is not ripe for conclusive decision; some of those who, as is supposed, might throw much light upon it, have hitherto maintained silence." It was in 1868 that the fourth volume—the Balaclava volume—of Mr. Kinglake's History was published. Since he wrote, singularly few of those who could throw light on obscure points of the battle have broken silence. Lord George Paget's Journal furnished little fresh information, since Mr. Kinglake had previously used it extensively. There is but a spark or two of new light in Sir Edward Hamley's more recent compendium. As the years roll on the number of survivors diminishes in an increasing ratio, nor does one hear of anything valuable left behind by those who fall out of the thinning ranks. The reader of the period, in default of any other authority, betakes himself to Kinglake. There are those who term Kinglake's volumes romance rather than history—or, more mildly, the romance of history. But this is unjust and untrue. It would be impertinent to speak of his style; that gift apart, his quest for accurate information was singularly painstaking, searching, and scrupulous. Yet it cannot

MAP OF BALACLAVA PLAIN.

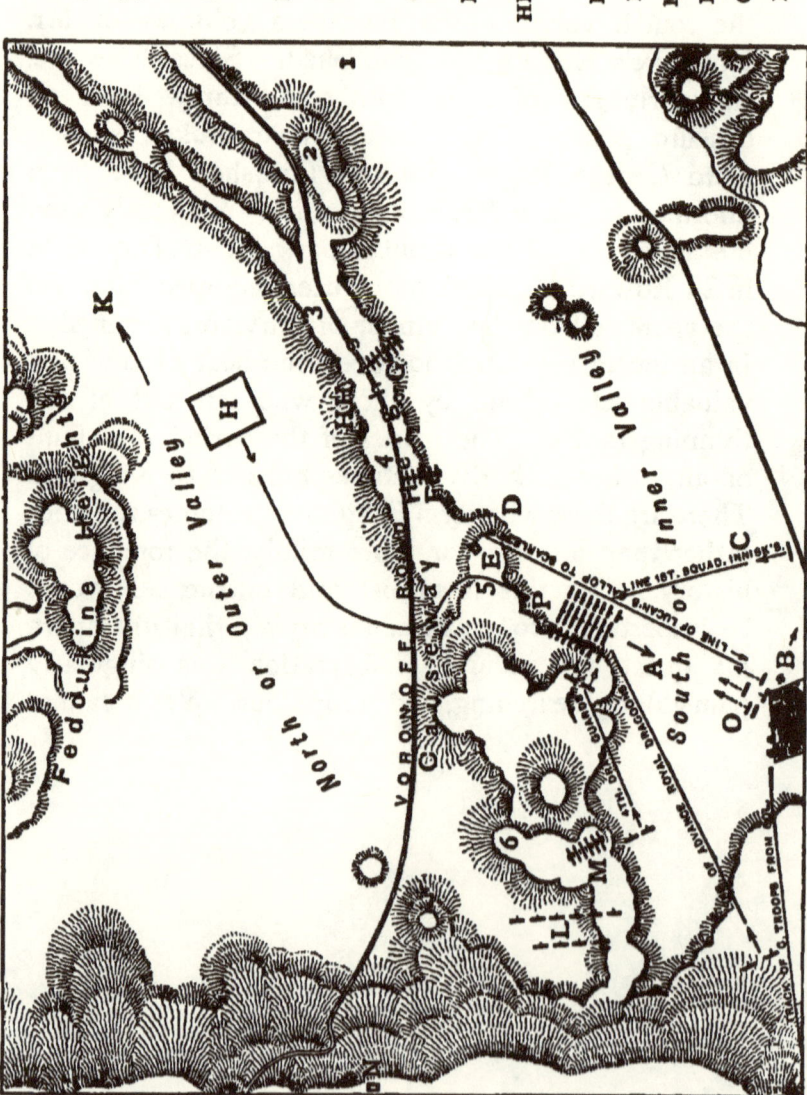

EXPLANATIONS.

Figures 1 to 6 indicate Redoubts.
A. Point of collision.
B. "C" Troop R.H.A.'s position during combat, in support Heavy Cavalry.
C. "C" Troop in action against fugitive Russian Cavalry about D., range about 750 yards.
E. Lord Lucan's position watching advance of Russian Cavalry mass.
F. Position "C" Troop when approached by Cardigan and Paget after Light Cavalry charge.
G. Position "C." Troop in support Light Cavalry charge.
H. Russian Cavalry mass advancing at trot up "North" valley.
HH. Russian Cavalry General and Staff trotting along Causeway heights, with view into both valleys.
K. Line of Light Cavalry charge.
L. Light Brigade during Heavy Cavalry charge.
M. "I" Troop R.H.A. during ditto.
N. Lord Raglan's position (approximate).
O. Scarlett's five squadrons beginning their advance.
P. Russian Cavalry mass halted.

be said that he was always well served. He had perforce to lean on the statements of men who were partisans, writing as he did so near his period that nearly all men charged with information were partisans. British officers are not given to thrusting on a chronicler tales of their own prowess. But *esprit de corps* in our service is so strong—and, spite of its incidental failings that are almost merits what lover of his country could wish to see it weakened?—that men of otherwise implicit veracity will strain truth, and that is a weak phrase, to exalt the conduct of their comrades and their corps. No doubt Mr. Kinglake occasionally suffered because of this propensity; and, with every respect, his literary *coup d'œil*, except as regards the Alma where he saw for himself, and Inkerman where no *coup d'œil* was possible, was somewhat impaired by his having to make his picture of battle a mosaic, each fragment contributed by a distinct actor concentrated on his own particular bit of fighting. If ever military history becomes a fine art we may find the intending historian, alive to the proverb that "onlookers see most of the game," detailing capable persons with something of the duty of the subordinate umpire of a sham fight, to be answerable each for a given section of the field, the historian himself acting as the correlative of the umpire-in-chief.

It is true that the battle of Balaclava was fought to "a gallery" consisting of the gazers who looked down into the plain from the upland of the Chersonese. But of close and virtually independent spectators of the battle's most thrilling episodes, so near the climax of the Heavy Cavalry charge that they heard the clash of the sabres, so close to the lip of the Valley of Death that they discerned the wounds of our stricken troopers who strewed its sward and could greet and be greeted by the broken groups that rode back out of the "mouth of hell," there was but one small body of people. This body consisted of the officers and men of "C" Troop, Royal Horse Artillery. "C" Troop had been encamped from 1st October until the morning of the battle close to the Light division, in that section of the British position known as the Right Attack. When the fighting began in the Balaclava plain on the morning of the 25th, it promptly started for the scene of action. Pursuing the nearest way to the plain by the Woronzoff road, at the point known as the "Cutting" it received an order from Lord Raglan to take a more circuitous route, as by the more direct one it was following it might become exposed to fire from Russian cannon on the Fedoukine heights. Pursuing the circuitous route it came out into the plain through the "Col" then known as the "Barrier," crossed the "South" or "Inner" valley, and reached the left rear of Scarlett's squadrons formed up for the Heavy Cavalry charge. Here it received an order from Brigadier-General Strangways, who commanded the Artillery, with which it could not comply; and thenceforward "C" Troop throughout the day acted independently, at the discretion of its enterprising and self-reliant commander. What it saw and what it did are recorded in a couple of chapters of a book entitled *From Coruña to Sevastopol*.[1] This volume

---

[1] *From Coruña to Sevastopol:* The History of "C" Battery, "A" Brigade (late "C" Troop), Royal Horse Artillery. W. H. Allen and Co.

was published some years ago, but the interesting and vivid details given in its pages of the Balaclava combats and the light it throws on many obscure incidents of the day have been strangely overlooked. The author of the chapters was an officer in the Troop whose experiences he shared and describes, and is a man well known in the service to be possessed of acute observation, strong memory, and implicit veracity. The present writer has been favoured by this officer with much information supplementary to that given in his published chapters, which is embodied in the following account throughout which the officer will be designated as "the 'C' Troop chronicler."

The "Plain of Balaclava" is divided into two distinct valleys by a low ridge known as the "Causeway Heights," which bisects it in the direction of its length and is everywhere easily practicable for all arms. The valley nearest to the sea and the town of Balaclava has been variously termed the "South" and the "Inner" valley; it was on the slope descending to it from the ridge that our Heavy Cavalry won their success; the valley beyond the ridge is the "North" or "Outer" valley, down which, their faces set eastward, sped to glorious disaster the "noble six hundred" of the Light Brigade. On the north the plain is bounded by the Fedoukine heights; on the west by the steep face of the Chersonese upland whereon was the allied main position before Sevastopol during the siege; on the south by the broken ground between the plain and the sea; on the east by the River Tchernaya and the Kamara hills. Our weakness in the plain invited attack. At Kadiköi, on its southern verge, Sir Colin Campbell covered Balaclava with a Scottish regiment, a Field battery, and some Turks. Near the western end of the South valley were the camps of the cavalry division. Straggled along the Causeway heights was a series of weak earthworks whose total armament consisted of nine iron guns, and among which were distributed some six or seven battalions of Turkish infantry. At daybreak of 25th October the Russian General Liprandi with a force of 22,000 infantry, 3300 cavalry, and 78 guns, took the offensive by driving the Turkish garrisons out of these earthworks in succession, beginning with the most easterly—No. 1, known as "Canrobert's Hill." The Turks holding it fought well and stood a storm and heavy loss before they were expelled. The other earthworks fell with less and less resistance, and the first three, with seven out of their nine guns, remained in the Russian possession.

During the morning, while the Russians were taking the earthworks along the ridge, our two cavalry brigades, in the words of General Hamley, had been manœuvring so as to threaten the flanks of any force which might approach Balaclava, without committing themselves to an action in which they would have been without the support of infantry. Ultimately, until his infantry should become available, Lord Raglan drew in the cavalry division to a position on the left of redoubt No. 6, near the foot of the Chersonese upland.

While it was temporarily quiescent there Liprandi was engaging in an operation of enterprise rare in the record of Russian cavalry. General Ryjoff at the head of a great body of horse started on an advance up the North valley. Presently he detached four squadrons to his left, which moved toward where Sir Colin Campbell was in position at the head of the Kadiköi gorge, was repulsed without difficulty by that soldier's fire, and rode back whence it had come. The main body of Russian horse, computed by unimaginative authorities to be about 2000 strong, continued up the valley till it was about abreast of redoubt No. 4,[1] when it halted; checked apparently, writes Kinglake, by the fire of two guns from a battery on the edge of the upland. The "C" Troop chronicler states that in addition to "a few" shots fired by this battery (manned by Turks), the guns of "I" troop R.H.A., temporarily stationed in a little hollow in front of the Light Brigade,[1] fired rapidly one round each, "haphazard," over the high ground in their front. General Hamley assigns no ground for the Russian halt, but mentions that just at the moment of collision between our Heavies and the Russian mass "three guns" on the edge of the upland were fired on the latter. From whatever cause, the Russian cavalry wheeled obliquely to the leftward, crossed the Causeway heights about redoubt No. 5, and began to descend the slope of the South valley. Kinglake heard of no ground for believing that the Russian horse thus wheeling southward, were cognisant of the presence of the Heavies in the valley they were entering. But the "C" Troop chronicler states that as the Troop was crossing the plain a few Russian horsemen were seen by it trotting fast along the top of the ridge,[1] who, when almost

[1] See Map.

immediately afterwards the head of the Russian column showed itself on the skyline, were set down as the General commanding it and his staff.

Kinglake observes that the Russians have declared their object in this operation to have been the destruction of a non-existent artillery park near Kadiköi, while some of our people imagined it to have been a real attempt on Balaclava. But up the centre of the North valley was neither the directest nor the safest way to Kadiköi, much less to Balaclava. Is it not more probable that the enterprise was of the nature merely of a sort of "snap-offensive"; while as yet the allied infantry visibly pouring down the slopes of the upland were innocuous because of distance and while the sole occupants of the plain were a couple of weak cavalry brigades and a single horse battery? Ryjoff on the ridge could see in his front at least portions of the Light Brigade; its fire told him the horse battery was thereabouts too, and there were those shots from the cannon on the upland. Is it not feasible that, looking down on his left to Scarlett's poor six squadrons—his two following regiments were then some distance off— and seeing those squadrons as yet without accompanying artillery, he should have judged them his easier quarry and ordered the wheel that should bring his avalanche down on them?

Kinglake recounts how, while our cavalry division yet stood intact near the foot of the upland, Lord Raglan had noticed the instability of the Turks under Campbell's command at Kadiköi and had sent Lord Lucan directions to move down eight squadrons of Heavies to support them; how Scarlett started with the Inniskillings, Greys, and Fifth Dragoon Guards, numbering six squadrons, to be followed by the two squadrons of the Royals; how the march toward Kadiköi was proceeding along the South valley, when all of a sudden Elliot, General Scarlett's aide-de-camp, glancing up leftward at the ridge " saw its top fretted with lances, and in another moment the skyline broken by evident squadrons of horse." Then, Kinglake proceeds, Scarlett's resolve was instantaneous; he gave the command " Left wheel into line!" and confronted the mass gathering into sight over against him. Soon after Scarlett had started Lord Lucan had learned of the advance up the North valley of the great mass of Russian cavalry, which he had presently descried himself, as also its change of direction southward across the Causeway ridge; and after giving Lord Cardigan "parting instructions" which that officer construed into compulsory inactivity on his part when a great opportunity presented itself, he had galloped off at speed to overtake Scarlett and give him directions for prompt conflict with the Russian cavalry. Thus far Kinglake.

The testimony of the "C" Troop chronicler differs from the above statement in every detail. He significantly points out that Kinglake does not, as is his custom, quote the words of Lord Raglan's order directing the march of the Heavies to Kadiköi. His averment is to the following effect. When the cavalry division after its manœuvring of the morning was retiring by Lord Raglan's command along the South valley toward the foot of the upland, it was followed as closely as they dared by some Cossacks who busied themselves in spearing and capturing the unfortunate Turks flying from the ridge toward Kadiköi athwart the rear of the British squadrons. Eventually the Cossacks reached the camp of the Light Brigade and set about stabbing and hacking at the sick and non-effective horses left standing at the picket-lines. Lord Raglan from his commanding position on the upland saw those Cossacks working mischief in our lines, and sent a message to Lord Lucan "to take some cavalry forward and protect the camp from being destroyed." The "C" Troop chronicler has in his possession a letter from the actual bearer of this message, to the effect that he duly delivered it to Lord Lucan and that consequent on it his lordship moved forward some heavy cavalry into the plain toward the picket-lines. Testimony to be presently noted will indicate the importance of this statement. The chronicler denies that Lord Lucan, as Kinglake states, galloped after Scarlett after having given Lord Cardigan his "parting instructions." No doubt he did give those instructions, when apprised by Lord Raglan's aide-de-camp of the threatening advance of Russian horse. But what he then did, assured as he was of the stationary attitude of the heavy squadrons sent out to protect the camp, was to ride forward along the ridge-line to discern for himself where, if indeed anywhere, the Russians were intending to strike. He most daringly remained at a forward and commanding point of the ridge[1] until actually chased off his ground by the van of the Russian wheel, and he then galloped straight down the slope to join Scarlett drawing out his

---

[1] See Map.

squadrons for the conflict with the Russian mass whose leading files Elliot's keen eye had discerned on the skyline.

If Kinglake were right as to his alleged movement of the Heavies toward Kadiköi and its sudden arrestment because of Elliot's discovery, "C" Troop, as it approached them, would have seen the squadrons still in motion. But the chronicler testifies that "C" Troop, while moving to the scene of action and when still more than a mile and a half distant (at least fifteen minutes at the pace the weakened gun-teams travelled), had a full view of the South valley. And it then saw five squadrons of heavy cavalry thus early halted in the plain near the cavalry picket-lines, fronting towards the ridge and apparently perfectly dressed—the Greys (two squadrons deep) in the centre, recognised by their bearskins; a helmeted regiment (also two squadrons deep) on the left (afterwards known to be the 5th Dragoon Guards); and one helmeted squadron on the right (2nd squadron Inniskillings). A sixth squadron (1st Inniskillings) was visible some distance to the right rear and it was also fronting towards the ridge. This force, so and thus early positioned, consisted, avers the chronicler, of the identical troops which Kinglake erroneously describes as straggling hurriedly into deployment under the urgency of Scarlett and Lucan to cope with the suddenly disclosed adversary.

When "C" Troop and its chronicler reached the rear of the formed-up squadrons they were found in the same formation as when first observed, but the whole had in the interval been moved somewhat to the right, farther into the plain, with intent no doubt to be clear of obstacles on the previous front. Kinglake speaks throughout of the force that first charged under Scarlett—"Scarlett's three hundred," as consisting of three squadrons ranked thus :—

2nd squad.	1st squad.	2nd squad. Inniskillings
Greys.		

And, although his words are not so clear as usual, he appears to believe that the 5th Dragoon Guards, whom in his plan he places some little distance to the left rear of the Greys, were actually the last to move to the attack, of all the five regiments participating in the heavy cavalry onslaught. The "C" Troop chronicler, noting details, be it remembered, from his position immediately in rear of the cavalry force which first charged, describes its composition and formation thus :—

Front squad. 5th Dr. Guards.	1st squad. Greys.	2nd squad. Inniskillings.
Rear squad. 5th Dr. Guards.	2nd squad. Greys.	

in all five squadrons, instead of Mr. Kinglake's three. Nor, according to the chronicler, did the three squadrons in first line start simultaneously, as Kinglake distinctly conveys. The leading squadron of the Greys moved off first, and just as it was breaking into a gallop was temporarily hampered by the swerving of the horse of Colonel Griffiths, who was struck in the head by a bullet from the halted Russians' carbine fire. Next moved, almost simultaneously, the 2nd squadron Inniskillings and the front squadron 5th Dragoon Guards ; thirdly, the

2nd squadron Greys, and finally the rear squadron 5th Dragoon Guards. Lord Lucan is represented as having been "personally concerned in or approving of everything connected with the five squadrons at this moment," galloping to each in succession, giving orders when and in what sequence it was to start, what section of the Russian front it was to strike, and exerting himself to the utmost to have everything fully understood. His errors were in omitting to call in the outlying regiments of the brigade, and either now—or earlier before he left the ridge, specifically to order Lord Cardigan to fall on the flank of the Russians at the moment when their front should be *aux prises* with Scarlett's heavy squadrons. "C" Troop's position was such that it could command, over the heads of the stationary Heavies, the gradual slope up to the Russian front, and every detail of the charge was under its eyes. Scarlett's burnished helmet and plain blue coat were conspicuous in front. The Troop also had the opportunity of making a deliberate study of the Russian cavalry both before and during the combat.

Its front had the appearance of three strong squadrons; its formation was either close or quarter distance column — probably the former, since the column could nowhere be seen through from front to rear; its depth halted was about the same as its breadth of front; its pace across the ridge was a sharp trot and its discipline was indicated by the smartness with which it took ground to the left. Kinglake describes the serried mass as encircled by a loose fringe of satellites, but the "C" Troop chronicler saw neither skirmishers, flankers, nor scouts; and no guns were discerned or heard, although General Hamley says that as the huge cohort swept down batteries darted out from it and threw shells against the troops on the upland. No Lancers were seen with the column, certainly none with pennons. The "partial deployment" of which Kinglake speaks, consisting of "wings or forearms" devised to cover the flanks or fold inwards on the front, did not make itself apparent to any observer of "C" Troop; and indeed the present writer never knew a Russian who had heard of it, the species of formation adumbrated, so far as he is aware, being confined to Zulu impis. It was noticed, and this is not rare, that on the halt the centre pulled up a little earlier than the flanks, so that the latter were somewhat prolonged and advanced. The halt was quite brief and a slower advance ensued without correction of the frontal dressing. Presently there was another halt and some pistol or carbine fire from the central squadron on the advancing first squadron of the Greys. Kinglake makes the Russian front meet our assault halted, but the "C" Troop chronicler declares that when the collision occurred the mass were actually moving forward but at "a pace so slow that it could hardly be called a trot." General Hamley describes "the impetus of the enemy's column carrying it on, and pressing our combatants back for a short space," and the chronicler speaks of the Russians as surging forward after the impact, but without bearing back our people.

It is extremely difficult for the reader of a detailed narrative of a combat that may become a landmark in the military history of a nation, to realise that it may have been fought and finished in no longer time than it has taken him to read the few paragraphs of introductory matter. Mr. Kinglake has devoted a whole volume to the battle of Balaclava, and four-fifths of it deals with the two cavalry fights—Scarlett's charge, and the charge of the Light Brigade. The latter deed was enacted from start to finish within the space of five-and-twenty minutes; as regards the former, from the first appearance of the Russian troopers on the skyline to their defeat and flight a period of eight minutes is the outside calculation. General Hamley, an eyewitness, says "some four or five minutes." During those minutes "C" Troop R.H.A. under Brandling's shrewd and independent guidance was moving slowly forward on the right of the ground that had been covered by the charging Heavies. There was no opportunity for its intervention while the melley lasted. Even when the Russian squadrons broke it could not for the moment act while the redcoats were still blended with the gray. But Brandling saw that his chance was nigh; he galloped forward to the point marked C on the map, unlimbered, and stood intent. Kinglake states that the fugitive Russians, hanging together as closely as they could, retreated by the way they had come and Hamley describes them as vanishing beyond the ridge. Kinglake also says that "I" Troop R.H.A. (accompanying the Light Brigade) fired a few shots at the retreating horsemen, against whom Barker's battery, from its position near Kadiköi, also came into action. The "C" Troop chronicler traverses those statements. His testimony is that the Russian line of retreat was by their left rear along the slope

G

of the South valley, and not immediately over the ridge; that the mass was spread over acres of ground; and that their officers were trying to rally the men and had actually got some ranks formed, when " C " Troop opened fire from about point C in the general direction of point D. " I " Troop was out of sight, he says, and Barker out of range; neither came into action; but " C " Troop, of whose presence in the field Kinglake apparently was unaware, fired forty-nine shot and shells, broke up the attempted rally, and punished the Russians severely. The range was about 750 paces.

At the time when the Light Brigade started on its "mad-brained" charge down the North valley, " C " Troop was halted dismounted on the slope of the South valley a little below redoubt No. 5. In rear of it was the Heavy Cavalry Brigade, halted on the scene of its recent victorious combat. Lord Lucan was some little distance to the front. " C " Troop presently saw him trot away over the ridge in the direction of the Light Brigade, a scrap of paper in his hand at which he kept looking—doubtless the memorable order which Nolan had just brought him—and a group of staff officers, among whom was Nolan, behind him. Out of curiosity Brandling with his trumpeter rode up to the crest, whence he commanded a view into the North valley. By and by some of the Heavies were moved over the crest, no doubt the Royals and Greys which Scarlett was to lead forward in support of the Light Brigade. All was still quiet but for an occasional shot from a Russian battery about redoubt No. 2, when suddenly Brandling came galloping back shouting "Mount! mount!" and telling his officers as he came in that the Light Cavalry had begun an advance on the other side of the ridge. But that he had happened to ride to the crest, the charge of the Light Brigade would have begun and ended without the knowledge of "C" Troop. No order from any source reached it, and Brandling, acting on his own initiative, took his guns rapidly to the front along the inner edge of the ridge and unlimbered at point G. He durst not fire into the bottom of the North valley where our light horsemen were mixed up with the enemy; all the diversion he could effect was to open on the Russian cannon-smoke directly in his front, about redoubt No. 2. Even from this he had soon to desist, being without support and threatened by the Russian cavalry, and he retired by the way he had advanced, to point F, where the troop halted near the Heavies, whose advance Lord Lucan had arrested resolving that they at all events should not be destroyed. These regiments had been moved toward the ridge out of the line of fire in the North valley, and were kept shifting their position and gradually retiring, suffering frequent casualties from the Russian artillery about redoubt No. 2 until they finally halted near the crest in the vicinity of "C" Troop's latest position at point F.

At this point only the left-hand gun of "C" Troop was on the crest, with a view into the North valley; the other guns were on the southern slope. But little had been previously seen of the terrible and glorious experiences of the Light Brigade; and now what was witnessed was not the glory but the horror of battle. For the wounded of the charge were passing to the rear, shattered and maimed, some staggering on foot, others reeling in their saddles, calling to the gunners and the Heavies to look at a "poor broken leg" or a dangling arm. Brandling and his officers held their flasks to the poor fellows' mouths as long as the contents lasted. The "C" Troop chronicler, whose narrative I have been following, tells how Captain Morris, who commanded the 17th Lancers, was carried past the front of the troop towards Kadiköi, dreadfully wounded about the head and calling loudly: "Lord, have mercy on my soul!" Kinglake gives a wholly different account of Captain Morris's removal from the field; but the "C" Troop chronicler is quite firm on his version, and explains that the 17th Lancers and "C" Troop having lain together shortly before the war all the people of the latter knew and identified Captain Morris.

Balaclava is rather an old story now, and some readers may require to be reminded that the Light Brigade charged in two lines, the first line being led by Lord Cardigan, the second by Lord George Paget; that the first line rode into the Russian batteries considerably in advance of the second, the latter having advanced at a more measured pace; and that the second line, with sore diminished ranks and accompanied by a couple of groups rather than detachments of the first, came back later than did the few survivors of Cardigan's regiments other than the groups referred to. The aspersion on Cardigan was that he returned prematurely, instead of remaining to share the fortunes of the second line of his brigade, and this he did not deny. Kinglake's statement is that "he rode back alone at a pace decorously slow, towards the spot where Scarlett was halted." He adds that General Scarlett maintained that Lord Lucan was present at the time; but Lord Lucan's averment was that Lord Cardigan did not approach him until afterwards when all was over. Kinglake relates further that when Lord George Paget came back at the head of the last detachment, some officers rode forward to greet him one of whom was Lord Cardigan. Seeing him approach composedly from the rear Lord George exclaimed: "Halloa, Lord Cardigan, weren't you there?" to which, according to one version of the story, Cardigan replied: "Wasn't I, though? Here, Jenyns, didn't you see me at the guns?"

The reasonable inferences from Kinglake are that Cardigan's first halt was made and that his earliest remarks were uttered when he reached Scarlett, and that he and Paget met after the charge for the first time when the alleged question and answer passed.

The "C" Troop chronicler's narrative of events is right in the teeth of these inferences. While the troop was halted at point F and after a great many wounded and disabled men had already passed it going to the rear, Lord Cardigan came riding by at a "quiet pace" close under the crest. He had passed the troop on his left for several horse-lengths, when he came back and halted within a yard or two of the left-hand gun, the only one fairly on the crest. He was not alone, but attended by Cornet Yates of his own old regiment the 11th Hussars, a recently commissioned ranker. " Lord Cardigan was in the full dress *pelisse* (buttoned) of the 11th Hussars, and he rode a chestnut horse very distinctly marked and of grand appearance. The horse seemed to have had enough of it, and his lordship appeared to have been knocked about but was cool and collected. He returned his sword, undid a little of the front of his dress and pulled down his underclothing under his waistbelt. Then, in a quiet way, as if rather talking to himself, he said, 'I tell you what it is: those instruments of theirs,' alluding to the Russian weapons, 'are deuced blunt; they tickle up one's ribs!' Then he pulled his revolver out of his holster as if the thought had just struck him, and said, 'And here's this d———d thing I have never thought of until now.' He then replaced it, drew his sword, and said, 'Well, we've done our share of the work!' and pointing up toward the Chasseurs d'Afrique on our left rear (ignorant of their opportune service), he added, 'It's time they gave those dappled gentry a chance.' Afterwards he asked, ' Has any one seen my regiment?' The men answered, 'No, sir.'" Brandling was holding aloof; and his lordship turned his horse and rode away farther back.

Just then a cheer was raised by some Heavies who had lately formed in front of "C" Troop. Cardigan, so the chronicler tells, looked backward to see the occasion, and saw the cheer was in compliment to the 8th Hussars coming back with Colonel Sewell in front and Colonel Mayow, the brigade-major, behind on the left. Cardigan wheeled, trotted back towards the 8th, turned round in front of Colonel Sewell, and took up the "walk." Then occurred something "painful to witness. It was seen from the left of 'C' Troop that the moment Cardigan's back was toward the 8th as he headed them, Colonel Mayow pointed toward him, shook his head, and made signs to the officers on the left of the Heavies as much as to say, 'See him; he has taken care of himself.'" Men in the ranks of the 8th also pointed and made signs to the troopers of the Heavies as they were passing left to left. There was, as well, a little excited undertalk from one corps to the other. Colonel Sewell neither saw nor took part in this wretched business; and of course Cardigan did not know that he was being thus ridiculed and disparaged while he was smiling and raising his sword to the cheers of the Heavies and the gunners.

Immediately after this episode the returning 4th Light Dragoons came obliquely across the North valley at a sharp pace, but fell into the "walk" as they came within a hundred yards of "C" Troop. Lord George Paget, who led what remained of the regiment, rode up to the flank of "C" Troop and halted on the very spot where Cardigan had stood a few minutes earlier. Lord George had the look of a man who had ridden hard, and was heated and excited. He exclaimed in rather a loud tone, "It's a d——d shame; there we had a lot of their guns and carriages taken, and received no support, and yet there's all this infantry about—it's a shame!" Meanwhile Lord Cardigan had come back and was close behind Lord George while he was speaking, without the other knowing it. He called out, "Lord George Paget!"; and on the latter turning round said to him in an undertone, "I am surprised!"; and "tossing his head in the air added some other remark which was not heard." Lord George lowered his sword to the salute, and, without speaking, turned his horse and rode on after his men. The "C" Troop chronicler is positive that both officers visited "C" Troop before going to any general or to any other command, and that they met there for the first time after the combat.

When Lord Raglan came down from the upland after all was over, the "C" Troop chronicler says that he went straight for Lucan then in front of the Heavy Cavalry brigade, having first sent for Cardigan to meet him. After a few moments the latter repassed the troop on his way toward the remnant of his brigade. "Then Lord Raglan took Lucan a little forward by himself out of hearing of the group of staff officers, and his gesticulations of head and arm were so suggestive of passionate anger, that the onlookers did not need to be told that the Commander-in-Chief did not charge the blame chiefly on Cardigan." Lord Raglan's subsequent interview with General Scarlett, which occurred in the hearing of "C" Troop, was of a different character. After complimenting the gallant old warrior his lordship said, "Now tell me all about yourself." Scarlett replied, "When the Russian column was moving down on me, sir, I began by sending first a squadron of the Greys at them, and——" but at the word "and" Lord Raglan struck in, saying, "And they knocked them over like the devil!" He then turned his horse away, as if he did not need to hear any more.

HOW I "SAVED FRANCE"

These be big words, my masters! I can only say they are not mine,—I am far too modest to utter any such high-sounding phrase on my own responsibility,—but they are the exact terms used by a high municipal dignitary in characterising the result of what he was pleased to term my "chivalrous conduct." My sardonic chum, on the contrary,—an individual wholly abandoned to the ignoble vice of punning,—asserts that my conduct was simply "barbarous." It will be for the reader to judge.

St. Meuse—let us call it St. Meuse—is a town of what is still French Lorraine; and to St. Meuse I came drifting up the Marne Valley, over the flat expanse of the plain of Châlons, and by St. Menehould, the proud stronghold of pickled pigs' feet, in the second week of September 1873. St. Meuse was one of the last of the French cities held in pawn by the Germans for the payment of the milliards. The last instalment of blood-money had been paid and the *Pickelhaubes* were about to evacuate St. Meuse as soon as the cash had been methodically counted, and after they should have leisurely filled their baggage trains and packed their portmanteaus. My intention in going to St. Meuse was to witness this evacuation scene, and to be a spectator of the return of light-heartedness to the French population of the place, on the withdrawal of the Teuton incubus which for three years had lain upon the safety-valve of their constitutional sprightliness. I had been a little out of my reckoning of time, and when I reached St. Meuse I found that I had a week to stay there before the event should occur which I had come to witness; but the interval could not be regarded as lost time, for St. Meuse is a very pleasant city and the conditions which were so soon to terminate presented a most interesting field of study.

You must know that St. Meuse is a fortress. It has a citadel or at least such fragments of a citadel as the bombardment had left, and the quaint old town is surrounded with bastions which are linked by curtains and flanked by lunettes, the whole being girdled by a ditch, beyond the counterscarp of which spreads a sloping glacis which makes a very pleasant promenade. The defensive strength of the place is reduced to zero in these days of far-reaching rifled siege artillery, for it lies in a cup and is surrounded on all sides by hills the summits of which easily command the fortifications. But the consciousness that it is obsolete as a fortress has not yet come home to St. Meuse. It has, in truth, a very good opinion of itself as a valorous, not to say heroic, place; nor can it be denied that its title to this self-complacency has been fairly earned. In the Franco-German war, spite of its defects, it stood a siege of over two months and succumbed only after a severe bombardment which lasted for several days. And while as yet it was not wholly beleaguered, it was very active in making itself disagreeable to the foreign invader. It was a patrolling party from St. Meuse that intercepted the courier on his way from the battlefield of Sedan to Germany, carrying the hurried lines to his wife which the Crown Prince of Prussia scrawled on the fly-leaf of an orderly book while as yet the last shots of the combat were dropping in the distance; carrying too the notes of the momentous battle which William Howard-Russell had jotted down in the heat of the action and had taken the same opportunity of despatching. St. Meuse, then, had balked the Princess of the first tidings of her husband's safety, and the great English newspaper of the earliest details of the most sensational battle of the age. It had fallen at last, but not ingloriously; and the iron of defeat had not entered so deeply into its soul as had been the case with some French fortresses, of which it could not well be said that they had done their honest best to resist their fate. Its self-respect, at least, was left to it, and it was something to know that when the German garrison should march away, it was bound to leave to St. Meuse the artillery and munitions of war of the fortress just as they had been found on the day of the surrender.

I came to like St. Meuse immensely in the course of the days I spent in it waiting for the great event of the evacuation. The company at the *table d'hôte* of the Trois Maures was varied and amusing. The Germans ate in a room by themselves, so that the obnoxious element was not present overtly at the general *table d'hôte*. But we had a few German officials in plain clothes—clerks in General Manteuffel's bureau, contractors, cigar merchants, etc., who spoke French even among themselves, and were painfully polite to the French habitués who were as painfully polite in return. There was a batch of Parisian journalists who had come to St. Meuse to watch the evacuation, and who wrote their letters in the café over the way to the accompaniment of *verres* of absinthe and bocks of beer. Then there was the gallant captain of gendarmes, who had arrived in St. Meuse with a trusty band of twenty-five subordinates to take over from the Germans the municipal superintendence of the place, and, later, the occupation of the fortress. He was the most polite man I ever knew, this captain of gendarmes, with a clever knack of turning you outside in in the course of half an hour's conversation, and the peculiar attribute of having, to all appearance, eyes in the back of his head. To him, as he placidly ate his food, there came, from time to time, quiet and rather bashful-looking men in civilian attire of a slightly seedy description. Sometimes they merely caught his eye and went out again without speaking; sometimes they handed to him little notes; sometimes they held with him a brief whispered conversation during which the captain's nonchalance was imperturbable. These respectable individuals who, if they saw you once in conversation with their chief, ever after bowed to you with the greatest empressement, were members of the secret police.

As for the inhabitants of St. Meuse, they appeared to await the hour of their delivery with considerable philosophy. Physically they are the finest race I ever saw in France; their men, tall, square, and muscular, their women handsome and comely. Numbers of both sexes are fair-haired, and the sandiness of hair which we are wont to associate with the Scottish Celt is by no means uncommon. A sardonic companion whom I had picked up by the way, attributed those characteristics to the fact that in the great war St. Meuse was a depôt for British prisoners of war who had in some way contrived to imbue the native population with some of their own physical attributes. He further prophesied a wave of Teuton characteristics as the result of the German occupation which was about to terminate; but his insinuations seemed to me to partake of the scurrilous, especially as he instanced Lewes, once a British depôt for prisoners of war, as a field in which similar phenomena were to be discerned. But, nevertheless, I unquestionably found a good deal of what may be called national hybridism in St. Meuse. I used to buy photographs of a shopkeeper over whose door was blazoned the Scottish name Macfarlane. Outwardly Macfarlane was a "hielanman" all over. He had a shock-head of bright red hair such as might have thatched the poll of the "Dougal cratur;" his cheek-bones were high, his nose of the Captain of Knockdunder pattern, and his mouth of true Celtic amplitude. One felt instinctively as if Macfarlane were bound to know Gaelic, and that the times were out of joint when he evinced greater fondness for *eau sucrée* than for Talisker. It was with quite a sense of dislocation of the fitness of things that I found Macfarlane could talk nothing but French. But although he had torn up the ancient landmarks, or rather suffered them to lapse, he yet was proud of his ancestry. His grandfather, it appeared, was a soldier of the "Black Watch" who had been a prisoner of war in St. Meuse, and who, when the peace came, preferred taking unto himself a daughter of the Amalekite and settling in St. Meuse, to going home to a pension of sevenpence a day and liberty to ply as an Edinburgh caddie.

As for the German "men in possession," they pursued the even tenor of their way in the precise yet phlegmatic German manner. Their guards kept the gates and bridges as if they meant to hold the place till the crack of doom, instead of being under orders to clear out within the week. The recruits drilled on the citadel esplanade, straightening their legs and pointing their toes as if their sole ambition in life was to kick their feet away into space, down to the very eve of evacuation. Their battalions practised skirmishing on the glacis with that routine assiduity which is the secret of the German military success. Old Manteuffel was living in the prefecture holding his levees and giving his stiff ceremonious dinner-parties, as if he had done despite to Dr. Cumming's warnings and taken a lease of the place. The German officers thronged their café, each man, after the manner of German officers, shouting at the pitch of his voice; and at the café of the under-officers tough old *Wachtmeisters* and grizzled sergeants with many medals played long quiet games at cards, or knocked the balls about on the chubby little pocketless tables with cues the tips of which were as large as the base of a six-pounder shell.

The French journalists insisted I should accept it

as an article of faith, that these two races dwelling together in St. Meuse hated each other like poison. They would have it that while discipline alone prevented the Germans from massacring every Frenchman in the place, it was only a humiliating sense of weakness that hindered the Frenchmen from rising in hot fury against the Germans who were their temporary masters. I am afraid the gentlemen of the Parisian press came rather to dislike me on account of my obdurate scepticism in such matters. That there was no great cordiality was obvious and natural. Some of the Germans were arrogant and domineering. For instance, having a respect for the Germans, it pained and indeed disgusted me to hear a colonel of the German staff, in answer to my question whether the evacuating force would march out with a rearguard as in war time, reply, " Pho, a field gendarme with a whip is rearguard enough against such *canaille !* " But in the mouths of Hans and Carl and Johann, the stout *Kerle* of the ranks, there were no such words of bitter scorn for their compulsory hosts. The honest fellows drew water for the goodwives on whom they were billeted, did a good deal of stolid love-making with the girls, and nursed the babies with a solicitude that put to shame the male parents of these youthful hopes of Troy. I take leave, as a reasonable person, to doubt whether it can lie in the heart of a family to hate a man who has dandled its baby and whether a man can be rancorous against a family whose baby he has nursed. But fashion's sway is omnipotent in emotion as in dress. Ever since the war, journalists, authors, and public opinion generally had hammered it into the French nation that if it were not to be a traitor to its patriotism, the first article of its creed must be hatred against the Germans ; and that the bitterer this hate the more fervent the patriotism. It was not indeed incumbent on Frenchmen and Frenchwomen to accept this creed, but it behoved them at least to profess it ; and it must be admitted that they did this for the most part with an intensity and vigour which seemed to prove that with many profession had deepened into conviction.

While as yet the evacuation had been a thing of the remote future, the people of St. Meuse had borne the yoke lightly, and indeed had, I believe, privily congratulated themselves on the substantial advantages in the way of money spent in the place and the immunity from taxation which were incidental to the foreign occupation. But as the day for the evacuation drew closer and closer, one became dimly conscious of an electrical condition of the social atmosphere which any trifle might stimulate into a thunderstorm. Blouses gathered and muttered about the street-corners, scowling at and elbowing the German soldiers as they strode to buy sausages to stay them in the homeward march. The gamins, always covertly insolent, no longer cloaked their insolence, and wagged little tricolour flags under the nose of the stolid German sentry on the Pont St. Croix. At the *table d'hôte* the painful politeness of the German civilians had no effect in thawing the studied coldness of the French habitués.

As for myself, I was a neutral, and professing to take no side, flattered myself that I could keep out of the vortex of the soreness. Soon after my arrival at St. Meuse I had called upon the Mayor at his official quarters in the Hôtel de Ville, and had received civil speeches in return for civil speeches. Then I had left my card on General Manteuffel, with whom I happened to have a previous acquaintance; and those formal duties of a benevolent neutral having been performed I had held myself free to choose my own company. Circumstances had some time before brought me into familiar contact with very many German officers, and I had imbibed a liking for their ways and conversation, noisy as the latter is. Several of the officers then in St. Meuse had been personal acquaintances in other days and it was at once natural and pleasant for me to renew the intercourse. I was made an honorary member of the mess; I spent many hours in the officers' casino; I rode out with the officers of the squadron of Uhlans. All this was very pleasant; but as the day of the evacuation became close I noticed that the civility of the French captain of gendarmes grew colder, that the cordiality of the French habitués of the *table d'hôte* visibly diminished, and that I encountered not a few unfriendly looks when I walked through the streets by myself. It began to dawn upon me that St. Meuse was getting to reckon me a German sympathiser, and as there was no half-way house, therefore not in accord with the emotions of France and St. Meuse.

On the afternoon immediately preceding the morning that had been fixed for the evacuation, there came to me a polite request that I should visit M. le Maire at the Hôtel de Ville. His worship was elaborately civil but obviously troubled in mind. He coughed nervously several times after the initiatory compliments had passed, and then he began to speak.

"Monsieur, you are aware that the Germans are going to-morrow morning?"

I replied that I had cognisance of this fact.

"Do you also know that the last of the German officials depart by the 5 A.M. train, not caring to remain here after the troops are gone?"

Of this also I was aware.

"Let me hope," continued the Mayor, "that you are going along with them, or at all events will ride away with Messieurs the officers?"

On the contrary, was my reply, I had come not only to witness the evacuation but to note how St. Meuse should bear herself in the hour of her liberation; I desired to witness the rejoicings; I was not less anxious to be a spectator of any disturbance if such unhappily should occur. Why should M. le Maire have conceived this desire to balk my natural curiosity?

M. le Maire was obviously not a little embarrassed; but he persevered and was candid. This deplorable occupation was now so nearly finished and happily, as yet, everything had been so tranquil, that it would be a thousand pities if any untoward event should occur to detract from the dignified attitude which the territory now to be evacuated had maintained. It was of critical importance in every sense that St. Meuse should not give way to riot or disorder on that occasion. He hoped and believed it would not—here M. le Maire laid his hand on his heart—but a spark, as I knew, fired tinder, and the St. Meuse populace were at present figurative tinder. I might be that spark.

"You much resemble a German," said M. le Maire, "with that great yellow beard of yours, and your broad shoulders, as if you had carried arms. Our citizens have seen you much in the society of Messieurs the German officers; they are not in a temper to draw fine distinctions of nationality; and, dear sir, I ask you to go away with the Germans lest perchance our blouses, reckoning you for a German, should not be very tender with you when the spiked helmets are out of the place. The truth is," said the worthy Maire with a burst of plain speaking, "I'm afraid that you will be mobbed and that there will be a row, and that then the Germans may come back and the evacuation be postponed, and I'll get wigged by the Prefect and the Minister of the Interior and bully-ragged in the newspapers, and St. Meuse will get abused and the fat will be generally in the fire!"

Here was an awkward fix. I could not comply with the Mayor's request; that was not to be thought of for reasons I need not mention here. I had no particular desire to be mobbed. Once before I had experienced the tender mercies of a French mob and I knew that they were very cruel. But stronger than the personal feeling was my sincere sympathy with the Mayor's critical position; and also my anxiety, by what means might be within my power, to contribute to the maintenance of a tranquillity so desirable. But, then, what means were within my power? I could not go; I could not promise to stop indoors, for it was incumbent on me to see everything that was to be seen. And if through me trouble came I should be responsible heaven knows for what!—with a skinful of sore bones into the bargain.

"If Monsieur cannot go,"—the Mayor broke in upon my cogitation,—"if Monsieur cannot go, will he pardon the exigency of the occasion if I suggest one other alternative? It is,"—here the Mayor hesitated—"it is the yellow beard which gives to Monsieur the aspect of a German. With only whiskers nobody could take Monsieur for anything but an Englishman. If Monsieur would only have the complaisance and charity to—to——"

Cut off my beard! Great powers! shear that mane that had been growing for years!—that cataract of hair that has been, so to speak, my oriflamme; the only physical belonging of which I ever was proud, the only thing, so far as I know, that I have ever been envied! For the moment the suggestion knocked me all of a heap. There came into my head some confused reminiscence of a story about a girl who cut off her hair and sold it to keep her mother from starving, or redeem her lover from captivity, or something of the kind. But that must have been before the epoch of parish relief, and kidnapping is now punishable by statute. What was St. Meuse to me that for her I should mow my hirsute glories? But then, if people grew savage, they might pull my beard out by the roots. And there had been lately dawning on me the dire truth that its tawny hue was becoming somewhat freely streaked with gray, a colour I abhor, except in eyes. I made up my mind.

"I'll do it, sir," said I to the Mayor, with a manly curtness. My heart was too full for many words.

He respected my emotion, bowed in silence over the hand which he had grasped, and only spoke to give me the address of his own barber.

This barber was a patriot of unquestioned zeal; but I am inclined to think his extraction was similar to that of Macfarlane, for he combined patriotism with profit in a most edifying manner. He shaved the German officers during the whole of their stay in St. Meuse; he accompanied them on their march to the frontier; he earned the last centime in Conflans; and then, driving forward to the frontier line, he unfurled the tricolour as the last German soldier stepped over it. It is seldom that one in this world sees his way to being so adroitly ambidextrous.

But this is a digression. In twenty minutes, shorn and shaven, I was back again in the Mayor's parlour. The tears of gratitude stood in his eyes. I learned afterwards that a decoration was contingent on his preservation of the public peace on the occasion of the evacuation.

Started by the Mayor, the report rapidly circulated through St. Meuse that I had cut off my beard rather than that it should be possible that any one should mistake me for a German. From being a suspect I became a popular idol. The French journalists entertained me to a banquet at night at which in libations of champagne eternal amity between France and England was pledged. Next morning the Germans went away and then St. Meuse kicked up its heels and burst into exuberant joy. The Mayor took me up to the station in his own carriage to meet the French troops, and introduced me to the colonel of the battalion as a man who had made sacrifices for *la belle France*. The colonel shook me cordially by the hand and I was embraced by the robust vivandière, who struck me as being in the practice of sustaining life on a diet of garlic. When we emerged from the station I was cheered almost as loudly as was the colonel, and a man waved a tricolour over my head all the way back to the town, treading at frequent intervals on my heels. In the course of the afternoon I happened to approach the civic band which was performing patriotic music in the Place St. Croix. When the bandmaster saw me he broke off the programme and struck up "Rule Britannia!" in my honour, to the clamorous joy of the audience, who were thwarted in their aim of carrying me round the Place shoulder-high only by the constancy with which I clung to the railings which surround Chevert's statue. But the crowning recognition of my sacrifice came at the banquet which the town gave to the French officers. The Mayor proposed the toast of "our English friend." "We had all," he said, "made sacrifices for *la Patrie*—he himself had sustained the loss of a wooden outhouse burned down in the bombardment; the gallant colonel on his right had spilt his blood at St. Privat. Them it behoved to suffer and they would do it again cheerfully, for it was, as he had said, for *la Patrie*. But what was to be said of an honourable gentleman who had sacrificed the most distinguishing ornament of his physical aspect without the holy stimulus of patriotism, and simply that there might be obviated the risk of an embroilment to the possible consequence of which he would not further allude? Would it be called the language of extravagant hyperbole, or would they not rather be words justified by facts, when he ventured before this honourable company to assert that his respected English friend had by his self-sacrifice saved France from a great peril?" The Mayor's question was replied to by a perfect whirlwind of cheering. Everybody in the room insisted upon shaking hands with me and I was forced to get on my legs and make a reply. Later in the evening I heard the Mayor and the town clerk discussing the project of conferring upon me the freedom of the city.

CHRISTMAS IN A CAVALRY REGIMENT

1875.

THE civilian world, even that portion of it which lives by the profusest sweat of its brow, enjoys an occasional holiday in the course of the year besides Christmas Day. Good Friday brings to most an enforced cessation from toil. Easter and Whitsuntide are recognised seasons of pleasure in most grades of the civilian community. There are few who do not compass somehow an occasional Derby day; and we may safely aver that the amount of work done on New Year's Day is not very great. But in all the year the soldier has but one real holiday—a holiday with all the glorious accompaniments of unwonted varieties of dainties and full liberty to be as jolly as he pleases without fear of the consequences. True, the individual soldier may have his day's leave, nay, his month's furlough; but his enjoyments resulting therefrom are not realised in the atmosphere of the barrack-room, but rather have their origin in the abandonment for the nonce of his military character and a *pro tempore* return into civilian life. Christmas Day is the great regimental merry-making, free to and appreciated by the veteran and the recruit alike; and as such it is looked forward to for many a month prior to its advent and talked of many a day after it is past and gone.

About a month before Christmas the observer skilled in the signs of the times may begin to notice the tokens of its approach. Self-deniant fellows, men who can trust themselves to carry a few shillings about with them without experiencing a chronic sensation that the accumulated pelf is burning a hole in their pockets, busy themselves in constructing "dimmocking bags" for the occasion, such being the barrack-room term for receptacles for money-hoarding purposes. The weak vessels, those who mistrust their own constancy under the varied temptations of dry throats, empty stomachs, and a scant allowance of tobacco, manage to cheat their fragility of "saving grace" by requesting their sergeant-major to put them "on the peg,"—that is to say, place them under stoppages, so that the accumulation takes place in his hands and cannot be dissipated by any premature weaknesses of the flesh. Everybody becomes of a sudden astonishingly sober and steady. There is hardly any going out of barracks now; for a walk involves the expenditure of at least "the price of a pint," and in the circumstances this extravagance is not allowable. The guard-room is unwontedly empty—nobody except the utterly reckless will get into trouble just now; for punishment at this season involves the forfeiture of certain privileges and the incurring of certain penalties—the former specially prized, the latter exceptionally disgusting at this Christmas season.

Slowly the days roll on with anxious expectancy, the coming event forming the one engrossing topic of conversation alike in barrack-room, in stable, in canteen, and in guard-room. The clever hands of the troop are deep in devising a series of ornamentations for the walls and roof of the common habitation. One fellow spends all his spare time on the top of a table with a bed on top of that again, embellishing the wall above the fireplace with a florid design in a variety of colours meant to be an exact copy of the device on the regiment's kettledrums, with the addition of the legend, "A Merry Christmas to the old Strawboots," inscribed on a waving scroll below. The skill of another decorator is directed to the clipping of sundry squares of coloured paper into wondrous forms—Prince of Wales's feathers, gorgeous festoons, and the like—with which the gas pendants and the edges of the window-frames are disguised out of their original nakedness and hardness of outline, so as to be almost unrecognisable by the eye of the matter-of-fact barrack-master himself. What is this felonious-looking band up to—these four determined rascals in the forbidden high-lows and stable overalls who go slinking mysteriously out at the back gate just at the gloaming? Are they Fenian sympathisers bound for a secret meeting, or are they deserters making off just at the time when there is the least likelihood of suspicion? Nay, they are neither; but, nevertheless, their errand is a nefarious one. Watch at the gate for an hour and you will see them come back again each man laden with the spoils of the shrubberies— holly, mistletoe, and evergreens—ruthlessly plundered under cover of the darkness. A couple of days before "the day," the sergeant-major enters the barrack-room, a smile playing upon his rubicund features. We all know what his errand is and he knows right well that we do ; but he cannot refrain from the customary short patronising harangue, " Our worthy captain—liberal gent you know—deputed me—what you like for dinner—plum-puddings, of course—a quart of beer a man ; make up your minds what you'll have—anything but game and venison ; " and so he vanishes grinning a saturnine grin. The moment is a critical one. We ought to be unanimous. What shall we have ? A council of deliberation is constituted on the spot and proceeds to the discussion of the weighty question. The suggestions are not numerous. The alternative lies between pork and goose. The old soldiers, for some inscrutable reason, go for goose to a man. The recruits have a carnal craving after the flesh of the pig. I did once hear a "carpet-bag"[1] recruit hesitatingly broach the idea of mutton, but he collapsed ignominiously under the concentrated stare of righteous indignation with which his heterodox suggestion was received. Goose *versus* pork is eagerly debated. As regards quantity the question is a level one, since the allowance from time immemorial has been a goose or a leg of pork among three men.

At length the point is decided during the evening stable-hour, according as old or young soldiers predominate in the room. The sergeant-major is

---

[1] "Carpet-bag" recruit is the barrack-room appellation of contempt for the young gentleman recruit who joins his regiment *omnibus impedimentis*—who, in fact, brings his baggage with him, to find it, of course, utterly useless.

informed of the conclusion arrived at, and in the evening the corporal of each room accompanies him on a marketing expedition into the town. Another important duty devolves upon the said corporal in the course of this marketing tour. The "dimmocking bags" have been emptied; the accumulations in the sergeant-major's hands have been drawn, and the corporal, freighted with the joint savings, has the task of expending the same in beer. In this undertaking he manifests a preternatural astuteness. He is not to be inveigled into giving his order at a public-house,—swipes from the canteen would do as well as that,—nor do the bottled-beer merchants tempt him with their high prices for dubious quality. No, he goes direct to the fountain-head. If there be a brewery in the place he finds it out and bestows his order upon it, thus triumphantly securing the pure article at the wholesale price. His purchasing calculation is upon the basis of two gallons per man. If, as is generally the case, the barrack-room he represents contains twelve men, he orders a twenty-four gallon barrel of porter—always porter; and if he has a surplus left he disburses it in the purchase of a bottle or two of spirits, for the behoof of any fair visitors who may haply honour the barrack-room with their presence.

It is Christmas Eve. The evening stable-hour is over and all hands are merrily engaged in the composition of the puddings; some stoning fruit, others chopping suet, beating eggs, and so forth. The barrel of beer is in the corner but it is sacred as the honour of the regiment! Nothing would induce the expectant participants in its contents to broach it before its appointed time shall come. So there is beer instead from the canteen in the tin pails of the barrack-room, and the work of pudding-compounding goes on jovially to the accompaniments of song and jest. Now, there is a fear lest too many fingers in the pudding may spoil it—lest a multitude of counsellors as to the proportions of ingredients and the process of mixing may be productive of the reverse of safety. But somehow a man with a specialty is always forthcoming, and that specialty is pudding-making. Most likely he has been the butt of the room—a quiet, quaint, retiring, awkward fellow who seemed as if he never could do anything right. But he has lit upon his vocation at last—he is a born pudding-maker. He rises with the occasion, and the sheepish "gaby" becomes the knowing practical man; his is now the voice of authority, and his comrades recant on the spot, acknowledge his superiority without a murmur, and perform "ko-tow" before the once despised man of undeveloped abilities. They pull out their clean towels with alacrity in response to his demand for pudding-cloths; they run to the canteen enthusiastically for a further supply on a hint from him that there is a deficiency in the ingredient of allspice. And then he artistically gathers together the corners of the cloths and ties up the puddings tightly and securely; whereupon a procession is formed to escort them into the cook-house, and there, having consigned them into the depths of the mighty copper, the "man of the time" remains watching the caldron bubble until morning, a great jorum of beer at his elbow the ready contribution of his now appreciative comrades.

The hours roll on; and at length out into the darkness of the barrack-square stalks the trumpeter on duty, and the shrill notes of the *réveille* echo through the stillness of the yet dark night. On an ordinary morning the *réveille* is practically negatived, and nobody thinks of stirring from between the blankets till the "warning" sounds quarter of an hour before the morning stable-time. But on this morning there is no slothful skulking in the arms of Morpheus. Every one jumps up, as if galvanised, at the first note of the *réveille*. For the fulfilment of a time-honoured custom is looked forward to—a remnant of the old days when the "women" lived in the corner of the barrack-room. The soldier's wife who has the cleaning of the room and who does the washing of its inmates—for which services each man pays her a penny a day, has from time immemorial taken upon herself the duty of bestowing a "morning" on the Christmas anniversary upon the men she "does for." Accordingly, about a quarter to six, she enters the room—a hard-featured, rough-voiced dame, perhaps, with a fist like a shoulder of mutton, but a soldier herself to the very core and with a big, tender heart somewhere about her. She carries a bottle of whisky—it is always whisky, somehow—in one hand and a glass in the other; and, beginning with the oldest soldier administers a calker to every one in the room till she comes to the "cruity," upon whom, if he be a pullet-faced, homesick, bit of a lad, she may bestow a maternal salute in addition, with the advice to consider the regiment as his mother now, and be a smart soldier and a good lad.

Breakfast is not an institution in any great acceptation in a cavalry regiment on Christmas morning. When the stable-hour is over a great many of the troopers do not immediately reappear in the barrack-room. Indeed they do not turn up until long after the coffee is cold; and, when they do return there is a certain something about them which, to the experienced observer, demonstrates the fact that, if they have been thirsty, they have not been quenching their drought at the pump. It is a standing puzzle to the uninitiated where the soldier in barracks contrives to obtain drink of a morning. The canteen is rigorously closed. No one is allowed to go out of barracks and no drink is allowed to come in. A teetotallers' meeting-hall could not appear more rigidly devoid of opportunities for indulgence than does a barrack during the morning. Yet I will venture to say, if you go into any barrack in the three kingdoms, accost any soldier who is not a raw recruit, and offer to pay for a pot of beer, that you will have an instant opportunity afforded you of putting your free-handed design into execution any time after 7 A.M. I don't think it would be exactly grateful in me to "split" upon the spots where a drop can be obtained in season; many a time has my parched throat been thankful for the cooling surreptitious draught and I refuse to turn upon a benefactor in a dirty way. Therefore suffice it to say that many a bold dragoon when he re-enters the barrack-room to get ready for church parade, has a wateriness about the eye and a knottiness in the tongue which tell of something stronger than the matutinal coffee. Indeed, when the trumpet sounds which calls the regiment to assemble on the parade-ground, there is dire misgiving in the mind of many a stalwart fellow, who is conscious that his face, as well as his speech, " berayeth him." But the lynx-eyed men in authority who another time would be down on a stagger like a card-player on the odd trick and read a flushed face as a passport to the guard-room, are genially blind this morning ; and so long as a man possesses the capacity of looking moderately straight to his own front and of going right-about without a flagrant lurch, he is not looked at in a critical spirit on the Christmas church parade. And so the regiment marches off to church, the band playing merrily in its front. I much fear there is no very abiding sense in the bosoms of the majority of the sacred errand on which they are bound.

But there are two of the inmates of each room who do not go to church. The clever pudding-maker and a sub of his selection are left to cook the Christmas dinner. This, as regards the exceptional dainties, is done at the barrack-room fire, the cook-house being in use only for the now despised ration meat and for the still simmering puddings. The handy man cunningly improvises a roasting-jack, and erects a screen consisting of bed-quilts spread on a frame of upright forms, for the purpose of retaining and throwing back the heat. He is a most versatile genius, this handy man. Now we see him in the double character of cook and salamander, and anon he develops a special faculty as a clever table-decorator as well. This latter qualification asserts itself in the face of difficulties which would be utterly discomfiting to one of less fertility of resource. There is, indeed, a large expanse of table in every barrack-room; but the War Department has not yet thought proper to consider private soldiers worthy to enjoy the luxury of table-linen. Yet bare boards at a Christmas feast are horribly offensive to the eye of taste. Something must be done; something has already been done. Ever since the last issue of clean sheets, one or two whole-souled fellows have magnanimously abjured these luxuries *pro bono publico*. Spartan-like they have lain in blankets, and saved their sheets in their pristine cleanliness wherewithal to cover the Christmas table. So now these are brought forth, not snow-white certainly, nor of a damask texture, being indeed somewhat sackclothy in their appearance, but still they are immeasurably in advance of the bare boards; and when the covers are laid, with each man's best knife and fork, with a little additional crockery-ware borrowed of a beneficent married woman and with the dainty sprigs of evergreen stuck on every available coign, the effect is triumphantly enlivening.

By the time these preparations are complete the men are back from church; and after a brief attendance at stables to water and feed they assemble fully dressed in the barrack-room, hungrily silent. The captain enters the room and *pro formâ* asks whether there are "any complaints?" A chorus of "No, sir," is his reply; and then the oldest soldier in the room with profuse blushing and stammering takes up the running, thanks the officer kindly in the name of his comrades for his generosity, and wishes him a " Happy Christmas and many of 'em " in return. Under cover of the responsive cheer the captain makes his escape, and a deputation visits the sergeant-major's quarters to fetch the allowance of beer which forms part of the treat. Then all fall to and eat ! Ye gods, how they eat ! Let the man who affirmed before the Recruiting Commission that the present scale of military rations was liberal enough show himself now, and then for ever hide his head ! The troopers seem to have become sudden converts to Carlyle's theory on the eloquence of silence. It reigns supreme, broken only by the rattle of knives and forks and by an occasional gurgle indicative of a man judiciously stratifying the solids and liquids, for a space of about twenty minutes, by which time—be the fare goose or pork—it is, barring the bones, only " a memory of the past." The puddings, turned out of the towels in which they have been boiled, then undergo the brunt of a fierce assault ; but the edge of appetite has been blunted by the first course and with most of the men a modicum of pudding goes on the shelf for supper. The soldier is very sensitive on the subject of his Christmas pudding. I remember once seeing a cook put on the table and formally " strapped " for allowing the pudding to stick to the bottom of the pot for lack of stirring.

At length dinner is over. Beds are drawn up from the sides of the room so as to form a wide circle of divans round the fire, and the big barrel's time has come at last. A clever hand whips out the bung, draws a pailful, and reinserts the bung till another pailful is wanted, which will be very soon. The pail is placed upon the hearthstone and its contents are decanted into the pint basins, which do duty in the barrack-room for all purposes from containing coffee and soup to mixing chrome-yellow and pipe-clay water. The married soldiers come dropping in with their wives, for whom the corporal has a special drop of "something short" stowed in reserve on the shelf behind his kit. A song is called for; another follows, and yet another and another. Now it is matter of notice that the songs of soldiers are never of the modern music-hall type. You might go into a hundred barrack-rooms or soldier's haunts and never hear such a ditty as "Champagne Charley" or "Not for Joseph." The soldier takes especial delight in songs of the sentimental pattern; and even when for a brief period he forsakes the region of sentiment, it is not to indulge in the outrageously comic but to give vent to such sturdy bacchanalian outpourings as the "Good Rhine Wine," "Old John Barleycorn," and "Simon the Cellarer." But these are only interludes. "The Soldier's Tear," "The White Squall," "There came a Tale to England," "Ben Bolt," "Shells of the Ocean," and other melodies of a lugubrious type, are the special favourites of the barrack-room. I remember once hearing a cockney recruit attempt "The Perfect Cure" with its accompanying gymnastic efforts; but he was not appreciated, and indeed, I think broke down in the middle for want of encouragement.

Songs and beer form the staple of the afternoon's enjoyment, intermingled with quiet chat consisting generally of reminiscences of bygone Christmases. Here and there a couple get together who are "townies," *i.e.* natives of the same district; and there is a good deal of undemonstrative feeling in the way they talk of the scenes and folks of boyhood. There is no speechifying. Your soldier is not an oratorical animal. Not but what he heartily enjoys a speech; but he somehow cannot make one, or will not try. I remember me, indeed, of a certain quiet Scotsman who one Christmastime being urgently pressed to sing and being unblessed with a tuneful voice, volunteered in utter desperation a speech instead. He referred in feeling language to the various troop-mates who had left us since the preceding Christmas, made a touching allusion to the happy home circle in which the Christmases of our boyhood had been spent, referred to the manner in which the old "Strawboots" had cut their way to glory through the dense masses of Russian horsemen on the hillside of Balaclava, and wound up appropriately by proposing the toast of "our noble selves." He created an immense sensation, was vociferously applauded, and, indeed, was the hero of the hour; but ere next Christmas he was among the "have beens" himself, and his mantle not having devolved upon any successor we had to content ourselves with the songs and the beer.

It is a lucky thing for a good many that there is no roll-call at the Christmas evening stable-hour. The non-commissioned officers mercifully limit their requirements to seeing the horses watered and bedded down by the most presentable of the roisterers, whose desperate efforts to simulate abject sobriety in order to establish their claim for strong-headedness are very comical to witness. It has often been matter of wonderment to me how the orders for the following day which are "read out" at the evening stable-hour, are realised on Christmas evening with clearness sufficient to ensure their being complied with next day without a hitch; but the truth is that, as we shall presently see, a certain order of things for the morning after Christmas has become stereotyped.

This interruption of the evening stable-hour over the circle re-forms round the fire, and the cask finally becomes a "dead marine." The cap is then sent round for contributions towards a further instalment of the foundation of conviviality, which is fetched from the canteen or the sergeant's mess; and another and yet another supply is sent for, as long as the funds hold out and somebody keeps sober enough to act as Ganymede. The orderly sergeant is not very particular to-night about his watch-setting report, for he knows that not many have the physical ability to be absent if they were ever so eager. And so the lights go out; the sun of the dragoon may be said to set in beer and he is left to do his best to sleep himself sober. For in the morning the reins of discipline are tightened again. The man who is foolish enough to revivify the drink which "is dying out in him" by a refresher is apt to find himself an inmate of the black-hole on very scant warning.

Headaches and thirst are curiously rife, and the consumption of "fizzers"—a temperance beverage of an effervescent character vended by an individual with the profoundest trust in human nature on the subject of deferred payments—is extensive enough to convert the regiment into a series of walking reservoirs of carbonic acid gas. The authorities display a demoniacal ingenuity in working the beer out of the system of the dragoon. The morning duty on the day following Christmas is invariably "watering order with numnahs," the numnah being a felt saddle-cloth without stirrups. Every man without exception rides out—no dodging is permitted—and the moment the malicious fiend of an orderly officer gets clear of the barracks he gives the word "Trot!" Six miles of it without a break is the set allowance; and it beats vinegar, pickles, tea smoked in a tobacco-pipe, or any other nostrum, as an effectual generator of sobriety. Six miles at the full trot without stirrups on a rough horse I can conscientiously recommend to the inebriated gentleman who fears to encounter a justly irate wife at two in the morning. I wont answer for the integrity of his cuticle when it is over; but I will stake my existence on the abject profundity of his sobriety. The process would extract the alcohol from a cask of spirits of wine, let alone dispel an average skinful of beer.

And thus evaporates the last vestige of the dragoon's Christmas festivity. It may be urged that the enjoyments of which I have endeavoured to give a faithful narrative are gross and have no elevating tendency. I fear the men of the spur and sabre must bow to the justice of the criticism; and I know of nothing to advance in mitigation save the old Scotch proverb: "It is ill to mak' a silk purse out o' a sow's ear."

THE MYSTERY OF MONSIEUR REGNIER

IN these modern days men live fast and forget fast; yet, since it was barely twenty-six years ago, numbers among us must still vividly remember the lurid autumn of 1870. Eastern and Northern France had been deluged with French and German blood. During the month of fighting from the 2nd of August to the 1st of September the regular armies of France had suffered defeat on defeat, and were now blockaded in Metz or were tramping from the catastrophe of Sedan to captivity in Germany. The Empire in France had fallen like a house of cards; Napoleon the Third was a prisoner of war in Cassel; the Empress and the ill-fated Prince Imperial were forlorn exiles in England. To the Empire had succeeded, at not even a day's notice—for in France a revolution is ever a summary operation—the Government of National Defence with the watchword of "War to the bitter end" rather than cede a foot of territory or one stone of a fortress. The Germans made no delay. The blood-tint had scarcely faded out of the waters of the Meuse, the unburied dead of Sedan yet festered in the sun-heat, and the blackened ruins of Bazeilles still smoked and stank, when their heads of columns set forth on the march to Paris. The troops were full of ardour; but in the Royal headquarters there was not a little disquietude. The old King made a long stay in the old cathedral city of Rheims, while men all over Europe were asking each other whether the catastrophe of Sedan had not virtually ended the war and were hoping for the white dove of peace to alight on the blood-stained land. But that happy consummation was not yet to be. When King Wilhelm crossed the frontier he had proclaimed that he warred not with the French nation but with its ruler. That ruler was now his prisoner; but Wilhelm had for adversary now the French nation, because it had taken up the quarrel which might have gone with the *Déchéance* and in effect had made it its own. In the absence of overtures there was no alternative but to march on Paris.

But Bismarck, although he carried a blithe front, was far from comfortable. He would fain have had peace—always on his own terms; but the question with him was with whom could he negotiate, capable, in the existing confusion, of furnishing adequate guarantees for the fulfilment of conditions? That requisite he could not discern in the self-constituted body which styled itself the Government of National Defence, but of which he spoke as "the gentlemen of the pavement." He had all the monarchical dislike and distrust of a republic, and before the German army had invested Paris he already had begun to ponder as to the possibility of reinstating the dethroned dynasty. Possibly indeed, he had already felt the pulse of Marshal Bazaine on this subject.

It was on the 23rd of September when the Royal headquarters was at Ferrières, Baron Rothschild's château on the east of Paris, that there either presented himself to Bismarck an intriguant, or that the Chancellor evoked for himself an instrument for whom the way was made open to penetrate the beleaguerment of Metz and submit to Bazaine certain considerations. In connection with this mission we heard a good deal at the time of a mysterious " Mons. M." and an equally mysterious " Mons. N." Both were myths: " M." and " N." were alike pseudonyms of the real go-between, a certain Edmond Regnier who died in Paris on the 23rd of January 1894, after a strange and varied career of which the episode to be detailed in this article is the most remarkable. In a now very rare pamphlet published by Regnier in November 1870, he describes himself as a French landed proprietor with financial interests in England yielding him an income of £800 per annum, and as having come to England with his family in the end of August of that year in consequence of the proximity of German troops to his French residence. The painstaking compilers of the indictment against Bazaine give rather a different account of the character and antecedents of M. Regnier. Their information is that he received an imperfect education, sufficiently proven by his extraordinary style and vicious orthography. He studied, with little progress, law and medicine; later he took up magnetism. He was curiously mixed up in the events of the revolution of 1848. He had some employment in Algeria as an assistant surgeon. Returning to France he developed a quarry of paving-stone, and afterwards married in England a wife who brought him a certain competence. "Regnier," continues the Report, "is a sharp, audacious fellow; his manners are vulgar—vain to excess he considers himself a profound politician. Was he induced to throw himself into the midst of events by one of the monomanias which are engendered by periods of storm and revolution? Was he simply an intriguer, plying his trade? It is difficult to tell. But however that may be, the established fact is that we find him in England in September 1870 besieging with his projects the *entourage* of the Empress."

Regnier's siege of the forlorn colony at Hastings took the form of a bombardment of letters, his principal victim being Madame Le Breton, the lady-in-waiting of the Empress and the sister of the unfortunate General Bourbaki, then in command of the Imperial Guard at Metz. He was about to have his passport viséd by the German Ambassador in London, rather an equivocal proceeding for a French subject; and on the 12th of September he wrote thus to Madame Le Breton, desiring that the letter should be communicated to Her Majesty:—

The Ambassador in London of the North German Confederation may possibly say, "I think the King of Prussia would prefer treating for peace with the Imperial Government rather than with the Republic." If so, I shall start to-morrow for Wilhelmshöhe, after having paid a visit to the Empress. The following are the propositions I intend to submit to the Emperor: (1) That the Empress-Regent ought not to quit French territory; (2) That the Imperial fleet *is* French territory; (3) That the fleet which greeted Her Majesty so enthusiastically on its departure for the Baltic, or at least a portion of it, however small, be taken by the Regent for her seat of government, thus enabling her to go from one to another of the French ports where she can count upon the largest number of adherents, and so prove that her government exists both *de facto* and *de jure*. Further, that the Empress-Regent issue from the fleet four proclamations—viz. to foreign governments, to the fleet, to the army, and to the French people.

It will suffice to quote two of those suggested proclamations :—

To foreign governments! To firmly insist upon the fact that the Imperial Government is the *actual* government, as it is the government by right. To the fleet! That just as the Emperor remained to the last in the midst of his army, sharing the chances of war, so also does the Regent, the only executive power legally existing, come with gladness to trust her political fortune to the Imperial fleet.

There followed a voluminous screed of irrelevant dissertation.

Regnier confessedly made no way with the Empress. He saw, indeed, Madame Le Breton on the 14th, but only to be told, in language worthy of a patriot sovereign, that "Her Majesty's feeling was that the interests of France should take precedence of those of the dynasty; that she would rather do nothing than incur the suspicion of having acted from an undue regard for dynastic interests, and that she has the greatest horror of any step likely to bring about a civil war." Those high-souled expressions ought to have given definite pause to Regnier's importunity; but that busybody was indefatigable. A second letter to Madame Le Breton for the Empress simply elicited from the gentlemen of her suite the information that Her Majesty, having read his communications, had expressed the greatest horror of anything approaching a civil war. A final letter from him, containing the following significant passage :—

I myself, or some other person, ought already to have been secretly and confidentially in communication with M. de Bismarck; our conditions for peace must be more acceptable than those to which the *soi-disant* Republican Government may have agreed; every action of theirs ought to be turned to our advantage—we ourselves must *act*,

evoked the ultimatum that "the Empress would not stir in the matter." Regnier then said that as he found no encouragement at Hastings he would probably go to Wilhelmshöhe, where he would perhaps be better understood; and he produced a photographic view of Hastings on which he begged that the Prince Imperial would write a line to his father. On the following morning the Prince's equerry returned him the photographic view at the foot of which were the simple and affectionate words: " Mon cher Papa, je vous envoie ces vues d'Hastings ; j'espère qu'elles vous plairont. Louis-Napoléon." I am personally familiar with the late Prince Imperial's handwriting and readily recognise it in this brief sentence. Regnier averred that it was with Her Majesty's consent that this paper was given him; but admitted that he was told she added : " Tell M. Regnier that there must be great danger in carrying out his project, and that I beg him not to attempt its execution." In other words, the Empress was willing that he should visit the Emperor at Cassel, authenticating him thus far by the Prince Imperial's little note; but she put her veto on his undertaking intrigues detrimental to the interests of France.

Regnier by no means took the road for Wilhelmshöhe. At 7 P.M. of Sunday the 18th he read in the special *Observer* that Jules Favre was next day to have an interview with Bismarck at Meaux. Eager to anticipate the Republican Foreign Minister he promptly took the night train for Paris. No trains were running beyond Amiens and he did not reach Meaux until midnight of the 19th, to learn that Bismarck and the headquarters had that day gone to Ferrières. At 10 A.M. of the 20th he reached that château and appealed to Count Hatzfeld, now German Ambassador in London, for an immediate interview with Bismarck, stating that he had come direct from Hastings. He was informed that the Chancellor had an appointment with Jules Favre at eleven and that it was improbable he could be received in advance. But Bismarck having been apprised of his arrival the fortunate Regnier was immediately ushered into his presence. Regnier congratulates himself on having anticipated the French Minister, ignorant of the circumstance that on the previous day the latter had two interviews with Bismarck and that their then impending interview was simply for the purpose of communicating to Favre the German King's final answer to the French proposals.

Regnier says that he drew from his portfolio the

photograph of Hastings with the Prince Imperial's little note to his father at its foot and handed the paper in silence to Bismarck; and that after the latter had looked at it for some moments, Regnier said, "I come, Count, to ask you to grant me a pass which will permit me to go to Wilhelmshöhe and give this autograph into the Emperor's hands." Why he should have applied to Bismarck for this is not apparent, since he might have gone direct from Hastings to Wilhelmshöhe without any necessity for invoking the Chancellor's offices. It seems extremely probable that the request for a pass was a mere pretext to gain an interview, and the more so since Bismarck made no allusion to the subject, but after a few moments, according to Regnier, addressed that person as follows:—

Sir, our position is before you; what can you offer us? with whom can we treat? Our determination is fixed so to profit by our present position as to render impossible for the future any war against us on the part of France. To effect this object, an alteration of the French frontier is indispensable. In the presence of two governments—the one *de facto*, the other *de jure*—it is difficult, if not impossible, to treat with either. The Empress-Regent has quitted French territory, and since then has given no sign. The Provisional Government in Paris refuses to accept this condition of diminution of territory, but proposes an armistice in order to consult the French nation on the subject. We can afford to wait. When we find ourselves face to face with a government *de facto* and *de jure*, able to treat on the basis we require, then we will treat.

Regnier suggested that Bazaine in Metz and Uhrich in Strasburg, if they should capitulate, might do so in the name of the Imperial Government. Bismarck replied that Jules Favre was assured that the garrisons of those fortresses were staunchly Republican; but that his own belief was that Bazaine's army of the Rhine was probably Imperialist. Then Regnier offered to go at once to Metz. "If you had come a week earlier," said Bismarck, "it was yet time; now, I fear, it is too late." Upon this the Chancellor went away to meet Jules Favre with the parting words to Regnier, "Be so good as to present my respectful homage to his Imperial Majesty when you reach Wilhelmshöhe." At a subsequent meeting the same evening Regnier repeated his anxiety to go at once to Metz and Strasburg and make an agreement that these places should be surrendered only in the Emperor's name. Bismarck was clearly not sanguine, but he said, "Do what you can to bring us some one with power to treat with us, and you will have rendered great service to your country. I will give orders for a 'general safe-conduct' to be given you. A telegram shall precede you to Metz, which will facilitate your entrance there. You should have come sooner." So these two parted; Regnier received his "safe-conduct" and started from Ferrières early on the morning of the 21st. But this indefatigable letter-writer could not depart without a farewell letter:—

I shall leave (he wrote to Bismarck) your advanced posts near Metz, giving orders for the carriage to await my return. I shall wrap myself in a shawl, which will hide a portion of my face. In the event of Marshal Bazaine acceding to my conditions, either Marshal Canrobert or General Bourbaki, acquainted with all that will be requisite for the success of my plans, may go out with my papers, dressed in my clothes, wrapped in my shawl, and depart for Hastings, after giving me his word of honour that for every one, except the Empress, he was to be simply Mons. Regnier. If everything succeeded according to my anticipation, he might then establish his identity, and place himself at the head of the army, with orders to defend the Chamber assembled, if possible, at a seaport town, where a loyal portion of the fleet should also be present. If the project should miscarry, the Marshal or the General would return and resume his post.

Bismarck must have smiled grimly as he read this strange farrago; yet, whatever may have been his motives, he furthered the errand on which Regnier was going to Metz.

That person reached the headquarters of Prince Frederick Charles at Corny, outside of Metz, on the afternoon of 23rd September and was promptly presented to the Prince, who said that Count Bismarck had informed him of his wish to enter Metz and had left it to him to decide as to the expediency of complying with it. This, said the Prince, he was prepared to do and he gave Regnier the requisite pass. The same evening that active individual presented himself at the French forepost line, and having stated that he had a mission to Marshal Bazaine and desired to see him immediately, he was driven to Ban-Saint-Martin where the Marshal was residing. Bazaine at once received him in his study. At the outset a discrepancy manifests itself in the subsequent testimony of the interlocutors. The Marshal states that Regnier said he came on the part of the Empress with the consent of Bismarck; while Regnier declares that he did not state to the Marshal that he had any mission from the Empress. On other points, with one important exception, the versions given of the interview by the two participants fairly agree, and Bazaine's account of it may be summarised. After Regnier had stated that his commission was purely verbal he went on to observe that it was to be regretted that a treaty of peace had not put an end to the war after Sedan; that the maintenance of the German armies on French territory was ruinous to the country; and that it would be doing France a great service to obtain an armistice preparatory to the conclusion of peace. That as regarded this, the French army under the walls of Metz—the only army remaining organised —would be in a position to give guarantees to the Germans if it were allowed its liberty of action; but that without doubt they would exact as a pledge the surrender of the fortress of Metz.

I replied (says Bazaine) that certainly if we—the "Army of the Rhine"—could extricate ourselves from the *impasse* in which we now were, with the honours of war—that is to say, with arms and baggage—in a word completely constituted as an army, we would be in a position to maintain order in the interior, and would cause the provisions of the convention to be respected; but a difficulty would occur as to the fortress of Metz, the governor of which, appointed by the Emperor, could not be relieved except by His Majesty himself.

One of Regnier's stated objects, continues the Marshal, was to bring it about that either Marshal Canrobert or General Bourbaki should go to England, inform the Empress of the situation at Metz, and place himself at her disposition. The departure of whichever of the two high officers should undertake this duty was to be surreptitious; and for this Regnier had provided with Prussian assistance. Seven Luxembourg surgeons who had been in Metz ever since the battle of Gravelotte had written to Marshal Bazaine for leave to go home through the Prussian lines. This letter, sent to the Prussian headquarters, was replied to in a letter carried into Metz by Regnier and by him given to Bazaine, to the effect that the *nine* surgeons were free to depart. As there were but seven surgeons, the implication is obvious that the safe-conduct was expanded to cover the incognito exit, along with the surgeons, of Regnier and the French officer bound for Hastings.

Regnier gave me (writes Bazaine) so many details of his *soi-disant* relations with the Empress and her *entourage* that, notwithstanding the strangeness of the apparition, I put faith in his mission, and believed that I ought not, in the general interest, to neglect the opportunity opened to me of putting myself in communication with the outside world. I consequently told him that he would be duly brought into relations with Marshal Canrobert and General Bourbaki, whom I would inform in regard to his proposals, and whom I would place at liberty to act as each might choose in the matter.

Finally Regnier produced the photograph of Hastings with the Prince Imperial's signature at the foot, and begged the Marshal to add his, which he did "as a souvenir of the interview" explained Regnier, according to the Marshal; according to Regnier, that he could exhibit the signature to

Bismarck in proof that he had the Marshal's assent to his proposals. Diplomacy conducted by chance signatures on casual photographs has a certain innocent simplicity, but is not in accordance with modern methods. Perhaps, however, the strangest thing in connection with this strange interview is Bazaine's final comment:—

All this which I have narrated was only a simple conversation to which I attached a merely secondary importance, since M. Regnier had no written authority from the Empress nor from M. de Bismarck. . . . This personage, therefore, appeared to act without the knowledge of the German military authorities, and it was not until considerably later that I became convinced of their cognisance, and of their mutual understanding as regards M. Regnier's visit to Metz.

And this in the face of General Stiehle's letter to him in his hand, brought in by Regnier, sanctioning the exit of the *nine* surgeons; and the Marshal's promise to Regnier that he and the officer who should accept the mission to Hastings should quit the camp incognito along with the Luxembourg surgeons.

Reference has been made to a discordance between the testimony of Marshal Bazaine and of Regnier on a very important point in regard to this interview. In his notes taken at the time the latter writes:—

The Marshal tells me of his excellent position, of the long period for which he can hold out; that he considers himself as the Palladium of the Empire. He speaks of the very healthy condition of the troops; and, if I may judge by his own rosy face, he is quite right. He tells of all the successful sallies he had made, and of the facility with which he can break through the besieging lines whenever he chooses to do so.

Later, he contradicts all this, explaining that finding himself in the Prussian lines and his papers liable to be read, he had written just the reverse of what he was told by the Marshal. He says that what Bazaine actually informed him was that the bread ration had been already diminished and would be necessarily further reduced in a few days; that the horses lacked forage and had to be used for food; and that in such conditions and taking into account the necessity of carrying four or five days' rations for the army and keeping a certain number of horses in condition to drag the guns and supplies, there would be great difficulty in holding out until the 18th of October. Bazaine, for his part, vehemently denied having given Regnier any such information, and it seems utterly improbable that he should have done so. It is nevertheless the fact that the 18th of October was the last day on which rations were issued to the army outside Metz. Regnier must have been a wizard; or Bazaine must have leaked atrociously; or there must have been lying on the Marshal's table during the interview with Regnier, the most recent state furnished by the French intendance, that of the 21st of September which specified the 18th of October as the precise date of the final exhaustion of the army's supplies.

At midnight of the 23rd Regnier went to the outposts and next morning to Corny, where he found a telegram from Bismarck authorising the departure for Hastings of a general from the army of Metz. He was back again at Ban-Saint-Martin on the afternoon of the 24th, when Marshal Canrobert and General Bourbaki were summoned to headquarters to meet him and the Luxembourg surgeons were assembled. Canrobert declined the proposed mission on the plea of ill-health. Bourbaki had to be searched for and was ultimately found at St. Julien with Marshal Lebœuf. As he dismounted at the headquarters he asked Colonel Boyer — they had both been of the intimate circle of the Empire — whether he knew the person walking in the garden with the Marshal?

"No," replied Boyer.

"What?" rejoined Bourbaki; "have you never seen him at the Tuileries?"

"No," said Boyer. "I forget names, but not faces — I never saw this fellow. He is neither a familiar of the Tuileries nor an employé." Whereupon the two aristocrats despised the bourgeois Regnier. But Bourbaki, nevertheless, had to endure the presentation to him of the "fellow," who promptly entered on a political discourse to the effect that the German Government was reluctant to treat with the Paris Government, which it did not consider so lawful as that of the Empress, and that if it treated with her the conditions would be less burdensome; that the intervention of the army of Metz was indispensable; that it was all-important that one of its chiefs should repair to the side of the Empress to represent the army with her; and that he, Bourbaki, was the fittest person to occupy that position on the declinature of Marshal Canrobert. Bourbaki turned from the man of verbiage to Bazaine and asked, "Marshal, what do you wish me to do?"

The Marshal answered that he desired him to repair to the Empress.

"I am ready," answered Bourbaki, "but on certain conditions: you will have the goodness to give me a written order; to announce my departure in army orders; not to place a substitute in my command; and to promise that, pending my return, you will not engage the Guard." His terms were accepted; he was told that he was to leave immediately and he went to his quarters to make his preparations.

It was understood that the general's departure was to be by way of being incognito, so that it should not get wind. He had no civilian clothes and Bazaine fitted him out in his; Regnier had obtained from one of the Luxembourger surgeons a cap with the Geneva Cross which completed the costume. At the Prussian headquarters General Stiehle, Prince Frederick Charles's chief of staff, desired to pay his respects to a man whose brilliant courage he admired. Bourbaki's bitter answer to Regnier who communicated to him Stiehle's wish, was that he would see "none of them, nor even eat a morsel of their bread," which, he said, would choke him. He presently started with the surgeons, travelling in Regnier's name and on Regnier's passport, on an enterprise which was to lead to the wreck of a fine career. At the same time Regnier quitted Corny on his return to Ferrières to report to Bismarck, having promised Bazaine that he would return to Metz within six days. His bolt was about shot. But he had not realised this fact. He maintains in his curious pamphlet that, to quote his own words, "the Minister had given me to understand that if I were backed by Bazaine and his army he would treat with me as if I were the representative of the Emperor or the Regent. I had obtained from the Marshal a capitulation with the honours of war, which the Minister—for the furtherance of our political ends—had consented to accord to him." He hurried expectant to Ferrières; there to be summarily disillusioned. Bismarck gave him an interview on the 28th, and crushed him in a few trenchant sentences:—

I am surprised and sorry (said the Chancellor) that you, who appeared to be a practical man, after having been permitted to enter Metz with the certainty of being able to leave it, a favour never before accorded, should have left it without some more formal recognition of your right to treat than merely a photograph with the Marshal's signature on it. But I, Sir, am a diplomatist of many years' standing, and this is not enough for me. I regret it; but I find myself compelled to relinquish all further communication with you till your powers are better defined.

Regnier expressed his regret at having been so cruelly deceived but thanked Bismarck for his kindness, whereupon the latter offered to give him a last chance. "I would certainly," he said, "have treated with you as to peace conditions, had you been able to treat in the name of a Marshal at the head of 80,000 men; as it is, I will send this telegram to the Marshal: 'Does Marshal Bazaine authorise M. Regnier to treat for the surrender of the army before Metz in accordance with the conditions agreed upon with the last-named?'" On the 29th came Bazaine's somewhat diffuse reply:—

I cannot reply definitely in the affirmative to the

question. Regnier announced himself the emissary of the Empress without written credentials. He asked the conditions on which I could enter into negotiations with Prince Frederick Charles. My answer was that I could only accept a convention with the honours of war, not to include the fortress of Metz. These are the only conditions which military honour permits me to accept.

Regnier bombarded the Chancellor with letters until the 30th, when Count Hatzfeld informed him that the Minister would listen to nothing more until Regnier could show full powers without evasion; that the matter must imperatively be conducted openly and above board; and that his Excellency hoped Regnier would be able to get clear of it with honour, and that soon.

So Regnier quitted Ferrières in great dejection. He gives vent ruefully to the belief that Bismarck regarded him as an unaccredited agent of the Empress, while, curiously enough, the partisans of the Empress took him for an emissary of Bismarck. Reaching Hastings on the 3rd of October he found that the Empress was now at Chislehurst. He had telegraphed in advance to "M. Regnier," the name which he had instructed General Bourbaki to pass under until the true Regnier should reach England. But Bourbaki had cast away the false name at the instigation of a brother officer while passing through Belgium. On arriving at Chislehurst he learned from the Empress that he had been made the victim of a mystification on the part of Regnier, and that she had never expressed the desire to have with her either Marshal Canrobert or himself. This intelligence, of which the newspapers had given him a presentiment, struck him to the heart. Although covered by his chief's order he found himself in a false position; and he wrote to the late Lord Granville, then Foreign Secretary, begging his good offices to obtain for him an authorisation to return to his post. An assurance was given that this would be accorded, and he hurried to Luxembourg there to await intimation of permission to re-enter Metz. Some delay occurred in the transmission of the Royal order to this effect and although Bourbaki was assured that the decision would shortly reach him, he became impatient, went into France, and placed himself at the disposition of the Provisional Government. But thenceforth he was a soured and dispirited man. The *ci-devant* aide-de-camp of an Emperor writhed under the harrow of Gambetta and Freycinet.

As for Regnier, on his return to England he seems to have haunted Chislehurst. Once, so he frankly writes, after waiting a full hour in expectation of an audience of the Empress Madame Le Breton came to tell him that Her Majesty was sorry to have kept him waiting so long, but that she had now definitely resolved not to receive him. Yet he hung on, and the same evening he tells that he was called somewhat abruptly into a room in which stood several gentlemen, when a lady suddenly rose from a couch and addressed him standing. At last he was face to face with the Empress. "Sir," said Her Majesty, "you have been persistent in wishing to speak with me personally; here I am; what have you to say?" Then Regnier, by his own account, harangued that august and unfortunate lady in a manner which in print seems extremely trenchant and dictatorial. It was all in vain, he confesses; he could not alter the convictions of the Empress. He says that "she feared that posterity, if she yielded, would only see in the act a proof of dynastic selfishness; and that dishonour would be attached to the name of whoever should sign a treaty based on a cession of territory." Probably Her Majesty spoke from a more lofty standpoint than Regnier was able to comprehend or appreciate.

Regnier's subsequent career during that troublous period was both curious and dubious. General Boyer states that on the 28th of October he found Regnier *tête-à-tête* with Prince Napoleon (Plon-Plon). Later he went to Cassel, where he busied himself in trying to implicate in political machinations sundry French officers who were prisoners there. Presently we find him at Versailles, figuring among the conductors of the *Moniteur Prussien*, Bismarck's organ during the German occupation of that city, in which journal he published a series of articles under the title of *Jean Bonhomme*. During the armistice after the surrender of Paris he betook himself to Brussels, where he told General Boyer that he had gone to Versailles to attempt a renewal of negotiations tending towards an Imperial restoration. He showed the general the original safe-conduct which Bismarck had given him at Ferrières, and a letter of Count Hatzfeld authorising him to visit Versailles. The last item during this period recorded of this strange personage — and that item one so significant as to justify Mrs. Crawford's shrewd suspicion "that Regnier played a double game, and that Prince

Bismarck, if he chose, could clear up the mystery which hangs over Regnier's curious negotiations"—is found in a page of the *Procès Bazaine*. This is the gem: "On the 18th of February 1871 he was in Versailles, where he met a person of his acquaintance, to whom he uttered the characteristic words—'I do not know whether M. de Bismarck will allow me to leave him this evening.'" He is said to have later been connected with the Paris police under the late M. Lagrange. Whether Regnier was more knave or fool—enthusiast, impostor, or "crank"—will probably be never known.

RAILWAY LIZZ

BY AN HOSPITAL MATRON

WE see many curious phases of humanity—we who administer to the sick in the great hospitals which are among the boasts of London. The mask worn by the face of the world is dropped before us. We see men as they are, and while the sight is often not calculated to enhance our estimate of human nature, there are occasionally strong reliefs which stand out from the mass of shadow. There are curious opinions entertained in the outer world as to the internal economy of hospitals, not a few " laymen " imagining that the main end of such establishments is that the doctors may have something to experiment upon for the advancement of their professional theories—something which, while it is human, is not very valuable in the social scale and therefore open to be hacked and hewn and operated upon with a freedom begotten of the knowledge that the subject is a mere vile corpus.

Nor is this the only delusion. Many people think that the hospital nurse is but another name for a heartless harpy, brimful of callous selfishness. Her attentions—kindness is an inadmissible word—are believed to be purely mercenary. Those who themselves can afford to fee her or who have friends able and willing to buy her services, may purchase civil treatment and careful nursing while the poor wretch who has neither money nor friends may languish unheeded. There is no greater mistake than this. Year by year the character of hospital nursing has improved. It is not to be denied that in times gone by there were nurses the mainsprings of whose actions may be said to have been money and gin; but these have long since been driven forth with contumely. I have seen a poor wretch of a discharged soldier without a single copper to bless himself with, nursed with as much tender assiduity and real feeling as if he were in a position to pay his nurses handsomely.

Indeed, in most hospitals now the practice of accepting money presents is altogether forbidden; and if the prohibition, as in the case of railway porters and guards, is sometimes looked upon in the light of a dead letter, there is, I sincerely believe, no such thing as any grasping after a guerdon nor any neglect in a case where it is evident no guerdon is to be expected. There is an hospital I could name in which the nurses are prohibited from accepting from patients any more substantial recognition of their services than a nosegay of flowers. The wards of this hospital are always gay with bright, fragrant posies, most of them the contributions of those who, having been carefully tended in their need, retain a grateful recollection of the kindness and now that they are in health again take this simple, pretty way of showing their gratitude. It is two years ago since a rough bricklayer's labourer got mended in the accident ward of this hospital of some curiously complicated injuries he had received by tumbling from the top of a house. Not a Sunday afternoon has there been since the house-surgeon told him one morning that he might go out, that he has not religiously visited the "Albert" ward and brought his thank-offering in the shape of a cheap but grateful nosegay.

Those nurses who thus devote themselves to the tending of sick have often curious histories if anybody would be at the trouble of collecting them. It is by no means always mere regard for the securing of the necessaries of life which has brought them to the thankless and toilsome occupation. We have all read of nunneries in which women immured themselves, anxious to sequester themselves from all association with the outer world and to devote themselves to a life of penance and devotion. After all their piety was aimless and of no utility to humanity. There was a concentrated selfishness in it which detracted from its ambitious aspiration. But in the modern nuns of our hospitals methinks we have women who, abnegating with equal solicitude the pleasures and dissipations of the world, find a more philanthropic opening for their exertions in their retirement than in sleeping on hair pallets, and in eating nothing but parched peas.

It was towards the autumn of a recent year that a modest-looking young woman applied to me for a situation on our nursing staff. She wore a widow's dress and seemed a self-contained, reserved little woman, with something weighing very heavily on her mind. Her testimonials of character were ample and of a very high order but they did not enlighten me with any great freedom as to her past history, and she for her part appeared by no means eager to supplement the meagre information furnished by them. However, people have a right to keep their own counsel if they please, and there was no sin in the woman's reticence. We happened to be very short of efficient nurses at the time and she was at once taken upon trial; her somewhat strange stipulation, which she made absolute, being agreed to—that she should not be compelled to reside in the hospital, but merely come in to perform her turn of nursing, and that over, be at liberty to leave the precincts when she pleased. I say the stipulation was a strange one, because attached to it there was a considerable pecuniary sacrifice as well as a necessity for entering a lower grade.

She made a very excellent nurse, with her quiet, reserved ways and her manner of moving about a ward as if she studied the lightness of every footfall. But she had her peculiarities. I have already said that she was not given to be communicative, and for the first three months she was in the place I do not believe she uttered a word to any one within the walls except on subjects connected with the performance of her duties. Then, too, she manifested a curious fondness for being on duty in the accident ward. Most nurses have very little liking for this ward—the work is very heavy and unremitting and frequently the sights are more than usually repulsive. But she specially made application to be placed in it, and the more terrible the nature of the accident the more eager was her zeal to minister to the poor victim. It seemed almost a morbid fondness which she developed for waiting, in particular, upon people injured by railway accidents. When some poor mangled plate-layer or a railway-porter crushed almost out of resemblance to humanity would be borne in and laid on an empty cot in the accident ward, this woman was at the bedside with a seemingly intuitive perception of what would best conduce to soothe and ease the poor shattered fellow; and she would wait on him "hand and foot" with an intensity of devotion far in excess of what mere duty, however conscientiously fulfilled, would have demanded of her. Indeed, her partiality for railway "cases" was so marked that it appeared to amount to a passion; and among the other nurses, never slow to fix upon any peculiarity and base upon it some not unfriendly nickname, our quiet friend went by the name of "Railway Lizz." Nobody ever got any clue to the reason, if there was one, for this predilection of hers. Indeed, nobody ever was favoured with the smallest scrap of her confidence. I confess to have felt much interest in the sad-eyed young widow and to have several times given her an opening which she might have availed herself of for narrating something of her past life; but she always retired within herself with a sensitiveness which puzzled me not a little, satisfied as I was that there was nothing in her antecedents of a character which would not bear the light.

There are few holidays within an hospital. Physical suffering is not to be mitigated by a gala day; the pressure of disease cannot be lightened by

L

jollity and merry-making. One New Year's Eve, when the world outside our walls was glad of heart, a poor shattered form was borne into the accident ward. It was a railway-porter whom a train had knocked down and passed over, crushing the young fellow almost out of the shape of humanity. Railway Lizz was by his side in a moment, wetting the pain-parched lips and smoothing the pillow of the half-conscious sufferer. The house-surgeon came and went with that silent shake of the head we know too surely how to interpret, and the mangled railway-porter was left in the care of his assiduous nurse. It was almost midnight when I again entered the accident ward. The night-lamp was burning feebly, shedding a dull dim light over the great room and throwing out huge grotesque shadows on the floor and the walls. I glanced toward the railway-porter's bed, and the tell-tale screen placed around it told me that all was over and that the life had gone out of the shattered casket. As I walked down the room toward the screen I heard a low subdued sound of bitter sobbing behind it; and when I stepped within it, there was the sad-faced widow-nurse weeping as if her heart would break. When she saw me she strove hard to repress her emotion and to resume the quiet, self-possessed demeanour which it was her wont to wear; but she failed in the attempt and the sobs burst out in almost convulsive rebellion against the effort to repress them. I put my arm round the neck of the poor young thing and stooping down kissed her wet cheek as a tear from my own eye mingled with her profuse weeping. The evidence of feeling appeared to overpower her utterly; she buried her head in my lap, and lay long there sobbing like a child. When the acuteness of the emotion had somewhat spent itself I gently raised her up, and asked of her what was the cause of a grief so poignant. I found that I was now at last within the intrenchments of her reserve; with a deep sigh she said, in her Scottish accent, that it was "a lang, lang story," but if I cared to hear it she would tell it. So sitting there, we two together in the dim twilight of the night-lamp, with the shattered corpse of the railway-porter lying there "streekit" decently before us, she told the following pathetic tale:—

"I am an Aberdeen girl by birth. My father was the foreman at a factory, a very stiff, dour man, but a gude father, and an upright, God-fearing man. When I was about eighteen, I fell acquainted with a railway-guard, a winsome, manly lad as ever ye would wish to see. If ye had kent my Alick, ye wadna wonder at me for what I did. My father was a proud man, and he couldna bear that I should marry a man that he said wasna my equal in station; and in his firm, masterful way he forbade Alick from coming about the house, and me from seeing him. It was a sair trial, and I dinna think ony father has a right to put doon his foot and mar the happiness of twa young folks in the way mine did. The struggle was a bitter ane, between a father's commands and the bidding of true luve; and at last, ae night coming home from a friend's house, Alick and I forgathered again, and he swore he would not gang till I had promised I would marry him afore the week was out.

"I'll not trouble ye with lang details of the battle that I fought with mysel', and how in the end Alick conquered. We were married in the West Kirk the Sunday after, and we twa set up our simple housekeeping in a single room in a house by the back of the Infirmary. Oh, mem, we were happy young things! Alick was the fondest, kindest man ye could ever think of. Sometimes he wad take me a jaunt the length of Perth in the van with him, and point out the places of interest on the road as we went flashing by them. Then on the Sunday, when he was off duty, we used to take a walk out to the Torry Lighthouse, or down by the auld brig o' Balgownie, and then hame to an hour's read of the Bible afore I put down the kebbuck and the bannocks. My father keepit hard and unforgiving; they tellt me he had sworn an oath I should never darken his door again, and at times I felt very sairly the bitterness of his feeling toward me, whan I was sitting up waiting for Alick's hame-coming whan he was on the night turn; but then he wad come in with his blithe smile and cheery greeting and every thought but joy at his presence wad flee awa as if by magic. Some of the friends I had kent when a lassie at home still keepit up the acquantance, and we used sometimes to spend an evening at one of their houses. The New Year time came, and Alick and myself got an invitation to keep our New Year's Eve at the house of a decent, elderly couple that lived up near the Kitty Brewster Station—quiet, retired folk that had been in business and made enough to live comfortable on. It was Alick's night for the late mail train from Perth, but he would be at Market Street

Station in time to get up among us to see the auld year out and the new ane in; and I was to spend the evening there and wait for his arrival.

"It was a vera happy time. The auld couple were as kind as kind could be, and their twa or three young folks keepit up the fun brisk and lively. I took a hand at the cairts and sang a lilt like the rest; but I was luiking for Alick's company to fill up my cup of happiness. The time wore on, and it was getting close to the hour at which he might be expectit. I kenna what ailed me, but I felt strangely uneasy and anxious for his coming. 'Here he is at last!' I said to myself, as my heart gave a jump at the sound of a foot on the gravel walk. As it came closer, I kent it wasna Alick's step, and a strange, cauld grip of fear and doubt caught me at the heart. Mr. Thomson, that was the name of our old friend, was called out, and I overheard the sound of a whispered conversation in the passage. Then he put his head in and called out his wife; I could see his face was as white as a sheet, and his voice shook in spite of himself. The boding of misfortune came upon me with a force it was in vain to strive against, and I rose up and gaed out into the passage amang them. The auld man was shakin' like an aspen leaf; the gudewife had her apron ower her face and was greeting like a bairn, and in the door stood Tam Farquharson, a railway-porter frae the station. I saw it aa' quicker nor I can tell it to you, leddy. I steppit up to Tam and charged him simple and straught.

"'Tam, what's happent to my Alick?'

"The wet tears stood in Tam's e'en as he

answered, 'Dinna speer, Lizzie, my puir lass, dinna speer, whan the answer maun be a waefu' ane.'

"'Tell me the warst, Tam,' says I; 'let me hear the warst, an' pit me oot o' my pain!'

"The words are dirlin' and stoonin' in my ears yet—

"'The engine gaed ower him, and he's lyin' dead at Market Street.'

"I didna faint, and I couldna greet. Something gied a crack inside my head, and my e'en swam for a minute; but the next I was putting on my bonnet and shawl and saying good-nicht to Mrs. Thomson. They tried to stop me. I heard Tam whisper to the auld man, 'She maunna see him. He is mangled oot o' the shape o' man.'

"But I wasna to be gainsaid, and Tam took my airm as we gaed doon through the toon to Market Street. There they tried hard to keep him oot frae my sight. They tellt me he wasna fit to be seen, but there's nae law that can keep a wife frae seeing her husband's corpse. He was lying in a waiting-room covered up with a sheet, and, oh me, he was sair, sair mangled—that puir fellow there is naething to him; but the winsome, manly face, with the sweet, familiar smile on it, was nane spoiled; and lang, lang, I sat there, us twa alane, with my hand on his cauld forehead, playing wi' his bonnie waving hair. They left me there, in their considerate kindliness, till the cauld light o' the New Year's morning began to break, and syne they came and tellt me I maun go. But I wadna gang my lane. He was mine, and mine only, sae lang as he was abune the mools; and I claimed my dead hame wi' me, to that hoose he had left sae brisk and sprichtly whan he kissed me in the morning. Four of the railway-porters carried him up to that hame which had lost its hame-look for me now. I keepit him to mysel' till they took him awa' frae me and laid him under a saugh tree in the Spittal Kirkyard."

She paused in her story, overcome by the bitter memory of the past, and I wanted no formal application now to give me the clue to her strange preference for the accident ward and her hitherto inexplicable fondness for "railway cases." Poor thing, with what inexpressible vividness must the circumstances in which this New Year's night was passing with her have recalled the sad remembrances of that other New Year's night the narrative of which she had just given me! Presently she recovered her voice, and briefly concluded the little history.

"Leddy, I was wi' bairn when my Alick was taken from me. Oh, how I used to pray that God would be gude to me, and give me a living keepsake of my dead husband! I troubled naebody. I never speered if my father would do anything for me; but I got work at the factory, and I lived in prayerful hope. My hour of trouble came, and a fatherless laddie was born into this weary world, the very picture o' him that was sleeping under the tree in the Spittal Kirkyard. I needna tell ye I christened him Alick, and the bairn has been my joy and comfort ever since God gifted me with him. I found the sichts and memories of Aberdeen ower muckle for me, sae I came up to London here, and ye ken the rest about me. It was because of being with my bairn that I wouldna agree to live in the hospital here like the rest of the nurses, and whan I gang hame noo to my little garret, he will waken up out of his saft sleep, rosy and fresh, and hold up his bonnie mou', sae like his father's, for 'mammie's kiss.'"

MY NATIVE SALMON RIVER

NONE of the greater rivers of Scotland makes so much haste to reach the ocean as does the turbulent and impatient Spey. From its parent lochlet in the bosom of the Grampians it speeds through Badenoch, the country of Cluny MacPherson, the chief of Clan Chattan, a region to this day redolent of memories of the '45. It abates its hurry as its current skirts the grave of the beautiful Jean Maxwell, Duchess of Gordon, who raised the 92nd Highlanders by giving a kiss with the King's shilling to every recruit, and who now since many long years

> Sleeps beneath Kinrara's willow.

But after this salaam of courtesy the river roars and bickers down the long stretch of shaggy glen which intervenes between the upper and lower Rocks of Craigellachie, whence the Clan Grant, whose habitation is this ruggedly beautiful strath, takes its slogan of "Stand fast, Craigellachie," till it finally sends its headlong torrent shooting miles out through the salt water of the Moray Firth. In its course of over a hundred miles its fierce current has seldom tarried; yet now and again it spreads panting into a long smooth stretch of still water when wearied momentarily with buffeting the boulders in its broken and contorted bed; or when a great rock, jutting out into its course, causes a deep black sullen pool whose sluggish eddy is crested with masses of yellow foam. Merely as a wayfaring pedestrian I have followed Spey from its source to its mouth; but my intimacy with it in the character of a fisherman extends over the five-and-twenty miles of its lower course, from the confluence of the pellucid Avon at Ballindalloch to the bridge of Fochabers, the native village of the Captain Wilson who died so gallantly in the recent fighting in Matabeleland. My first Spey trout I took out of water at the foot of the cherry orchard below the sweet-lying cottage of Delfur. My first grilse I hooked and played with trout tackle in "Dalmunach" on the Laggan water, a pool that is the rival of "Dellagyl" and the "Holly Bush" for the proud title of the best pool of lower Spey. My first salmon I brought to the gaff with a beating heart in that fine swift stretch of water known as "The Dip," which connects the pools of the "Heathery Isle" and the "Red Craig," and which is now leased by that good fisherman, Mr. Justice North. I think the Dundurcas water then belonged to the late Mr. Little Gilmour, the well-known welter-weight who went so well to hounds season after season from Melton Mowbray, and who was as keen in the water on Spey as he was over the Leicestershire pastures. A servant of Mr. Little Gilmour was drowned in the "Two Stones" pool, the next below the "Holly Bush;" and the next pool below the "Two Stones" is called the "Beaufort" to this day—named after the present Duke, who took many a big fish out of it in the days when he used to come to Speyside with his friend Mr. Little Gilmour.

In those long gone-by days brave old Lord Saltoun, the hero of Hougomont, resided during the fishing season in the mansion-house of Auchinroath, on the high ground at the mouth of the Glen of Rothes. One morning, some five-and-forty years ago, my father drove to breakfast with the old lord and took me with him. Not caring to send the horse to the stable, he left me outside in the dogcart when he entered the house. As I waited rather sulkily—for I was mightily hungry—there came out on to the doorstep a very queer-looking old person, short of figure, round as a ball, his head sunk between very high and rounded shoulders, and with short stumpy legs. He was curiously attired in a whole-coloured suit of gray; a droll-shaped jacket the great collar of which reached far up the back of his head, surmounted a pair of voluminous breeches which suddenly tightened at the knee. I imagined him to be the butler in morning dishabille; and when he accosted me good-naturedly, asking to whom the dogcart and myself belonged, I answered him somewhat shortly and then ingenuously suggested that he would be doing me a kindly act if he would go and fetch me out a hunk of bread and meat, for I was enduring tortures of hunger.

Then he swore, and that with vigour and fluency, that it was a shame that I should have been left outside; called a groom and bade me alight and come indoors with him. I demurred—I had got the paternal injunction to remain with the horse and cart. "I am master here!" exclaimed the old person impetuously; and with further strong language he expressed his intention of rating my father soundly for not having brought me inside along with himself. Then a question occurred to me, and I ventured to ask, "Are you Lord Saltoun?" "Of course I am," replied the old gentleman; "who the devil else should I be?" Well, I did not like to avow what I felt, but in truth I was hugely disappointed in him; for I had just been reading Siborne's *Waterloo*, and to think that this dumpy old fellow in the duffle jacket that came up over his ears was the valiant hero who had held Hougomont through cannon fire and musketry fire and hand-to-hand bayonet fighting on the day of Waterloo while the post he was defending was ablaze, and who had actually killed Frenchmen with his own good sword, was a severe disenchantment. When I had breakfasted he asked leave of my father to let me go with him to the waterside, promising to send me home safely later in the day. When he was in Spey up to the armpits—for the "Holly Bush" takes deep wading from the Dundurcas side—the old lord looked even droller than he had done on the Auchinroath doorstep, and I could not reconcile him in the least to my Hougomont ideal. He was delighted when I opened on him with that topic, and he told me with great spirit of the vehemence with which his brother-officer Colonel Macdonnell, and his men forced the French soldiers out of the Hougomont courtyard, and how big Sergeant Graham closed the door against them by main force of muscular strength. Before he had been in the water twenty minutes the old lord was in a fish;

his gillie, old Dallas, who could throw a fine line in spite of the whisky, gaffed it scientifically, and I was sent home rejoicing with a 15 lb. salmon for my mother and a half-sovereign for myself wherewith to buy a trouting rod and reel. Lord Saltoun was the first lord I ever met, and I have never known one since whom I have liked half so well.

Spey is a river which insists on being distinctive. She mistrusts the stranger. He may be a good man on Tweed or Tay, but until he has been formally introduced to Spey and been admitted to her acquaintance, she is chary in according him her favours. She is no flighty coquette, nor is she a prude; but she has her demure reserves, and he who would stand well with her must ever treat her with consideration and respect. She is not as those facile demi-mondaine streams, such as the Helmsdale or the Conon, which let themselves be entreated successfully by the chance comer on the first jaunty appeal. You must learn the ways of Spey before you can prevail with her, and her ways are not the ways of other rivers. It was in vain that the veteran chief of southern fishermen, the late Francis Francis, threw his line over Spey in the *veni, vidi, vici* manner of one who had made Usk and Wye his potsherd, and who over the Hampshire Avon had cast his shoe. Russel, the famous editor of the *Scotsman*, the Delane of the north country, who, pen in hand, could make a Lord Advocate squirm, and before whose gibe provosts and bailies trembled, who had drawn out leviathan with a hook from Tweed, and before whom the big fish of Forth could not stand—even he, brilliant fisherman as he was, could "come nae speed ava" on Spey, as the old Arndilly water-gillie quaintly worded it.

Yet Russel of the *Scotsman* was perhaps the most whole-souled salmon fisher of his own or any other period. His piscatorial aspirations extended beyond the grave. Who that heard it can ever forget the peroration, slightly profane perhaps, but entirely enthusiastic, of his speech on salmon fishing at a Tweedside dinner? "When I die," he exclaimed in a fine rapture, "should I go to heaven, I will fish in the water of life with a fly dressed with a feather from the wing of an angel; should I be unfortunately consigned to another destination, I shall nevertheless hope to angle in Styx with the worm that never dieth." To his editorial successor Spey was a trifle more gracious than she had been to Russel; but she did not wholly open her heart to this neophyte of her stream, serving him up in the pool of Dellagyl with the ugliest, blackest, gauntest old cock-salmon of her depths, owning a snout like the prow of an ancient galley.

Spey exacts from those who would fish her waters with success a peculiar and distinctive method of throwing their line, which is known as the "Spey cast." In vain has Major Treherne illustrated the successive phases of the "Spey cast" in the fishing volume of the admirable Badminton series. It cannot be learned by diagrams; no man, indeed, can become a proficient in it who has not grown up from childhood in the practice of it. Yet its use is absolutely indispensable to the salmon angler on the Spey. Rocks, trees, high banks, and other impediments forbid resort to the overhead cast. The essence and value of the Spey cast lies in this—that his line must never go behind the caster; well done, the cast is like the dart from a howitzer's mouth of a safety rocket to which a line is attached. To watch it performed, strongly yet easily, by a skilled hand is a liberal education in the art of casting ; the swiftness, sureness, low trajectory, and lightness of the fall of the line, shot out by a dexterous swish of the lifting and propelling power of the strong yet supple rod, illustrate a phase at once beautiful and practical of the poetry of motion. Among the native salmon fishermen of Speyside, *quorum ego parva pars fui*, there are two distinct manners which may be severally distinguished as the easy style and the masterful style. The disciples of the easy style throw a fairly long line, but their aim is not to cover a maximum distance. What they pride themselves on is precise, dexterous, and, above all, light and smooth casting. No fierce switchings of the rod reveal their approach before they are in sight; like the clergyman of Pollok's *Course of Time* they love to draw rather than to drive. Of the masterful style the most brilliant exponent is a short man, but he is the deepest wader in Spey. I believe his waders fasten, not round his waist, but round his neck. I have seen him in a pool, far beyond his depth, but "treading water" while simultaneously wielding a rod about four times the length of himself, and sending his line whizzing an extraordinary distance. The resolution of his attack seems actually to hypnotise salmon into taking his fly ; and, once hooked, however hard they may fight for life, they are doomed fish.

Ah me! These be gaudy, flaunting, flashy days!

Our sober Spey, in the matter of salmon fly-hooks, is gradually yielding to the garish influence of the times. Spey salmon now begin to allow themselves to be captured by such indecorous and revolutionary fly-hooks as the "Canary" and the "Silver Doctor." Jaunty men in loud suits of dittoes have come into the north country, and display fly-books that vie in the variegated brilliancy of their contents with a Dutch tulip bed. We staunch adherents to the traditional Spey blacks and browns, we who have bred Spey cocks for the sake of their feathers, and have sworn through good report and through evil report by the pig's down or Berlin wool for body, the Spey cock for hackle, and the mallard drake for wings, have jeered at the kaleidoscopic fantasticality of the leaves of their fly-books turned over by adventurers from the south country and Ireland; and have sneered at the notion that a self-respecting Spey salmon would so far demoralise himself as to be allured by a miniature presentation of Liberty's shop-window. But the salmon has not regarded the matter from our conservative point of view; and now we, too, ruefully resort to the "canary" as a dropper when conditions of atmosphere and water seem to favour that gaudy implement. And it must be owned that even before the "twopence-coloured" gentry came among us from distant parts, we, the natives, had been side-tracking from the exclusive use of the old-fashioned sombre flies into the occasional use of gayer yet still modest "fancies." Of specific Spey hooks in favour at the present time the following is, perhaps, a fairly correct and comprehensive list: purple king, green king, black king, silver heron, gold heron, black dog, silver riach, gold riach, black heron, silver green, gold green, Lady Caroline, carron, black fancy, silver spale, gold spale, culdrain, dallas, silver thumbie, Sebastopol, Lady Florence March, gold purpie, and gled (deadly in "snawbree"). The Spey cock—a cross between the Hamburg cock and the old Scottish mottled hen—was fifty years ago bred all along Speyside expressly for its feathers, used in dressing salmon flies; but the breed is all but extinct now, or rather, perhaps, has been crossed and re-crossed out of recognition. It is said, however, to be still maintained in the parish of Advie, and when the late Mr. Bass had the Tulchan shootings and fishings his head keeper used to breed and sell Spey cocks.

Probably the most extensive collection of salmon fly-hooks ever made was that which belonged to the late Mr. Henry Grant of Elchies, a property on which is some of the best water in all the run of Spey. His father was a distinguished Indian civil servant and of later fame as an astronomer; and his elder brother, Mr. Grant of Carron, was one of the best fishermen that ever played a big fish in the pool of Dellagyl. Henry Grant himself had been a keen fisherman in his youth, and when, after a chequered and roving life in South Africa and elsewhere, he came into the estate, he set himself to build up a representative collection of salmon flies for all waters and all seasons. His father had brought home a large and curious assortment of feathers from the Himalayas; Mr. Grant sent far and wide for further supplies of suitable and distinctive material, and then he devoted himself to the task of dressing hundred

M

after hundred of fly-hooks of every known pattern and of every size, from the great three-inch hook for heavy spring water to the dainty little "finnock" hook scarcely larger than a trout fly. A suitable receptacle was constructed for this collection from the timber of the "Auld Gean Tree of Elchies"—the largest of its kind in all Scotland—whose trunk had a diameter of nearly four feet and whose branches had a spread of over twenty yards. The "Auld Gean Tree" fell into its dotage and was cut down to the strains of a "lament," with which the wail and skirl of the bagpipes drowned the noise of the woodmen's axes. Out of the wood of the "Auld Gean Tree" a local artificer constructed a handsome cabinet with many drawers, in which were stored the Elchies collection of fly-hooks classified carefully according to their sizes and kinds. The cabinet stood—and, I suppose, still stands—in the Elchies billiard-room; but I fear the collection is sadly diminished, for Henry Grant was the freest-handed of men and towards the end of his life anybody who chose was welcome to help himself from the contents of the drawers. Yet no doubt some relics of this fine collection must still remain; and I hope for his own sake that Mr. Justice A. L. Smith the present tenant of Elchies, is free of poor Henry's cabinet.

It is a popular delusion that Speyside men are immortal; this is true only of distillers. But it is a fact that their longevity is phenomenal. If Dr. Ogle had to make up the population returns of Strath Spey he could not fail to be profoundly astonished by the comparative blankness of the mortality columns. Frederick the Great, when his fellows were rather hanging back in the crisis of a battle, stung them with the biting taunt, "Do you wish to live for ever?" If his descendant of the present day were to address the same question to the seniors of Speyside, they would probably reply, "Your Majesty, we ken that we canna live for ever; but, faith, we mak' a gey guid attempt!" A respected relative of mine died a few years ago at the age of eighty-five. Had he been a Southron, he would have been said to have died full of years; but of my relative the local paper remarked in a touching obituary notice that he "was cut off prematurely in the midst of his mature prime." When I was young, Speyside men mostly shuffled off this mortal coil by being upset from their gigs when driving home recklessly from market with "the maut abune the meal;" but the railways have done away in great measure with this cause of death. Nowadays the centenarians for the most part fall ultimate victims to paralysis. In the south it is understood, I believe, that the third shock is fatal; but a Speyside man will resist half a dozen shocks before he succumbs, and has been known to walk to the kirk after having endured even a greater number of attacks.

Among the senior veterans of our riverside I may venture to name two most worthy men and fine salmon fishers. Although both have now wound in their reels and unspliced their rods, one of them still lives among us hale and hearty. "Jamie" Shanks of Craigellachie is, perhaps, the father of the water. He himself is reticent as to his age and there are legends on the subject which lack authentication.

It is, however, a matter of tradition that Jamie was out in the '45; and that, cannily returning home when Charles Edward turned back at Derby, he earned the price of a croft by showing the Duke of Cumberland the ford across Spey near the present bridge of Fochabers, by which the "butcher duke" crossed the river on his march to fight the battle of Culloden. It is also traditioned that Jamie danced round a bonfire in celebration of the marriage of "bonnie Jean," Duchess of Gordon, an event which occurred in 1767. Apart from the Dark Ages one thing is certain regarding Jamie, that the great flood of 1829 swept away his croft and cottage, he himself so narrowly escaping that he left his watch hanging on the bed-post, watch and bed-post being subsequently recovered floating about in the Moray Firth. The greatest honour that can be conferred on a fisherman—the Victoria Cross of the river—has long belonged to Jamie; a pool in Spey bears his name, and many a fine salmon has been taken out of "Jamie Shanks's Pool," the swirling water of which is almost at the good old man's feet as he shifts the "coo" on his strip of pasture or watches the gooseberries swelling in his pretty gárden. His fame has long ago gone throughout all Speyside for skill in the use of the gaff: about eight years ago I was witness of the calm, swift dexterity with which he gaffed what I believe was his last fish. In the serene evening of his long day he still finds pleasant occupation in dressing salmon flies; and if you speak him fair and he is in good humour "Jamie" may let you have half a dozen as a great favour.

The other veteran of our river of whom I would

say something was that most worthy man and fine salmon fisher Mr. Charles Grant, the ex-schoolmaster of Aberlour, better known among us who loved and honoured the fine old Highland gentleman as "Charlie" Grant. Charlie no longer lives; but to the last he was hale, relished his modest dram, and delighted in his quiet yet graphic manner to tell of men and things of Speyside familiar to him during his long life by the riverside. Charles Grant was the first person who ever rented salmon water on Spey. It was about 1838 that he took a lease from the Fife trustees of the fishing on the right bank from the burn of Aberlour to the burn of Carron, about four miles of as good water as there is in all the run of Spey. This water would to-day be cheaply rented at £250 per annum; the annual rent paid by Charles Grant was two guineas. A few years later a lease was granted by the Fife trustees of the period of the grouse shootings of Benrinnes, the wide moorlands of the parishes of Glass, Mortlach, and Aberlour, including Glenmarkie the best moor in the county, at a rent of £100 a year with four miles of salmon water on Spey thrown in. The letting value of these moors and of this water is to-day certainly not less than £1500 a year.

Charles Grant had a great and well-deserved reputation for finding a fish in water which other men had fished blank. This was partly because from long familiarity with the river he knew all the likeliest casts; partly because he was sure to have at the end of his casting-line just the proper fly for the size of water and condition of weather; and partly because of his quiet neat-handed manner of dropping his line on the water. There is a story still current on Speyside illustrative of this gift of Charlie in finding a fish where people who rather fancied themselves had failed—a story which Jamie Shanks to this day does not care to hear. Mr. Russel of the *Scotsman* had done his very best from the quick run at the top of the pool of Dalbreck, down to the almost dead-still water at the bottom of that fine stretch, and had found no luck. Jamie Shanks, who was with Mr. Russel as his fisherman, had gone over it to no purpose with a fresh fly. They were grumpishly discussing whether they should give Dalbreck another turn or go on to Pool-o-Brock the next pool down stream, when Charles Grant made his appearance and asked the waterside question, "What luck?" "No luck at all, Charlie!" was Russel's answer. "Deevil a rise!" was Shanks's sourer reply. In his demure purring way Charles Grant—who in his manner was a duplicate of the late Lord Granville—remarked, "There ought to be a fish come out of that pool." "Tak' him out, then!" exclaimed Shanks gruffly. "Well, I'll try," quoth the soft-spoken Charlie; and just at that spot, about forty yards from the head of the pool, where the current slackens and the fish lie awhile before breasting the upper rapid, he hooked a fish. Then it was that Russel in the genial manner which made provosts swear, remarked, "Shanks, I advise you to take a half year at Mr. Grant's school!" "Fat for?" inquired Shanks sullenly. "To learn to fish!" replied the master of sarcasm of the delicate Scottish variety.

Respectful by nature to their superiors, the honest

working folk of Speyside occasionally forget themselves comically in their passionate ardour that a hooked salmon shall be brought to bank. Lord Elgin, now in his Indian satrapy, far away from what Sir Noel Paton in his fine elegy on the late Sir Alexander Gordon Cumming of Altyre called

> The rushing thunder of the Spey,

one day hooked a big fish in the "run" below "Polmet." The fish headed swiftly down stream, his lordship in eager pursuit, but afraid of putting any strain on the line lest the salmon should "break" him. Down round the bend below the pool and by the "Slabs" fish and fisherman sped, till the latter was brought up by the sheer rock of Craigellachie. Fortunately a fisherman ferried the Earl across the river to the side on which he was able to follow the fish. On he ran, keeping up with the fish, under the bridge, along the margin of "Shanks's Pool," past the "Boat of Fiddoch" pool and the mouth of the tributary; and he was still on the run along the edge of the croft beyond when he was suddenly confronted by an aged man, who dropped his turnip hoe and ran eagerly to the side of the young nobleman. Old Guthrie could give advice from the experience of a couple of generations as poacher, water-gillie, occasional water-bailiff, and from as extensive and peculiar acquaintance with the river as Sam Weller possessed of London public-houses. And this is what he exclaimed: "Ma Lord, ma Lord, gin ye dinna check him, that fush will tak' ye doun tae Speymouth—deil, but he'll tow ye oot tae sea! Hing intil him, hing intil him!" His lordship exerted himself accordingly, but did not secure the old fellow's approval. "Man! man!" Guthrie yelled, "ye're nae pittin' a twa-ounce strain on him; he's makin' fun o' ye!" The nobleman tried yet harder, yet could not please his relentless critic. "God forgie me, but ye canna fush worth a damn! Come back on the lan', an' gie him the butt wi' pith!" Thus adjured, his lordship acted at last with vigour; the sage, having gaffed the fish, abated his wrath, and, as the salmon was being "wetted," tendered his respectful apologies.

In my time there have been three lairds of Arndilly, a beautiful Speyside estate which is margined by several miles of fishing water hardly inferior to any throughout the long run of the river. Many a man, far away now from "bonnie Arndilly" and the hoarse murmur of the river's roll over its rugged bed, recalls in wistful recollection the swift yet smooth flow of "the Dip;" the thundering rush of Spey against the "Red Craig," in the deep, strong water at the foot of which the big red fish leap like trout when the mellowness of the autumn is tinting into glow of russet and crimson the trees which hang on the steep bank above; the smooth restful glide into the long oily reach of the "Lady's How," in which a fisherman may spend to advantage the livelong day and then not leave it fished out; the turbulent half pool, half stream, of the "Piles," which always holds large fish lying behind the great stones or in the dead water under the daisy-sprinkled bank on which the tall beeches cast their shadows; the "Bulwark Pool;" the "Three Stones," where the grilse show their silver sides in the late May evenings; "Gilmour's" and "Carnegie's," the latter now, alas! spoiled by gravel; the quaintly named "Tam Mear's Crook" and the "Spout o' Cobblepot;" and then the dark, sullen swirls of "Sourdon," the deepest pool of Spey.

The earliest of the three Arndilly lairds of my time was the Colonel, a handsome, generous man of the old school, who was as good over High Leicestershire as he was over his own moors and on his own water, and who, while still in the prime of life, died of cholera abroad. Good in the saddle and with the salmon rod, the Colonel was perhaps best behind a gun, with which he was not less deadly among the salmon of the Spey than among the grouse of Benaigen. His relative, old Lord Saltoun, was hard put to it once in the "Lady's How" with a thirty-pound salmon which he had hooked foul, and which, in its full vigour, was taking all manner of liberties with him, making spring after spring clean out of the water. The beast was so rebellious and strong that the old lord found it harder to contend with than with the Frenchmen who fought so stoutly with him for the possession of Hougomont. The Colonel, fowling-piece in hand, was watching the struggle, and seeing that Lord Saltoun was getting the worst of it awaited his opportunity when the big salmon's tail was in the air after a spring, and, firing in the nick of time, cut the fish's spine just above the tail, hardly marking it elsewhere. The Colonel occasionally fished the river with cross-lines, which are still legal although their use is now considered rather the "Whitechapel game." He resorted to the cross-lines, not in greed for fish but for the sake of the shooting practice they afforded him. When the hooked fish were struggling and in their struggles showing their tails out of water, he several times shot two right and left breaking the spine in each case close to the tail.

The Colonel was succeeded by his brother, who had been a planter in Jamaica before coming to the estate on the death of his brother. Hardly was he home when he contested the county unsuccessfully on the old never-say-die Protectionist platform against the father of the present Duke of Fife; on the first polling-day of which contest I acquired a black eye and a bloody nose in the market square of a local village at the hands of some gutter lads, with whose demand that I should take the Tory rosette out of my bonnet I had declined to comply. Later, this gentleman became an assiduous fisher of men as a lay preacher, but he was as keen after salmon as he was after sinners. He hooked and played—and gaffed—the largest salmon I have ever heard of being caught in Spey by an angler—a fish weighing forty-six pounds. The actual present laird of Arndilly is a lady, but in her son are perpetuated the fishing instincts of his forbears.

My reminiscences of Spey and Speyside are drawing to an end, and I now with natural diffidence approach a great theme. Every Speyside man will recognise from this exordium that I am about to treat of "Geordie." It is quite understood throughout lower Speyside that it is the moral support which Geordie accords to Craigellachie Bridge, in the immediate vicinity of which he lives, that chiefly maintains that structure; and that if he were to withdraw that support, its towers and roadway would incontinently collapse into the depths of the sullen pool spanned by the graceful erection. The best of men are not universally popular, and it must be said that there are those who cast on Geordie the aspersion of being "some thrawn," for which the equivalent in south-country language is perhaps "a trifle cross-grained." These, however, are envious people, who are jealous of Geordie's habitual association with lords and dukes, and who resent the trivial stiffness which is no doubt apparent in his manner to ordinary people for the first few days after the illustrious persons referred to have reluctantly permitted him to withdraw from them the light of his countenance. For my own part I have found Geordie, all things considered, to be wonderfully affable. That his tone is patronising I do not deny; but then there is surely a joy in being patronised by the factotum of a duke.

I have never been quite sure, nor have I ever dared to ask Geordie, whether he considers the Duke to be his patron, or whether he regards himself as the patron of that eminent nobleman. From the "aucht-and-forty daugh" of Strathbogie to the Catholic Braes of Glenlivat where fifty years ago the "sma' stills" reeked in every moorland hollow, across to beautiful Kinrara and down Spey to the fertile Braes of Enzie, his Grace is the benevolent despot of a thriving tenantry who have good cause to regard him with esteem and gratitude. The Duke is a masterful man, whom no factor need attempt to lead by the nose; but on the margin of Spey, from the blush-red crags of Cairntie down to the head of tide water, he owns his centurion in Geordie, who taught him to throw his first line when already he was a minister of the Crown, and who, as regards aught appertaining to salmon fishing, saith unto his Grace, Do this and he doeth it.

Geordie is a loyal subject, and when a few years ago he had the opportunity of seeing Her Majesty during her momentary halt at Elgin station, he paid her the compliment of describing her as a "sonsie wife." But the heart-loyalty of the honest fellow goes out in all its tender yet imperious fulness towards the Castle family, to most of the members of which, of both sexes, he has taught the science and practice of killing salmon. Hint the faintest shadow of disparagement of any member of that noble and worthy house, and you make a life enemy of Geordie. On no other subject is he particularly touchy, save one—the gameness and vigour of the salmon of Spey. Make light of the fighting virtues of Spey fish—exalt above them the horn of the salmon of Tay, Ness, or Tweed—and Geordie loses his temper on the instant and overwhelms you with the strongest language. There is a tradition that among Geordie's remote forbears was one of Cromwell's Ironsides who on the march from Aberdeen to Inverness fell in love with a Speyside lass of the period, and who, abandoning his Ironside appellation of "Hew-Agag-in-Pieces," adopted the surname which Geordie now bears. This strain of ancestry may account for Geordie's smooth yet peremptory skill as a disciplinarian. It devolves upon him during the rod-fishing season to assign to each person of the fishing contingent his or her particular stretch of water, and to tell off to each as guide one of his assistant attendants.

It is a great treat to find Geordie in a garrulous humour and to listen to one of his salmon-fishing stories, told always in the broadest of north-country Doric. His sense of humour is singularly keen, notwithstanding that he is a Scot; and it is not in his nature to minimise his own share in the honour and glory of the incident he may relate. One of Geordie's stories is vividly in my recollection, and may appropriately conclude my reminiscences of Speyside and its folk. There was a stoup of "Benrinnes" on the mantelpiece and a free-drawing pipe in Geordie's mouth. His subject was the one on which he can be most eloquent—an incident of the salmon-fishing season, on which the worthy man delivered himself as follows :—

"Twa or three seasons back I was attendin' Leddy Carline whan she was fushin' that gran' pool at the brig o' Fochabers. She's a fine fusher, Leddy Carline : faith, she may weel be, for I taucht her mysel'. She hookit a saumon aboot the midst o' the pool, an' for a while it gied gran' sport; loupin' and tumblin', an' dartin' up the watter an' doon the watter at sic a speed as keepit her leddyship muvin' gey fast tae keep abriesht o't. Weel, this kin' o' wark, an' a ticht line, began for tae tak' the spunk oot o' the saumon, an' I was thinkin' it was a quieston o' a few meenits whan I wad be in him wi' the gaff; but my birkie, near han' spent though he was, had a canny bit dodge up the sleeve o' him. He made a bit whamlin' run, an' deil tak' me gin he didna jam himself intil a neuk atween twa rocks, an' there the dour beggar bade an' sulkit. Weel, her leddyship keepit aye a steady drag on him, an' she gied him the butt wi' power; but she cudna get the beast tae budge—no, nae sae muckle as the breadth o' my thoomb-nail. Deil a word said Leddy Carline tae me for a gey while, as she vrought an' vrought tae gar the saumon quit his neuk. But she cam nae speed wi' him; an' at last she says, says she, 'Geordie, I can make nothing of him: what in the world is to be done?' 'Gie him a shairp upward yark, my leddy,' says I; 'there canna be muckle strength o' resistance left in him by this time!' Weel, she did as I tellt her—I will say this for Leddy Carline, that she's aye biddable. But, rugg her hardest, the fush stuck i' the neuk as gin he waur a bit o' the solid rock, an' her leddyship was becomin' gey an' exhaustit. 'Take the rod yourself, Geordie,' says she, 'and try what you can do; I freely own the fish is too many for me.' Weel, I gruppit the rod, an' I gied a shairp, steady, upward drag; an' up the brute cam, clean spent. He hadna been sulkin' aifter aa'; he had been fairly wedged atween the twa rocks, for whan I landit him, lo an' behold! he was bleedin' like a pig, an' there was a muckle gash i' the side o' him, that the rock had torn whan I draggit him by main force up an' oot. The taikle was stoot, ye'll obsairve, or else he be tae hae broken me; but tak' my word for't, Geordie is no the man for tae lippen tae feckless taikle.

"Weel, I hear maist things; an' I was tellt that same nicht hoo at the denner-table Leddy Carline relatit the haill adventur', an' owned, fat was true aneuch, that the fush had fairly bestit her. Weel, amo' the veesitors at the Castle was the Dowager Leddy Breadanham; an' it seemed that whan Leddy Carline was through wi' her narrateeve, the dowager be tae gie a kin' o' a scornfu' sniff an' cock her neb i' the air; an' she said, wha but she, that she didna hae muckle opingin o' Leddy Carline as a saumon fisher, an' that she hersel' didna believe there was a fush in the run o' Spey that she cudna get the maistery ower. That was a gey big word, min' ye; it's langidge I wadna venture for tae make use o' mysel', forbye a south-countra dowager.

"Weel, I didna say muckle; but, my faith, like the sailor's paurot, I thoucht a deevil o' a lot. The honour o' Spey was in my hauns, an' it behuvit me for tae hummle the pride o' her dowager leddyship. The morn's mornin' cam, an' by that time I had decided on my plan o' operautions. By guid luck I fand the dowager takin' her stroll afore brakfast i' the floor-gairden. I ups till her, maks my boo, an' says I, unco canny an' respectfu', 'My leddy, ye'll likely be for the watter the day?' She said she was, so says I, 'Weel, my leddy, I'll be prood for tae gae wi' ye mysel', an' I'll no fail tae reserve for ye as guid water as there is in the run o' Spey!' She was quite agreeable, an' so we sattlit it.

"The Duke himsel' was oot on the lawn whan I was despatchin' the ither fushin' folk, ilk ane wi' his or her fisherman kerryin' the rod. ''Geordie,' said his Grace, 'with whom will you be going yourself?' 'Wi' the Dowager Leddy Breadanham, yer Grace!' says I. 'And where do you think of taking her ladyship, Geordie?' speers he. ''N'odd, yer Grace,' says I, 'I am sattlin in my min' for tae tak' the leddy tae the "Brig o' Fochabers" pool;' an' wi' that I gied a kin' o' a respectfu' half-wink. The Duke was no' the kin' o' man for tae wink back, for though he's aye grawcious, he's aye dignifeed; but there was a bit flichter o' humour roun' his mou' whan he said, says he, 'I think that will do very well, Geordie!'

"Praesently me an' her leddyship startit for the 'Brig o' Fochabers' pool. She cud be vera affauble whan she likit, I'll say that muckle for the dowager; an' me an' her newsed quite couthie-like as we traivellt. I saftened tae her some, I frankly own; but than my hert hardent again whan I thoucht o' the duty I owed tae Spey an' tae Leddy Carline. Of coorse there was a chance that my scheme wad miscairry; but there's no a man on Spey frae Tulchan tae the Tug Net that kens the natur' o' saumon better nor mysel'. They're like sheep—fat ane daes, the tithers will dae; an' gin the dowager hookit a fush, I hadna muckle doobt fat that fush wad dae. The dowager didna keep me vera lang in suspense. I had only chyngt her fly ance, an' she had maist fushed doon the pool a secont time, whan in the ripple o' watter at the head o' the draw abune the rapid a fush took her 'Riach' wi' a greedy sook, an' the line was rinnin' oot as gin there had been a racehorse at the far end o't, the saumon careerin' up the pool like a flash in the clear watter. The dowager was as fu' o' life as was the fush. Odd, but she kent brawly hoo tae deal wi' her saumon—that I will say for her! There was nae need for me tae bide closs by the side o' a leddy that had boastit there was na a fush in Spey she cudna maister, sae

I clamb up the bank, sat doun on ma doup on a bit hillock, an' took the leeberty o' lichtin' ma pipe. Losh! but that dowager spanged up an' doun the waterside among the stanes aifter that game an' lively fush; an' troth, but she was as souple wi' her airms as wi' her legs; for, rinnin' an' loupin' an' spangin' as she was, she aye managed for tae keep her line ticht. It was a dooms het day, an' there wasna a ruffle o' breeze; sae nae doobt the fush was takin' as muckle oot o' her as she was takin' oot o' the fush. In aboot ten meenits there happent juist fat I had expectit. The fush made a sidelins shoot, an' dairted intil the vera crevice occupeed by Leddy Carline's fush the day afore. 'Noo for the fun!' thinks I, as I sat still an' smokit calmly. She was certently a perseverin' wummun, that dowager—there was nae device she didna try wi' that saumon tae force him oot o' the cleft. Aifter aboot ten meenits mair o' this wark, she shot at me ower her shouther the obsairve, 'Isn't it an obstinate wretch?' 'Aye,' says I pawkily, 'he's gey dour; but he's only a Spey fush, an' of coorse ye'll maister him afore ye've dune wi' him!' I'm thinkin' she unnerstude the insinivation, for she uttert deil anither word, but yokit tee again fell spitefu' tae rug an' yark at the sulkin' fush. At last, tae mak a lang story short, she was fairly dune. 'Geordie,' says she waikly, 'the beast has quite worn me out! I'm fit to melt—there is no strength left in me; here, come and take the rod!' Weel, I deleeberately raise, poocht ma pipe, an' gaed doun aside her. 'My leddy,' says I, quite solemn, an' luikin' her straucht i' the face—haudin' her wi' my ee, like—'I hae been tellt fat yer leddyship said yestreen, that there wasna a saumon in Spey ye cudna maister. Noo, I speer this at yer leddyship—respectfu' but direck; div ye admit yersel clean bestit—fairly lickit wi' that fush, Spey fush though it be? Answer me that, my leddy!' 'I do own myself beaten,' says she, 'and I retract my words.' 'Say nae mair, yer leddyship!' says I—for I'm no a cruel man—' say nae mair, but maybe ye'll hae the justice for tae say a word tae the same effeck in the Castle whaur ye spak yestreen?' 'I promise you I will,' said the dowager —'here, take the rod!' Weel, it was no sae muckle a fush as was Leddy Carline's. I had it oot in a few meenits, an' by that time the dowager was sae far revived that she was able to bring it in aboot tae the gaff; an' sae, in the hinner end, she in a sense maistert the fush aifter aa'. But I'm thinkin' she will be gey cautious in the futur' aboot belittlin' the smeddum o' Spey saumon!

THE CAWNPORE OF TO-DAY

THE traveller up the country from Calcutta does not speedily reach places the names of which vividly recall the episodes of the great Mutiny. It is a chance if, as the train passes Dinapore, he remembers the defection of the Sepoy brigade stationed there which Koer Singh seduced from its allegiance. Arrah may possibly recall a dim memory of Wake's splendid defence of Boyle's bungalow and of Vincent Eyre's dashingly executed relief of the indomitable garrison. Benares is a little off the main line—Benares, on the parade ground of which Neill first put down that peremptory foot of his, where Olpherts was so quick with those guns of his, and where Jim Ellicott did his grim work with noose and cross-beam until long after the going down of the summer sun. But when the traveller's eye first rests on the gray ramparts of Akbar's hoary fortress in the angle where the Ganges and the Jumna meet and blend one with another, the reality of the Mutiny begins to impress itself upon him. Allahabad was the scene of a terrible tragedy; it was also the point of departure whence Havelock set forward on Cawnpore with his column, not indeed of rescue, but of retribution. 'The journey from Allahabad to Cawnpore, although perchance performed in the night, is not one to be slept through by any student of the story of the great rebellion. The Indian moon pours her flood of light on the little knoll hard by Futtehpore, where Havelock stood when Jwala Pershad's first round shot came lobbing through his staff in among the camp kettles of the 64th. That village beyond the mango tope is Futtehpore itself, whence the rebel sowars swept headlong down the trunk road till Maude's guns gave them the word to halt. The pools are dry now through which, when Hamilton's voice had rung out the order—"Forward, at the double!" the light company of the Ross-shire Buffs splashed recklessly past the abandoned Sepoy guns, in their race with the grenadier company of the 64th that had for its goal the Pandy barricade outside the village. In that cluster of mud huts—its name is Aoong—the gallant Rénaud fell with a shattered thigh, as he led his "Lambs" up to the *épaulement* which covered its front. One fight a day is fair allowance anywhere, but those fellows whom Havelock led were gluttons for fighting. Spanning that deep rugged nullah there, down which the Pandoo flows turbulently in the rainy season, is the bridge across which in the afternoon of the morning of Aoong, Stephenson with his Fusiliers dashed into the Sepoy battery and bayoneted the gunners before they could make up their minds to run away. And it was in the gray morning following the day of that double battle (the 15th of July) that the General, having heard for the first time that there were still alive in Cawnpore a number of women and children who had escaped the massacre of the boats, told his men what he knew. "With God's help," shouted Havelock, with a break in his voice that was like a sob, as he stood with his hat off and his hand on his sword—"with God's help, men, we will save them, or every man die in the attempt!" One answer came back in a great cheer; but a sadder answer to the aspiration, a bitter truth that made that aspiration futile and hopeless, had lain ever since the evening of the day before in the Beebeegur, and almost as the chief was speaking the Well was receiving its dead inmates. Where the train begins to slacken its pace on approaching the station, it is passing over the field of the first—the creditable—battle of Cawnpore. Fresh from the butchery Nana Sahib (Dhoondoo Punth) himself had come out to aid in the last stand against the avengers. Yonder is the mango tope which formed the screen for Hamilton's turning movement. It needs little imagination to recall the scene. Close by, at the cross-roads, stands the Sepoy battery, and those horsemen still nearer are reconnoitring sowars. Beyond the road the Highlanders are deploying on the plain as they clear the sheltering flank of the mango trees, amidst a grim silence broken only by the crash of the bursting shells and the cries of the bullock-drivers as the guns rattle on to open fire from the reverse flank. The flush rises in Hamilton's face and the eyes of him begin to sparkle, as he shouts "Ross-shire Buffs, wheel into line!" and then "Forward!" Quick as lightning the trails of the Sepoy guns are swung round and shot and shell come crashing through the ranks, while the rebel infantry, with a swiftness which speaks well for their British drill, show a front against this inroad on their flank. In silent grim imperturbability the Highland line stalks steadily on with the long springy step to be learned only on the heather. Now they are within eighty yards of the muzzles of the guns, and they can see the colour of the mustaches of the men plying and supporting them. Then Hamilton, with his sword in the air and his face all ablaze with the fighting blood in him, turns round in the saddle, shouts "Charge!" and bids the pipers to strike up. Wild and shrill bursts over that Indian plain the rude notes of the Northern music. But louder yet, drowning them and the roll of the artillery, rings out that Highland war-cry that has so often presaged victory to British arms. The Ross-shire men are in and over the guns ere the gunners have time to drop their lint-stocks and ramming-rods; they fall with bayonets at the charge upon the supporting infantry, and the supporting infantry go down where they huddle together, lacking the opportunity to break and run away in time. But the battle rages all day, and the white soldiers, as they fight their way slowly forward, hear the bursts of military music that greet the Nana as he moves from place to place, *not* in the immediate front. Barrow and his handful of cavalry volunteers crash into the thick of them with the informal order to his men, "Give point, lads; damn cuts and guards." Young Havelock, mounted by the side of the gallant and ill-fated Stirling trudging forward on foot, brings the 64th on at the double against the great 24-pounder on the Cawnpore road that is vomiting grape at point-blank range. The night falls and the battle ceases, but among the wearied fighting men there is none of the elation of victory; for through the ranks, after the going down of the sun, had throbbed the bruit, originating no one knew where, that the women and children in Cawnpore had been butchered on the afternoon of the day before, while Stephenson and his Fusiliers were carrying the bridge of the Pandoo Nuddee.

The railway station of Cawnpore is distant more than a mile from the cantonment. Close to the road and not far from the station, the explorer easily finds the massive pile of the " Savada House," now allotted as residences for railway officials. English children play now in the corridors once thronged by the minions of the Nana, for here were his headquarters during part of the siege. Its verandas all day long were full of ministers, diviners, courtiers, and creatures. Here strolled the supple, pantherlike Azimoolah, the self-asserted favourite of home society in the pre-Mutiny days. Teeka Sing, the Nana's war minister, had his "bureau" in a tent under the peepul tree there. In that other clump of trees, where an ayah is tickling a white baby into laughter, was the pavilion of the Nana himself, who inherited the Mahratta preference for canvas over bricks and mortar. And here, while the crackle of the musketry fire and the din of the big guns came softened on the ear by distance, sat the adopted son of the Peishwa while Jwala Pershad came for orders about the cavalry, and Bala Rao, his brother, explained his devices for harassing the sahibs, and Tantia Topee, Hoolass Sing, Azimoolah, and the Nana himself devised the scheme of the treachery. But the Savada House has even a more lurid interest than this. Hither the women and children whom an unkind fate had spared from dying with the men were brought back from the Ghaut of Slaughter. You may see the two rooms into which 125 unfortunates were huddled after that march from before the presence of one death into the presence of another. As they plodded past the intrenchment so long held, and across the plain to the Nana's pavilion, "I saw," says a spectator, "that many of the ladies were wounded. Their clothes had blood upon them. Two were badly hurt and had their heads bound up with handkerchiefs; some were wet, covered with mud and blood, and some had their dresses torn; but all had clothes. I saw one or two children without clothes. There were no men in the party, but only some boys of twelve or thirteen. Some of the ladies were barefoot." Hither, too, were sent later the women of that detachment of the garrison which had got off from the ghaut in the boat defended by Vibart, Ashe, Delafosse, Bolton, Moore, and Thomson, and which had been captured at Nuzzufghur by Baboo Ram Bux. It had been for those people a turbulent departure from the Suttee Chowra Ghaut, but it was a yet more fearful returning. "They were brought back," testified a spy; "sixty sahibs, twenty-five memsahibs, and four children. The Nana ordered the sahibs to be separated from the memsahibs, and shot by the 1st Bengal Native Infantry. . . . 'Then,' said one of the memsahibs, 'I will not leave my husband. If he must die I will die with him.' So she ran and sat down behind her husband, clasping him round the waist. Directly she said this, the other memsahibs said, 'We also will die with our husbands,' and they all sat down each by her husband. Then their husbands said, 'Go back,' and they would not. Whereupon the Nana ordered his soldiers, and they went in, pulling them forcibly away." . . .

The drive from the railway station to the European cantonments is pleasant and shaded. At a bend in the road there comes into view a broad, flat, treeless parade ground. This plain lies within a circle of foliage, above which, on the south-eastern side, rise the balconies and flat tops of a long range of barracks built in detached blocks, while around the rest of the circle the trees shade the bungalows of the cantonment. Near the centre of this level space there is an irregular enclosure defined by a shallow sunk wall and low quickset hedge, and in the middle of this enclosure rises the ornate and not wholly satisfactory structure known as the "Memorial Church." It is built on the site of the old dragoon hospital, which was the very focus of the agony of the siege. It is impossible to analyse the mingled emotions of amazement, pride, pity, wrath, and sorrow which fill the visitor to this shrine of British valour, endurance, and constancy. The heart swells and the eyes fill as one, standing here with all the arena of the heroism lying under one's eyes, recalls the episodes of the glorious, piteous story. The blood stirs when one remembers the buoyant valour of the gallant Moore, who, "wherever he passed, left men something more courageous and women something less unhappy," the reckless audacity of Ashe, the cool daring of Delafosse, the deadly rifle of Stirling, the heroic devotion of Jervis. And a great lump grows in the throat when one bethinks him of the beautiful constancy and fearful sufferings of the women; of British ladies going barefoot and giving up their stockings as cases for grape-shot; of Mrs. Moore's journeys across to No. 2 Barrack; of the hapless gentlewomen, "unshod, unkempt, ragged, and squalid, haggard and emaciated, parched with drought, and faint with hunger, sitting waiting to hear that they were widows." And what a place it was which the garrison had to defend! Not a foot of all the space bomb-proof, an apology for an intrenchment such as "an active cow might jump over." The imagination has to do much work here, for most of the landmarks are gone. The outline of the world-famous earthwork is almost wholly obliterated; only in places is it to be dimly recognised by brick-discoloured lines, and a low raised line on the smooth *maidan*. The enclosure now existing has no reference to the outlines of the intrenchment. That enclosure merely surrounds the graveyard, in the midst of which stands the "Memorial Church," a structure that cannot be commended from an architectural point of view. But the space enclosed around its gaunt red walls is pregnant with painful interest. We come first on a railed-in memorial tomb, bearing an inscription in raised letters, on a cross let into the tessellated pavement: "In three graves within this enclosure lie the remains of Major Edward Vibart, 2nd Bengal Cavalry, and about seventy officers and soldiers, who, after escaping from the massacre at Cawnpore on the 27th June 1857, were captured by the rebels at Sheorapore, and murdered on the 1st July." The inmates of these graves were originally buried elsewhere, and were removed hither when the enclosure was formed. In another part of the enclosure is a raised tomb, the slab of which bears the inscription : " This stone marks a spot which lay within Wheeler's intrenchment, and covers the remains and is sacred to the memory of those who were the first to meet their death when beleaguered by mutineers and rebels in June 1857." Two only lie in this grave, Mr. Murphy and a lady who died of fever. These two perished on the first day of the siege and had the exclusive privilege of being decently interred within the precincts of the intrenchment. After the first day of the siege there was scant leisure for funeral rites. To find the last resting-place of the remaining dead of this siege, we must quit the enclosure and walk across the *maidan* to a spot among the trees by the roadside under the shadow of No. 4 Barrack. There was an empty well here when the siege begun ; three weeks after, when the siege ended, this well contained the bodies of 250 British people. With daylight the battle raged around that sepulchre, but when the night came the slain of the day were borne thither with stealthy step and scant attendance. Now the well is filled up, and above it, inside a small ornamental enclosure formed by iron railings, there rises a monument which bears the following inscription : " In a well under this enclosure were laid by the hands of their fellows in suffering the bodies of men, women, and children, who died hard by during the heroic defence of Wheeler's intrenchment when beleaguered by the rebel Nana." Below the inscription is this apposite quotation from Psalm cxli. 7 : " Our bones are scattered at the grave's mouth, as when one cutteth and cleaveth wood upon the earth. But mine eyes are unto Thee, O God the Lord." At the corners of the flower-plot are small crosses bearing individual names. One commemorates Sir George Parker, the cantonment magistrate; a second, Captain Jenkins; a third, Lieutenant Saunders and the men of the 84th Regiment; a fourth, Lieutenant Glanville and the men of the Madras Fusiliers; and here, too, lies stout-hearted yet tender-hearted John MacKillop of the Civil Service the hero of another well, that from which the team of buffaloes are now drawing water to make the mortar for the Memorial Church. Thence was procured the water for the garrison and it was a target also for the rebel artillery, so that the appearance of a man with a pitcher by day and by night the creaking of the tackle, was the signal for a shower of grape. But John MacKillop, "not being a fighting-man," made himself useful as he modestly put it, for a week as captain of the Well, till a grape-shot sent him to that other well thence never to return.

The Memorial Church is in the form of a cross, and now that it has been finished is not destitute of beauty as regards its interior. Perhaps it is in place, but the noblest monument that could commemorate Cawnpore would have been the maintenance, for the wonder of the world unto all time, of the intrenchment and what it surrounded, as nearly as possible in the condition in which they were left on the evacuation of the garrison. The grandest monument in the world is the Residency of Lucknow, which remains and is kept up substantially in the condition in which it was left when Sir Colin Campbell brought out its garrison in November 1857; and the Cawnpore intrenchment would have been a still nobler memorial as the abiding testimony to a defence even more wonderful, although unfortunately unsuccessful, than that of Lucknow. But the Memorial Church of Cawnpore will always be interesting by reason of its site and of the memorial tablets on the walls of its interior. In the left transept is a tablet "To the memory of the Engineers of the East Indian Railway, who died and were killed in the great insurrection of 1857; erected in affectionate remembrance by their brother Engineers in the North-West Provinces." On the left side of the nave are several tablets. One is to the memory of poor young John Nicklen Martin, killed in the battle at Suttee Chowra Ghaut. Another commemorates three officers, two sergeants, two corporals, a drummer, and twenty privates of the 34th Regiment, killed at the (second) Battle of Cawnpore on the 28th November 1857; the day on which the Gwalior Contingent, seduced into rebellion by Tantia Topee, made itself so unpleasant to General Windham, the "Cawnpore Runners," and other regiments of that officer's command. A third tablet is "To the memory of A. G. Chalwin, 2nd Light Cavalry, and his wife Louisa, who both perished during the siege of Cawnpore in July 1857. These are they which came out of great tribulation." A fourth commemorates Captain Gordon and Lieutenant Hensley, of the 82nd Foot, also victims of the Gwalior Contingent. In the right of the nave there is a tablet "Sacred to the memory of Philip Hayes Jackson, who, with Jane, his wife, and her brother Ralf Blyth Croker, were massacred by rebels at Cawnpore on 27th June." Another is to Lieutenant Angelo, of the 16th Grenadiers Bengal Native Infantry, who also fell in the boat massacre; and a third is to the memory of the gallant Stuart Beatson, who was Havelock's adjutant-general, and who, dying as he was of cholera, did his work at Pandoo Nuddee and Cawnpore in a *dhoolie*. In the right transept are tablets in memory of the officers of the Connaught Rangers, and of the officers and men of the 32nd Cornwall Regiment "who fell in defence of Lucknow and Cawnpore and subsequent campaign"—fourteen officers and 448 "women and men." And here, too, is perhaps the most affecting memorial of any—a tablet "In memory of Mrs. Moore, Mrs. Wainwright, Miss Wainwright, Mrs. Hill, forty-three soldiers' wives and fifty-five children, murdered in Cawnpore in 1857."

It is easy enough now to follow the footsteps of Mrs. Moore, dangerous as was that journey of hers, from the intrenchment to the corner of No. 2 Barrack, which she was wont to make when her husband went on duty there to strengthen the hands of Mowbray Thomson. There is no trace now and the very memory of its whereabouts is lost, of the bamboo hut in a sheltered corner which the garrison of this exposed post built for the brave gentlewoman. But No. 2 Barrack, except that it is finished and tenanted, stands now very much as it did when Glanville first, and when he fell then Mowbray Thomson, defended with a success which seems so wonderful when we look at the place defended and its situation. The garrison was not always the same. "My sixteen men," writes Thomson, "consisted in the first instance of Ensign Henderson of the 56th Native Infantry, five or six of the Madras Fusiliers, two plate-layers, and some men of the 84th. The first instalment was soon disabled. The Madras Fusiliers were all shot at their posts. Several of the 84th also fell, but in consequence of the importance of the position, as soon as a loss in my little corps was reported, Captain Moore sent us over a reinforcement from the intrenchment. Sometimes a soldier, sometimes a civilian, came. The orders given us were not to surrender with our lives, and we did our best to obey them." And in a line with No. 2 Barrack is No. 4 Barrack, held with equal stanchness by a party of Civil Engineers who had been employed on the East Indian Railroad, and who had for their commander Captain Jenkins. Seven of the engineers perished in defence of this post.

There is nothing more to see on the *maidan*, and one feels his anger rising at the obliteration of everything that might help towards the localisation of associations. Let us leave the scene of the defence and follow the track of the defenders as they marched down to the scene of the great treachery. The distance from the intrenchment to the ghaut is barely a mile. Think of that stirrup-cup—that *doch an dhorras*—of cold water, in which the hapless band pledged one another. The noble Moore cheerily leads the way down the slope to the bridge with the white rails with an advance guard of a handful of his 32nd men. The palanquins with the women, the children, and the wounded follow, the latter bandaged up with strips of women's gowns and petticoats, and fragments of shirt-sleeves. And then come the fighting-men— a gallant, ragged, indomitable band. A martinet colonel would stand aghast—for save a regimental button here and there, he would find it hard to recognise the gaunt, hairy, sun-scorched squad for British soldiers. But let who might incline to disown these few war-worn men in their dirty flannel rags and fragmentary nankeen breeches, their foes know them for what they are, and make way for the white sahibs with no dressing indeed in their ranks, but each man with his rifle on his shoulder, the deadly revolver in his belt, and the fearless glance in the hollow eye. The wooden bridge with the white rails spans at right angles a rough irregular glen which widens out as it approaches the river, some three hundred yards distant from the bridge. It is a mere footpath that leaves the road on the hither side of the bridge, and skirting the dry bed of the nullah touches the river close to the old temple. By this footpath it was that our countrymen and countrywomen passed down to the cruel ambush which had been laid for them in the mouth of the glen. There are few to whom the details of that fell scene are not familiar. What a contrast between the turmoil and devilry of it and the serene calmness of the all but solitude the ghaut now presents! On the knolls of the farther side snug bungalows nestle among the trees, under the veranda of one of which a lady is playing with her children. The village of Suttee Chowra on the bluff on the left of the ghaut, where Tantia Topee's sepoys were concealed, no longer exists; a pretty bungalow and its compound occupy its site. The little temple on the water's edge by the ghaut is slowly mouldering into decay; on the plaster of the coping of its river wall you may still see the marks of the treacherous bullets. The stair which, built against its wall, led down to the water's edge, has disappeared. Tantia Topee's dispositions for the perpetration of the treachery could not now succeed, for the Ganges has changed its course and there is deep water close in shore at the ghaut. In the stream nearest to the Oude side the river has cast up a long narrow dearah island, in the fertile mud of which melons are cultivated where once whistled the shot from the guns on the Oude side of the river. A Brahmin priest is placidly sunning himself on the river platform of the temple over the dome of which hangs the foliage of a peepul tree. A dhobie is washing the shirts of a sahib in the stream that once was dyed with the blood of the sahibs. There is no monument here, no superfluous reminder of the terrible tragedy. The man is not to be envied whose eyes are dry, and whose heart beats its normal pulsations, while he stands here alone on this spot so densely peopled by associations at once so tragic and so glorious.

The scene of the final massacre lies some distance higher up the river. As we cross the Ganges canal, the native city lying on our left, there rises up before us the rich mass of foliage that forms the outer screen of the beautiful Memorial Gardens. The hue of the greenery would be sombre but for the blossoms which relieve it, emblem of the divine hope which mitigated the gloom of despair for our countrywomen who perished so cruelly in this balefully historic spot. Of the Beebeeghur, the term by which among the natives is known the bungalow where the massacre was perpetrated, not one stone now remains on another but neither its memory nor its name will be lost for all time. Natives are strolling in the shady flower-bordered walks of the Memorial Gardens, the prohibition which long debarred their entrance having been wisely removed. In the centre of the garden rises, fringed with cypresses, a low mound, the summit of which is crowned by a circular screen, or border, of light and beautiful open-work architecture. The circular space enclosed is sunken, and from the centre of this sunken space there rises a pedestal on which stands the marble presentment of an angel. There is no need to explain what episode in the tragic story this monument commemorates; the inscription round the capital of the pedestal tells its tale succinctly indeed, but the words burn. "Sacred," it runs, "to the perpetual memory of the great company of Christian people, chiefly women and children, who near this spot were cruelly massacred by the followers of the rebel, Nana Doondoo Punth of Blithoor; and cast, the dying with the dead, into the well below, on the 15th day of July 1857." A few paces to the north-west of the monument is the spot where stood the bungalow in which the massacre was done; and now, where the sight they saw maddened our countrymen long ago to a frenzy of revenge, there bloom roses and violets. And a step farther on, in a thicket of arbor vitæ trees and cypresses, is the Memorial Churchyard, with its many nameless mounds, for here were buried not a few who died during the long occupation of Cawnpore, and in the combats around it. Here there is a monument to Thornhill, the Judge of Futtehghur, Mary his wife, and their two children, who perished in the massacre. Thornhill was one of the males brought out from the bungalow and shot earlier in the afternoon than when the women's time came. Another monument bears this inscription: "Sacred to the memory of the women and children of the 32nd, this monument is raised by twenty men of the same regiment, who were passing through Cawnpore, 21st Nov. 1857." And among the tombstones are those of gallant Douglas Campbell of the 78th, Woodford of the 2nd Battalion Rifle Brigade, and Young of the 4th Bengal Native Infantry.

BISMARCK

BEFORE AND DURING THE FRANCO-GERMAN WAR

THE ex-Chancellor of the German Empire owed nothing of his unique career to adventitious advantages. Otto von Bismarck-Schoenhausen, who for more than a generation was the most prominent and most powerful personality of Europe, was essentially a self-made man. He was a younger son of a cadet family of a knightly and ancient but somewhat decayed house, ranking among the lesser nobility of the Alt Mark of Brandenburg. The square solid mansion in which he was born, embowered among its trees in the region between the Elbe and the Havel, might be taken by an Englishman for the country residence of a Norfolk or Somersetshire squire of moderate fortune. But memories cling around the massive old family place of Schoenhausen, such as can belong to no English residence of equal date. In the library door of the Brandenburg mansion are seen to this day three deep fissures made by the bayonet points of French soldiers fresh from the battlefield of Jena, who in their brutal lawlessness pursued the young and beautiful chatelaine of the house and strove to crush in the door which the fugitive had locked behind her. The lady thus terrified and outraged was the mother of Bismarck; and the story told him in boyhood of his loved mother's narrow escape from worse than death, and of his father's having to conceal her in the depth of the adjoining forest, may well have inspired their son with the ill-feeling against the French nation which he never cared to disguise.

The Bismarcks had been fighting men from time immemorial, and the combatant nature of the great scion of their race displayed itself in frequent duels during his university career at Göttingen. In the series of some eight-and-twenty duels in which he engaged during his first three terms, he was wounded but twice—once in the leg and again on the cheek, the mark of which latter wound he bears to this day. At one time he seems to have all but decided to embrace the military career but for family reasons he became a country gentleman, and if Europe had remained undisturbed by revolution he might have lived and died a bucolic squire, "Dyke Captain" of his district, with a seat in the Provincial Diet, a liking for history and philosophy, a propensity to rowdyism and drinking bouts of champagne and porter, and a character which defined itself in his local appellation of "Mad Bismarck." *Dis aliter visum.* The Revolution of 1848 swept over Europe and Bismarck rallied to the support of his sovereign. When in 1851 the young Landwehr lieutenant was sent to Frankfort by that sovereign as the representative of Prussia in the German Diet, he carried with him a reputation for unflinching devotion to the Crown, for a conservatism which had been styled not only "mediæval" but "antediluvian," and for startling originality in his views as well as fearlessness in expressing them. The latter attribute he displayed when, in reply to a remark of a French diplomat on a question of policy, "*Cette politique va vous conduire à Jena*," Bismarck significantly retorted, "*Pourquoi pas à Leipsic ou à Waterloo?*" During his tenure of office at Frankfort his conviction steadfastly strengthened that Prussia could become a great nation only by shaking herself free from the Austrian supremacy in Germany. "It is my conviction," he placed on record in a despatch soon after the Crimean War, "that at no distant time we shall have to fight with Austria for our very existence;" and he was yet more emphatic when he wrote just before leaving Frankfort to take up his new position as German Ambassador to Russia in the beginning of 1859: "I recognise in our relations with the Bund a certain weakness affecting Prussia, which, sooner or later, we shall have to cure *ferro et igni*"—with fire and sword—words which embodied the first distinct enunciation of that policy of "blood and iron" which was destined ultimately to bring about the unification of Germany. His disgust was so strong that Prussia did not assert herself against Austria in 1858 when the latter's hands were full in Italy, that his continued presence at Frankfort was considered unadvisable. He remained "in ice"—to use his own expression—at St. Petersburg until early in 1862; and in September of that year, after a few months of service as Prussian Ambassador at Paris, he was appointed by King Wilhelm to the high and onerous post of Minister-President with the portfolio of Foreign Secretary.

It was then that his great career as a European statesman really began.

The impression is all but universal that King Wilhelm throughout the eventful years which followed was but the figure-head of the ship at the helm of which stood Bismarck, strong, shrewd, subtle, cynical, and unscrupulous. This conception I believe to be utterly wrong. I hold Wilhelm to have been the virtual maker of the united Germany and the creator of the German Empire; and that the accomplishment of both those objects, the former leading up to the latter, was already quietly in his mind long before he mounted the throne. I consider him to have possessed the shrewdest insight into character. I believe him to have been quite unscrupulous, when once he had brought himself to cross the threshold of a line of action. I discern in him this curious, although not very rare, phase of character, that although resolutely bent on a purpose he was apt to be irresolute and even reluctant in bringing himself to consent to measures whereby that purpose was to be accomplished. He was that apparent contradiction in terms, a bold hesitator; he habitually needed, and knew that he needed, to have his hand apparently forced for the achievement of the end he was most bent upon. He knew full well that his aspirations could be fulfilled only at the bayonet point; and recognising the defects of the army, he had while still Regent set himself energetically to the task of making Prussia the greatest military power of Europe. He it was who had put into the hands of Prussian soldiers the weapon that won Königgrätz. With his clear eye for the right man he had found Moltke and placed the premier strategist of his day at the head of the General Staff. Roon he picked out as if by intuition from comparative obscurity, and assigned to him the work of preparing and carrying out that scheme of army reform which all continental Europe has copied.

And then, constant in the furtherance of his purposes, Wilhelm deliberately invented Bismarck. He had steadfastly taken note of the man whom he chose to be his minister from the big Landwehr lieutenant's first commission to the Frankfort Diet in 1851; probably, indeed, earlier, when Bismarck was a rare but forcible speaker in Frederick Wilhelm's "quasi-Parliament." In Bismarck Wilhelm saw precisely the man he wanted—the complement of himself; arbitrary as he was, unscrupulous as he was, but bolder and at the same time more wise. Knowing where he himself was lacking, he recognised the man who, when he himself should have the impulse to balk and hesitate, was of that hardier nature— "grit" the Americans call it—to take him hard by the head and force him over the fence which all the while he had been longing to be on the other side of. To a monarch of this character Bismarck was simply the ideal guide and support—the man to urge him on when hesitating, to restrain him when over-ardent. Wilhelm had all along thoroughly realised that war with Austria was among the inevitables between him and the accomplishment of his aims, and had accepted it as such when it was yet afar off; but when confronted full with it his nerve failed him, and Bismarck —engaged among other things for just such an emergency—had to act as the spur to prick the side of his master's intent. The spur having done its work Wilhelm was himself again; he really enjoyed Königgrätz and would fain have dictated peace to Austria from the Hofburg of Vienna. In his zeal for promoting German unity at Prussia's bayonet point he lost his head a little, and on Bismarck devolved, in his own words, "the ungrateful duty of diluting the wine of victory with the water of moderation." One of the beads on the surface of the former fluid was certainly thus early the Imperial idea; but the time for its fulfilment Bismarck wisely judged not yet ripe. As it approached four years later, the diary of the Crown Prince depicts with unconscious humour the amusing progress of the "weakening" of Wilhelm's opposition to the Kaisership; it weakened in good time quite out of the sort of existence it had ever had, and Wilhelm was ready for the Kaisership before the Kaisership was ready for him.

Bismarck as Premier began as he meant to go on, with uncompromising masterfulness. The Chamber and the nation might probably have fallen in willingly with Wilhelm's scheme for the reorganisation and reinforcement of the army, had it been possible to divulge the intent in furtherance of which the increased armament was being created. But since neither monarch nor minister could even hint at the objects in view, the nation was set against that increased armament for which it could discern no apparent use. So the Chamber, session after session, went through the accustomed formula of rejecting the military reorganisation bill as well as the military expenditure estimates. "No surrender" was the steadfast motto of Bismarck and his royal master. The constitution, such as it was, in effect was suspended. The Upper House voted everything it was asked to vote; loans were duly effected, the revenues were collected and the military disbursements were made, right in the teeth of the popular will and the veto of the representatives of the nation. Bismarck became the best-hated man in Prussia. He was compared to Catiline and Strafford; he was threatened with impeachment; the House and the nation clamoured to the King for his dismissal and for the sovereign's return to the path of constitutional government.

But the long "conflict-time" was drawing near its close, and the triumph of the monarch and his minister over the constitution was approaching. The policy of doing political evil that national advantage might come was, for once at least, to stand vindicated. War with Austria as the outcome of Bismarck's astute if unscrupulous statecraft was imminent when the hostile parliament was dissolved; and a general election took place amidst the fervid outburst of enthusiasm which the earlier victories of the Prussian arms in the "Seven Weeks' War" stirred throughout the nation. The prospect of war had been unpopular in the extreme, but the tidings of the first success kindled the flame of patriotism. Bismarck lost for ever the title of the "best-hated man in Prussia" in the loud volume of the enthusiastic greetings of the populace, and on the day of Münchengrätz and Skalitz Prussia now rejoiced to put her stubborn neck under the great minister's foot.

The mingled truculence and tortuousness of the diplomacy by which Bismarck sapped up to the short but decisive war, the issue of which gave to Prussia the virtual headship of Germany and contributed so greatly toward the unification of the Fatherland, constitute a striking illustration of his methods in statecraft. He was fairly entitled to say, "*Ego qui feci.*" He had achieved his aim in defiance of the nation. The Court threw its weight into the scale against the war; to the Crown Prince the strife with Austria was notoriously repugnant. The King himself, as the crisis approached, evinced marked hesitation. How triumphantly the event vindicated the policy of the great Premier, is a matter of history. He has frankly owned that if the decisive battle should have resulted in a Prussian defeat, he had resolved not to survive the shipwreck of his hopes and schemes. And there was a period in the course of the colossal struggle of Königgrätz, when to many men it seemed that the wielders of the needle-gun were having the worst of the battle. An awful hour for Bismarck, conscious of the load of responsibility which he carried. With great effort he could indeed maintain a calm visage, but his heart was beating and every pulse of him throbbing. In his torture of suspense he caught at straws. Moltke asked him for a cigar. As Bismarck handed him his cigar case he snatched a shred of comfort from the inference that if matters were very bad Moltke could hardly care to smoke. But Moltke was not only in a frame for tobacco but Bismarck watched with what deliberate coolness the great strategist inspected and smelt at cigar after cigar before making his final selection; and he dared to infer that the man who best understood the situation was in no perturbation as to the ultimate outcome. The opportune arrival of the Crown

Prince's army on the Austrian right flank decided the business, and that arrival Bismarck was the first to discern. Lines were dimly visible on the hither slope of the Chlum heights; but they were pronounced to be ploughed ridges. Bismarck closed his field-glasses with a snap and exclaimed, "No, these are not plough furrows; the spaces are not equal; they are marching lines!" And he was right.

Eighteen days after the victory of Königgrätz the Prussian hosts were in line on the historic Marchfeld whence the spires of Vienna could be dimly seen through the heat-haze. The soldiers were eager for the storm of the famous lines of Florisdorf and King Wilhelm was keen to enter the Austrian capital. But now the practical wisdom of Bismarck stepped in and his arguments for moderation prevailed. The peace which ended the Seven Weeks' War revolutionised the face of Germany. Austria accepted her utter exile from Germany, recognised the dissolution of the old Bund, and consented to non-participation in the new North German Confederation of which Prussia was to have the unquestioned military and diplomatic leadership. Prussia annexed Hanover, Electoral Hesse, Nassau, Sleswig and Holstein, Frankfort-on-Main, and portions of Hesse-Darmstadt and Bavaria. Her territorial acquisitions amounted to over 6500 square miles with a population exceeding 4,000,000, and the states with which she had been in conflict paid as war indemnity sums reaching nearly to £10,000,000 sterling. In a material sense, it had not been a bad seven weeks for Prussia; in a sense other than material, she had profited incalculably more. She was now, in fact as in name, one of the "Great Powers" of Europe. The nation realised at length what manner of man this Bismarck was and what it owed to him. When the inner history of the period comes to be written, it will be recognised that at no time of his extraordinary career did Bismarck prove himself a greater statesman than during the five days of armistice in July 1866, when he fought his diplomatic Königgrätz in the Castle of Nikolsburg and assuaged the wounds of the Austrian defeat by terms the moderation of which went far to obliterate the memory of the rancour of the recent strife.

He had been wily enough to secure by vague non-committal half-promises the neutrality of France during the weeks while Prussia was crushing the armed strength of Austria in Bohemia. But the issue of Königgrätz startled Napoleon and set France in ferment. Bismarck dared to refuse point-blank the demand which the French Emperor made for the fortress of Mayence, made though that demand was under threat of war. The Prussian commanders would have liked nothing better than a war with France, and Roon indeed had warned for mobilisation 350,000 soldiers to swell the ranks of the forces already in the field; but Bismarck was wise and could wait. He allowed Napoleon to exercise some influence in the negotiations in the character of a mediator; and to French intervention was owing the stipulation that the South German States should be at liberty to form themselves into a South German Confederation of which Napoleon hoped to be the patron. But Bismarck was a better diplomatist than Napoleon. While he formed and knit together the North German Confederation in which Prussia was dominant, he quietly negotiated an alliance offensive and defensive with each of the Southern States separately. No Southern bund was ever formed, and when the Franco-German War broke out in 1870 Napoleon saw the shipwreck of his abortive devices in the spectacle of the troops of Bavaria and Würtemberg marching on the Rhine in line with the battalions of Prussia.

The unity of Germany was not yet; that consummation and the Kaisership—the two greatest triumphs of Bismarck's life—required another and a greater war to bring about their accomplishment. During the interval between 1866 and 1870, while the armed strength of Northern Germany was being quietly but sedulously perfected, Bismarck with dexterous caution was smoothing the rough path toward the ultimate unification. He would not have his hand forced by the enthusiasts for "the consummation of the national destiny." "No horseman can afford to be always at a gallop" was the figure with which he met the clamourers of the Customs Parliament. He invoked the terms of the treaty of Prague against the spokesmen of the Pan-German party inveighing vehemently against the policy of delay. He was staunch in his conviction that the South for its own safety's sake would come into the union the moment that the North should engage in war. He was a few weeks out in his reckoning; the Southern States waited until Sedan had been fought, when the prospect of the spoils of victory was assured; and this measured delay on their part was the best justification of Bismarck's sagacious deliberateness. The negotiations were tedious, but at length, on the evening of 23rd November 1870 the Convention with Bavaria was signed, and the unity of Germany was an accomplished fact. Busch vividly depicts the great moment:—

> The Chief came in from the salon, and sat down at the table. "Now," he exclaimed excitedly, "the Bavarian business is settled and everything is signed. *We have got our German Unity and our German Emperor.*" There was silence for a moment. "Bring a bottle of champagne," said the Chief to a servant, "it is a great occasion." After musing a little, he remarked, "The Convention has its defects, but it is all the stronger on account of them. I count it the most important thing that we have accomplished during recent years."

Notwithstanding that there was still before Bismarck a period of twenty years of virtual omnipotence, it was in the memorable years of 1870 and 1871 that the apostle of blood and iron attained the zenith of his extraordinary career. Germany was his wash-pot; over France had he cast his shoe. The years of *Sturm und Drang* were behind him, during which he had wrought out the military supremacy of Prussia in spite of herself; and in 1870 he had no misgivings as to the ultimate result. So confident indeed was he that before he crossed the French frontier on the second day after the twin victories of Wörth and Spicheren, he had already resolved on annexing to the Fatherland the old German province of Alsace which had been part of France for a couple of centuries.

Bismarck was at his best in 1870 in certain attributes; in others he was at his worst, and a bitter bad worst that worst was. He was at his best in clear swift insight, in firm masterful grasp of every phase of every situation, in an instinctive prescience of events, in lucid dominance over German and European policy. If patriotism consists in earnest efforts to advantage and aggrandise one's native land *per fas aut nefas*, than Bismarck during the Franco-German War there never was a grander patriot. His hands were clean, he wanted nothing for himself except, curiously enough, the only thing that his old master was strong enough to deny him, the rank of Field Marshal when that military distinction was conferred on Moltke. He was at his worst in many respects. He had, or affected, a truculence which was simply brutal, its savagery intensified rather than mitigated by a bluff, boisterous bonhomie. Jules Favre complained to him that the German cannon in front of Paris fired upon the sick and blind in the Blind Institute. Bismarck in those days of swaggering prosperity had a fine turn of badinage. "I don't know what you find so hard in that," he retorted, "you do far worse; you shoot at our soldiers who are hale and useful fighting men." It is to be hoped that Favre had a sense of humour; he needed it all to relish the grim pleasantry.

I do not suppose, if he had had a free hand, that Bismarck would have exhibited the courage of his opinions; but if his sentiments as expressed count for anything he would fain have seen the methods of warfare in the Dark Ages reverted to. "Prisoners! more prisoners!" he once exclaimed at Versailles, after one of Prince Frederick Charles's victories in the Loire country—"What the devil do we want with prisoners? Why don't they make a battue of them?" His motto, especially as regarded Francs-tireurs, was "No quarter," forgetful of the swarms of free companions and volunteer bands whose gallant services in Prussia's War of Liberation are commemorated to this day in song and story. It was told him that among the French prisoners taken at Le Bourget were a number of Francs-tireurs—by the way, they were the volunteers *de la Presse* and wore a uniform. "That they should ever take Francs-tireurs prisoners!" roared Bismarck in disgust. "They ought to have shot them down by files!" Again, when it was reported that Garibaldi with his 13,000 "free companions" had been taken prisoners, the Chancellor exclaimed, "Thirteen thousand Francs-tireurs, who are not even Frenchmen, made prisoners! Why on earth were they not shot?" And when he heard that Voights Rhetz having experienced some resistance from the inhabitants of the open town of Tours, had shelled it into submission, Bismarck waxed wrath because the General had ceased firing when the white flag went up. "I would have gone on," said he, "throwing shells into the town till they sent me out 400 hostages." The simple truth is that in spite of his long pedigree and good blood Bismarck was not quite a gentleman in our sense of the word; and as this accounts for his ferocious bluster and truculent bloodthirsty utterances when he was in power in the war time, so it was the keynote to his more recent undignified attitude and howls of querulous impatience of his altered situation.

P

It must be said of him, however, that he was a man of cool and undaunted courage. I have seen him perfectly impassive under heavy fire. In Bar-le-Duc, in Rheims, and over and over again in Versailles, I have met him walking alone and unarmed through streets thronged with French people who recognised him by the pictures of him, and who glared and spat and hissed in a cowed, furtive, malign fashion that was ugly to see.

I vividly remember the first occasion on which I saw Bismarck. It was on the little tree-shaded *Place* of St. Johann, the suburb of Saarbrücken, in the early evening of the 8th August, the next day but one after the battle of the Spicheren. Saarbrücken was full to the door-sills with the wounded of the battle and stretcher-parties were continually tramping to the "warriors' trench" in the cemetery, carrying to their graves soldiers who had died of their wounds. The Royal Headquarters had arrived a couple of hours earlier, and I was staring with all my eyes at a fresh-faced, white-haired old gentleman who was sitting in one of the windows of Guepratt's Hotel and whom I knew from the pictures to be King Wilhelm. Two officers in general's undress uniform were walking up and down under the pollarded lime-trees, talking as they walked. Presently from out a house opposite the hotel there emerged a very tall burly man of singularly upright carriage and with a certain air of swashbucklerism in his gait. A long cavalry sabre trailed and clanked on the rough pavement as he advanced to join the two sauntering officers under the trees. He wore the long blue double-breasted frockcoat with yellow cuffs and facings and white cap which I knew to be the undress uniform of the Bismarck Cuirassiers, but he was only partially in undress since the long cuirassier thigh-boots in which he strode were conventionally full uniform. The wearer of this costume was Bismarck; nor did I ever see him otherwise attired except on four occasions—at the Château Bellevue on the morning after Sedan, in the Galerie des Glaces in the Château of Versailles on 18th January, in the Place de la Concorde of capitulated Paris, and in the triumphal entry into Berlin; when he appeared in full uniform. Saluting His Majesty and then the two officers whom I recognised as Moltke and Roon, he joined the pedestrian couple, taking post between them and joining in their promenade and conversation. We heard his voice and laugh above the rumble of the waggon wheels on the causeway; the other two spoke little—Moltke, as he moved with bent head and hands clasped behind his back, scarcely anything.

One would have imagined that those three men, the chief makers of that empire which was soon to come to the grand but not brilliant old gentleman in the window-seat, were on the most intimate and cordial terms. In reality they were jealous of each other with an inconceivable intensity. Bismarck had umbrage with Moltke because the great strategist withheld from the great statesman the military information which the latter held he ought to share. Moltke has roundly disclosed in his posthumous book his conviction that Roon's place as Minister of War was at home in Germany, not on campaign, embarrassing the former's functions. Roon envied Moltke because of the latter's more elevated military position, and disliked Bismarck because that outspoken man made light of Roon's capacity. I have known the headquarter staff of a British army whose members were on bad terms one with the other, and the result, to put it mildly, was unsatisfactory. But those three high functionaries, each with bitterness in his heart against his fellows, nevertheless co-operated earnestly and loyally in the service of their sovereign and for the advantage of their country. Their common patriotism had the mastery in them of their mutual hatred and jealousy. Ardt's line: "*Sein Vaterland muss grösser sein!*" was the watchword and inspiration of all three, and dominated their discordancies.

On the 17th August, the day of comparative quietude intervening between the day of Mars-la-Tour and the day of Gravelotte I was wandering about among the hamlets and farmsteads to the southward of Mars-la-Tour, waiting the arrival in their appointed bivouacs about Puxieux of my early friends of the Saxon Army Corps. Since in the battle of the previous day some 32,000 men had fallen killed or wounded within a comparatively small area, it may be imagined—or rather, without having seen the horror of carnage it cannot be imagined— how shambles-like was the aspect of this Aceldama. Scrambling up through the Bois la Dame with intent to obtain a wider view from the plateau above it, I found in a farmyard in the hamlet of Mariaville a number of wounded men under the care of a single and rather helpless surgeon. The water supply was very short and I volunteered to carry some bucketsful from the stream below. The surgeon told me that among his patients was Count Herbert Bismarck, the Chancellor's eldest son, who—as was also his younger brother Count "Bill"—was a volunteer private in the 2nd Guard Dragoons, and who had been shot in the thigh in the desperate charge made by that fine regiment to extricate from annihilation the Westphalian regiments which had suffered so severely near Bruville. A little later I saw Bismarck who had left the King on the Flavigny height, and who was riding about, as I assumed, in quest of his wounded son's whereabouts. I ventured to inform him on this point and he thanked me with some emotion. He was greatly moved at the meeting with his son but their interview was short; then he addressed himself to reproving the surgeon for not having had the Mariaville poultry killed for the use of the wounded, and presently rode away to order up a supply of water in barrels. I remember thinking him an exceedingly practical man.

The English Warwick was styled the "Kingmaker"; but it was for the Prussian Bismarck to be Emperor-breaker and Emperor-maker within the same six months. The most wretched morning of Napoleon's life was that following the fatal day of Sedan, spent in and before the weaver's cottage on the Donchery road with Bismarck by his side, telling him in stern if courteous terms that as a prisoner of war his power to exercise the Imperial functions had fallen from him. It has been said that "the egg from which was hatched the German Empire was laid on the battlefield of Sedan." But, not to speak of the offer of the Imperial Crown to King Frederick

Wilhelm by the Frankfort Parliament in 1848, Bismarck more than a year before the Austro-Prussian war had spoken to Lord Augustus Loftus, then British Ambassador to Prussia, of his ultimate intention that the King of Prussia should become the Emperor of an united Germany. The *Kaiserthum* permeated the air of Northern Germany throughout the years from 1866 to 1870. But Bismarck had the true statesman's sense of the proper sequence of things. He would move no step toward the Kaisership until German unity was in near and clear sight. Then, and not till then, in spite of the Crown Prince's ardour, was the Imperial project brought forward, discussed, and finally carried through by Bismarck's tact and diplomacy.

On the 18th January 1871, the anniversary of the coronation of the first king of his house, Wilhelm was proclaimed German Emperor in the Galerie des Glaces of the Château of Versailles. Behind the grand old monarch on the dais were ranged the regimental colours which had been borne to victory at Wörth and the Spicheren, at Mars-la-Tour, Gravelotte, and Sedan. On Wilhelm's right was his handsome and princely son; to right and to left stood potentates and princes and the leaders of the hosts of United Germany. Stalwart and square, somewhat apart on the extreme left of the great semicircle of which his sovereign was the centre, with a face of deadly pallor—for he had risen from a sick-bed—stood Bismarck in full cuirassier uniform leaning on his great sword, the man of all others who might that day most truly say, "*Finis Coronat Opus.*" His strong massive features were calm and self-possessed, yet elevated as it were by some internal power which drew all eyes to the great immobile figure with the indomitable lineaments instinct with will—force and masterfulness. After the solemn religious service His Majesty in a loud yet broken voice proclaimed the re-establishment of the German Empire, and that the Imperial dignity so revived was vested in him and his descendants for all time in accordance with the unanimous will of the German people. Bismarck then stood forward and read in sonorous tones the proclamation which the Emperor addressed to the German nation. As his final words rang through the hall the Grand Duke of Baden strode forward and shouted with all his force, "Long live the Emperor Wilhelm!" With a tempest of cheering, amidst waving of swords and of helmets the new title was acclaimed, and the Emperor with streaming tears received the homage of his liegemen. The first on bended knees to kiss his sovereign's hand was the Crown Prince, the second was Bismarck. The band struck up the National Anthem. Louder than the music, heard above the clamour of the cheering, sounded the thunder of the French cannon from Mont Valérien, the *Ave Cæsar* from the reluctant lips of worsted France. Bismarck, impassive as he seemed, must have had his emotions as he quitted this scene of triumph for the banquet-table of the Kaiser of his own making. He knew himself for the most conspicuous man in Europe, the greatest subject in the world. It was the proudest day of his life.

There were many proud days still to occur in his long life. One of those was on the occasion of the

German entry into Paris during the armistice which resulted in peace. The war had been of his making, and he chose to witness with his own eyes the actual triumph of his craft. It was a strange spectacle. There, helmet on head and sword on thigh, he sat in the shadow of the crape-shrouded statue of Strasburg on the Place de la Concorde. About him had gathered a group of extremely sinister French of the Belleville type. They had recognised him, and their lurid upward glances at the massive form on the great war-horse were charged with baleful meaning. Bismarck once or twice looked down on them with a grim smile under his moustache. At length the most daring of the "patriots" emitted a tentative hiss. With a little polite wave of his gloved hand Bismarck bent over his holster and requested "Monsieur" to oblige him with a light for his cigar. The man writhed as he compelled himself to comply. Little doubt that in his heart he wished the lucifer were a dagger and that he had the courage to use it.

THE INVERNESS "CHARACTER" FAIR

1873

" *THURSDAY.*—Gathering, hand-shaking, brandy and soda and drams.

" *Friday.*—Drinking, dandering, and feeling the way in the forenoon ; the ordinary in the afternoon ; at night a spate of drink and bargaining.

" *Saturday.*—Bargaining and drink.

" *Sunday morning.*—Bargains, drink, and the kirk."

Such was the skeleton programme of the Inverness "Character" Fair given by a farmer friend to me, who happened to be lazily rusticating in the north of Scotland during the pleasant month of July. My friend asked me to accompany him in his visit to this remarkable institution and the programme was too tempting for refusal. As we drove to the station he handed me Henry Dixon's *Field and Fern*, open at a page which gave some particulars of the origin and character of the great annual sheep and wool market of the north. "Its Character Market," wrote "The Druid,"—no longer, alas! among us—" is the great bucolic glory of Inverness. The Fort-William market existed before, but the Sutherland

and Caithness men, who sold about 14,000 sheep and 15,000 stones of wool annually so far back as 1816, did not care to go there. They dealt with regular customers year after year, and roving woolstaplers with no regular connection went about and notified their arrival on the church door. Patrick Sellar, 'the agent for the Sutherland Association,' saw exactly that some great *caucus* of buyers and sellers was wanted at a more central spot; and on 27th February 1817 that meeting of the clans was held at Inverness which brought the fair into being. Huddersfield, Wakefield, Halifax, Burnley, Aberdeen, and Elgin signified that their leading merchants were favourable and ready to attend. Sutherland, Caithness, Wester Ross, Skye, the Orkneys, Harris, and Lewis were represented at the meeting; Bailie Anderson also 'would state with confidence that the market was approved of by William Chisholm, Esq., of Chisholm, and James Laidlaw, tacksman, of Knockfin;' and so the matter was settled for ever and aye, and the *Courier* and the *Morning Chronicle* were the London advertising media. This Highland Wool Parliament was originally held on the third Thursday in June, but now it begins on the second Thursday of July and lasts till the Saturday; and Argyllshire, Nairnshire, and High Aberdeenshire have gradually joined in. The plain-stones in front of the Caledonian Hotel have always been the scene of the bargains, which are most truly based on the broad stone of honour; not a sheep or fleece is to be seen and the buyer of the year before gets the first offer of the cast or clip. The previous proving and public character of the different flocks are the purchasers' guide far more than the sellers' description."

Thus far "The Druid"; and my companion as we drove supplemented his information. It is from the circumstance that not a head of sheep or a tait of wool is brought to the market but that everything is sold and bought unseen and even unsampled, that the market derives its appellation of "character" fair. Of the value of the business transacted, the amount of money turned over, it is impossible to form with confidence even an approximate estimate since there is no source for data; but none with whom I spoke put the turnover at a lower figure than half a million. In a good season such as the past, over 200,000 sheep are disposed of exclusive of lambs, and of lambs about the same number. The stock sold from the hills are for the most part Cheviots and Blackfaces; from the low grounds half-breds, being a cross between Leicester and Cheviot and crosses between the Cheviot and Blackface. All the sales of sheep and lambs are by the "clad score" which contains twenty-one. The odd one is thrown in to meet the contingency of deaths before delivery is effected. Established when there was a long and wearing journey for the flocks from the hills where they were reared down to their purchasers in the lowlands or the south country, the altered conditions of transit have stimulated farmers to efforts for the abolition of the "clad score." Now that sheep are trucked by railway instead of being driven on foot or conveyed from the islands to their destination in steamers specially chartered for the purpose, the farmers grudge the "one in" of the "clad score."

In 1866 they seized the opportunity of an exceptionally high market and keen competition to combine against the old reckoning and in a measure succeeded. But next year was as dull as '66 had been brisk, and then the buyers and dealers had their revenge and re-established the "clad score" in all its pristine firmness of position. The sheep-farmers wean their lambs about the 24th of August and delivery of them is given to the buyers as soon as possible thereafter. The delivery of ewes and wethers is timed by individual arrangement. A large proportion of the old ewes—no ewes are sold but such as are old—go to England where a lamb or two is got from them before they are fattened. Most of the lambs are bought by sheep-farmers who, not keeping a ewe flock, are not themselves breeders, and are kept till they are three years old—"three shears" as they are technically called—and sold fat into the south country. There they get what Mr. M'Combie called the last dip and the butcher sells them as "prime four-year-old wedder mutton."

The size of some of the Highland sheep farms is to be reckoned by miles not by acres; and the stock, as in Australia, by the thousand. The largest sheep-owner, perhaps, that the Highlands ever knew was Cameron of Corrichollie, now dead. He was once examined before a Committee of the House of Commons, and came to be questioned on the subject of his ownership of sheep. "You may have some 1500 sheep, probably, sir?" quoth the interrogating M.P. "Aiblins," was Corrichollie's quiet reply as he took a pinch of snuff; "aiblins I have a few more nor that." "Two thousand, then?" "Yes, I pelieve I have that and a few more forpye," calmly responded the Highlander with another pinch. "Five thousand?" "Oh, ay, and a few more." "Twenty thousand, sir?" cried the M.P., capping with a burst his previous bid. "Oh, ay, and some more forpye," was the imperturbable response. "In Heaven's name how many sheep have you, man?" burst out the astonished catechist. "I'm no very sure to a thousan' or two," replied Corrichollie in his dry laconic way and with an extra big pinch; "but I'm owner of forty thousan' sheep at the lowest reckoning." Lochiel, known to the Sassenach as Mr. Cameron, M.P., is perhaps the largest living sheep-owner in Scotland. He has at least 30,000 sheep on his vast tracks of moorland on the braes of Lochaber. In the Island of Skye Captain Cameron of Talisker has a flock of some 12,000; and there are several other flocks both in the islands and on the mainland of more than equal magnitude. Sheep-farming, at least in many instances, is an hereditary avocation, and some families can trace a sheep-farming ancestry very far back. The oldest sheep-farming family in Scotland are the Mackinnons of Corrie in Skye. They have been on Corrie for four hundred years and they were holding sheep-farms elsewhere even earlier. The Macraes of Achnagart in Kintail, paid rent to Seaforth for two hundred years. For as long before they had held Achnagart on the tenure of a bunch of heather exigible annually and their fighting services as good clansmen. Two hundred years ago an annual rental of £5 was substituted for the heather "corve"; the clansmen's service continuing and being rendered up till the '45.

Now clanship is but a name : a Seaforth Mackenzie is no longer chief in Kintail, and the Macrae who has succeeded his forbears in Achnagart finds the bunch of heather and the £5 alike superseded by the very far other than nominal rent of £1000. The modern Achnagart with his broad shoulders and burly frame, looks as capable as were any of his ancestry to render personal service to his chief if a demand were made upon him ; and very probably would be quite prepared to accept a reduction of his money rental if an obligation to perform feudal clan-service were substituted. Achnagart with his £1000 a year rental by no means tops the sheep-farming rentals of his county. Perhaps Robertson of Achiltie, whose sheep-walks stretch up on to the snow-patched shoulders of Ben Wyvis and far away west to Loch Broom, pays the highest sheep-farming rental in Ross-shire, when the factor has pocketed his half-yearly check for £800.

Part of this I learn from my friend as we drive to the station ; part I gather afterwards from other sources. The station for which we are bound is Elgin, the county town of Morayshire. Between Elgin and Inverness, it is true, we shall see but few of the great sheep-farmers and flock-masters of the west country, who converge on the annual tryst from other points of the compass and by various routes— by the Skye railway, by that portion of the Highland line which extends north of Inverness, through Ross into Sutherland, by the Caledonian Canal, etc. But it is promised to me that I shall see many of the notable agriculturists of Moray land, who go to the market as buyers ; and a contingent of sheep-breeders are sure to join us at Forres, coming down the Highland line from the Inverness-shire Highlands on Upper Strathspey. There is quite an exceptional throng on the platform of the Elgin station, of farmers, factors, lawyers, and ex-coffee-planters—all very plentiful in Elgin; tanners bound for investments in prospective pelts; and men of no avocation yet as much bound to visit Inverness to-day as if they meant to invest thousands. In a corner towers the mighty form of Paterson of Mulben, famous among breeders of polls with his tribe of "Mayflowers." From beneath a kilt peep out the brawny limbs of Willie Brown of Linkwood and Morriston, nephew of stout old Sir George who commanded the light division at the Alma, son to a factor whose word in his day was as the laws of the Medes and Persians over a wide territory, and himself the feeder of the leviathan cross red ox and the beautiful gray heifer which took honours so high at one of the recent Smithfield Christmas Shows. There is the white beard and hearty face of Mr. Collie, late of Ardgay, owner erstwhile of "Fair Maid of Perth" and breeder of "Zarah." Here, too, is a fresh, sprightly gentleman in a kilt whom his companions designate "the Bourach." Requesting an explanation of the term I am told that "Bourach" is the Gaelic for "through-other," which again is the Scottish synonym for a kind of amalgam of addled and harum-scarum. A jolly tanner observes: "I'll get a compartment to oursels." The reason of the desire for this exclusive accommodation is apparent as soon as we start. A "deck" of cards is produced and a quartette betake themselves to whist with half-crown stakes on the rubber and sixpenny points. This was mild speculation to that which was engaged in on the homeward journey after the market, when a Strathspey sheep-farmer won £8 between Dalvey and Forres. As my friends shuffle and deal, I look out of window at the warm gray towers of the cathedral, beautiful still spite of the desecrating hand of the "Wolf of Badenoch." Our road lies through the fertile "Laigh of Moray," one of the richest wheat districts in the Empire and as beautiful as fertile. At Alves we pick up a fresh, hale gentleman, who is described to me as "the laird of three properties," bought for more than £100,000 by a man who began life as the son of a hillside crofter. We pass the picturesque ruins of Kinloss Abbey and draw up at Forres station, whose platform is thronged with noted agriculturists bound for the "Character" Fair. Here is that spirited Englishman Mr. Harris of Earnhill, whose great cross ox took the cup at the Agricultural Hall seven or eight years ago; and the brothers Bruce—he of Newton Struthers, whose marvellous polled cow beat everything in Bingley Hall at the '71 Christmas Show and but for "foot and mouth" would have repeated the performance at the Smithfield Show; and he of Burnside who likewise has stamped his mark pretty deeply in the latter arena. At Forres we first hear Gaelic; for a train from Carr Bridge and Grantown in Upper Strathspey has come down the Highland Railway to join ours, and the red-haired Grants around the Rock of Craigellachie—where a man whose name is not Grant is regarded as a *lusus naturæ*—are Gaelic speakers to a man. No witches accost us, and speaking personally I feel no "pricking of the thumbs" as we skirt the blasted heath on which Macbeth met the witches; the most graphic modern description of which on record was given to Henry Dixon in the following quaint form of Shakespearean annotation: "It's just a sort of eminence; all firs and ploughed land now; you paid a toll near it. I'm thinking, it's just a mile wast from Brodie Station."

Nairn is that town by the citation of a peculiarity of which King Jamie put to shame the boastings of the Southrons as to the superior magnitude of English towns. "I have a town," quoth the sapient James, "in my ancient kingdom of Scotland, whilk is sae lang that at ane end of it a different language is spoken from that whilk prevails at the other." To this day the monarch's words are true; one end of Nairn is Gaelic, the other Sassenach. Here we obtain a considerable accession of strength. The attributes of one kilted chieftain are described to me in curious scraps of illustrative patchwork. "A great litigant, an enthusiastic agriculturist, a dealer in Hielan' nowt—something of a Hielan' nowt himself, a semi-auctioneer, a great hand as chairman at an agricultural dinner, a visitor to the Baker Street Bazaar when the Smithfield Shows were held there and where the Cockneys mistook him for one of the exhibits and began pinching and punching him." Stewart of Duntalloch swings his stalwart form into our carriage—a noted breeder of Highland cattle and as fine a specimen of a Highlander as can be seen from Reay to Pitlochrie. "Culloden! Culloden!" chant the porters in that curious sing-song peculiar to the Scotch platform porter. The whistle of the engine and the talk about turnips and cattle contrast harshly with that bleak, lonely, moorland swell yonder—the patches of green among the brown heather telling where moulders the dust of the chivalrous clansmen. It is but little longer than a century and a quarter ago since Charles Stuart and Cumberland confronted each other over against us there; and here are the descendants of the men that fought in their tartans for the "King over the Water," who are discussing the right proportion of phosphates in artificial manures and of whom one asks me confidentially for my opinion on the Leger favourite.

Here we are at Inverness at length; that city of the Clachnacudden stone. There is quite a crowd in the spacious station of business people who have been awaiting the arrival of the train from the east, and the buyers and sellers whom it has conveyed find themselves at once among eager friends. Hurried announcements are made as to the conditions and prospects of the market. The card-players have plunged suddenly *in medias res* of bargaining. The man who had volunteered to stand me a seltzer and sherry has forgotten all about his offer, and is talking energetically about clad scores and the price of lambs. I quit the station and walk up Union Street through a gradually thickening throng, till I reach Church Street and shoulder my way to the front of the Caledonian Hotel. I am now in "the heart of the market," standing as I am on the plain-stones in front of the Caledonian Hotel and looking up and down along the crowded street. What physique, what broad shoulders, what stalwart limbs, what wiry red beards and high cheek-bones there are everywhere! You have the kilt at every turn, in every tartan, and often in no tartan at all. Other men wear whole-coloured suits of inconceivably shaggy tweed, and the breadth of the bonnets is only equalled by that of the accents. Every second man has a mighty plaid over his shoulder. It may serve as a sample of his wool, for invariably it is home made. Some carry long twisted crooks such as we see in old pastoral prints; others have massive gnarled sticks grasped in vast sinewy hands on the back of which the wiry red hairs stand out like prickles. There is falling what in the south we should reckon as a very respectable pelt of rain, but the Inverness Wool Fair heeds rain no more than thistledown. Hardly a man has thought it worth his pains to envelop his shoulders in his plaid, but stands and lets the rain take its chance. There is a perfect babel of tongues; no bawling or shouting, however, but a perpetual gruff *susurrus* of broad guttural conversation accentuated every now and then by a louder exclamation in Gaelic. Quite half of the throng are discoursing in this language. It is possible to note the difference in the character of the Celt and Teuton. The former gesticulates, splutters out a perfect torrent of alternately shrill, guttural, and intoned Gaelic; he shrugs his shoulders, he throws his arms about, he thrills with vivacity. The Teuton expresses quiet, sententious canniness in every gesture and every utterance; he is a cold-blooded man and keeps his breath to cool his porridge.

On the plain-stones there are a number of benches on which men sit down to gossip and chaffer. Scraps of dialogue float about in the moist air. If you care to be an eavesdropper you must have a knowledge of Gaelic to be one effectively. "It's to be a stout market," remarks stalwart Macrae of Invershiel, come of a fine old West Highland stock and himself a very large sheep-farmer. "Sixteen shillings is my price. I'll come down a little if you like," says the tenant of Belmaduthy to keen-faced Mr. Mackenzie of Liverpool, one of the largest wool-dealers and sheep-buyers visiting the market. "You'll petter juist pe coming down to it at once." "I could not meet you at all." "I'm afraid I'll pe doing what they'll pe laughing at me for." "We can't agree at all," are the words as a couple separate, probably to come together again later in the day. "An do reic thu na 'h'uainn fhathast, Coignasgailean?" "Cha neil fios again'm lieil thusa air son tavigse thoirtorra, Cnocnangraisheag?" "Thig gus ain fluich sin ambarfan." Perhaps I had better translate. Two sheep-farmers are in colloquy, and address each other by the names of their farms, as is all but universal in the north. Cnocnangraisheag asks Coignasgailean, "Have you sold your lambs?" The cautious reply is, "I don't know; are you inclined to give me an offer?" and the proposal ensues, "Come and let us take a drink on the transaction." Let us follow the two worthies into the Caledonian. Jostling goes for nothing here and you may shove as much in reason as you choose, taking your chance of reprisals from the sons of Anak. The lobbies of the Caledonian are full of men drinking and bargaining with books in hand. There is no sitting-room in all the house and we follow the Cnocnangraisheag and his friend into the billiard-room, where we are promptly served standing. What keenness of business-discussion mingled with what galore of whisky there is everywhere! The whisky seems to make no more impression than if it were ginger-beer; and yet it is over-proof Talisker, as my throat and eyes find to their cost when I recklessly attempt to imitate Coignasgailean and take a dram neat. As I pass the bar going out Willie Brown is bawling for soda with something in it, and Donald Murray of Geanies, one of the ablest men in the north of Scotland, brushes by with quick decisive step. In the doorway stands the sturdy square-built form of Macdonald of Balranald, the largest breeder of Highland cattle in the country. Over the heathery pasture-land of North Uist 1500 head and more of horned newt of his range in half-wild freedom. The Mundells and the Mitchells seem ubiquitous. The ancestors of both families came from England as shepherds when the Sutherland clearances were made toward the end of last century, and between them they now hold probably the largest acreage—or rather mileage, of sheep-farming territory in all Scotland.

It is a "very dour market," that all admit. Everybody is holding back, for it is obvious prices are to be "desperate high" and everybody wants to get the full benefit of the rise. The predetermination of the Southern dealers to "buy out" freely at big prices had been rashly revealed over-night by one of the fraternity at the after-dinner toddy-symposium in the Caledonian. He had been sedulously plied with drink by "Charlie Mitchell" and some others of the Ross and Sutherland sheep-farmers, till reticence had departed from his tongue. Ultimately he had leaped on the table, breaking any quantity of glass-ware in the saltatory feat, and had asserted with free swearing his readiness to give 50s. all round for every three-year-old wedder in the north of Scotland. His horror-stricken partners rushed upon him and bundled him downstairs in hot haste, but the murder was out and the "dour market" was accounted for. Fancy 50s. a head for beasts that do not weigh 60 lb. apiece as they come off the hill! No wonder that we townsmen have to pay dear for our mutton.

I push my way out of the heart of the market to find the outlying neighbourhood studded all over with conversing groups. There is an all-pervading smell of whisky, and yet I see no man who has "turned a hair" by reason of the strength of the Talisker. A town-crier ringing a bell passes me. He halts, and the burden of his cry is, "There is a large supply of fresh haddies in the market!" The walls are placarded with advertisements of sheep smearing and dipping substances; the leading ingredients of which appear to be tar and butter. A recruiting sergeant of the Scots Fusilier Guards is standing by the Clachnacudden Stone, apparently in some dejection owing to the little business doing in his line. Men don't come to the "Character" Fair to 'list. It strikes me that quite three-fourths of the shops of Inverness are devoted to the sale of articles of Highland costume. Their fronts are hidden by hangings of tartan cloth; the windows are decked with sporrans, dirks, cairngorm plaid-brooches, ram's-head snuff-boxes, bullocks' horns and skean dhus. If I chose I might enter the emporium of Messrs. Macdougall in my Sassenach garb and re-emerge in ten minutes outwardly a full-blown Highland chief, from the eagle's feather in my bonnet to the buckles on my brogues. Turning down High Street I reach the quay on the Ness bank, where I find in full blast a horse fair of a very miscellaneous description, and totally destitute of the features that have earned for the wool market the title of "Character" Fair. There are blood colts running chiefly to stomach, splints and bog spavins; ponies with shaggy manes, trim barrels, and clean legs; and slack-jointed cart-horses nearly asleep—for "ginger" is an institution which does not seem to have come so far north as Inverness. Business is lively here, the chronic "dourness" of a market being discounted by the scarcity of horseflesh.

At four o'clock we sit down to the market ordinary in the great room of the Caledonian. A member of Parliament occupies the chair, one of the croupiers is a baronet, the other the chief of the clan Mackintosh. There is a great collection of north-country notabilities, and tables upon tables of sheep-farmers and sheep-dealers. We have a considerable *cacoethes* of speech-making, among the orators being Professor Blackie of Edinburgh, whose quaint comicalities convulse his audience. It is pretty late when the Professor rises to speak, and the whisky has been flowing free. Some one interjects a whiskyfied interruption into the Professor's speech, who at once in stentorian tones orders that the disturber of the harmony of the evening shall be summarily consigned to the lunatic asylum. I see him ejected with something like the force of a stone from a catapult and have no reasonable doubt that he will spend the night an inmate of "Craig Duncan." The speeches over bargaining recommences moistened by toddy, which fluid appears to exercise an appreciable softening influence on the "dourness" of the market. Till long after midnight seasoned vessels are talking and dealing, booking sales while they sip their tenth tumbler.

I have to leave on the Saturday morning, but I make no doubt that the skeleton programme given at the beginning of this paper will have its bones duly clothed with flesh.

THE WARFARE OF THE FUTURE

AT first sight the proposition may appear startling and indeed absurd ; yet hard facts, I venture to believe, will enforce the conviction on unprejudiced minds that the warfare of the present when contrasted with the warfare of the past is dilatory, ineffective, and inconclusive.

Present, or contemporary warfare may be taken to date from the general adoption of rifled firearms; the warfare of the past may fairly be limited for purposes of comparison or contrast, to the smooth-bore era ; indeed, for those purposes there is no need to go outside the present century. Roughly speaking the first five and a half decades of the century were smooth-bore decades ; the three and a half later decades have been rifled decades, of which about two and a half decades constitute the breech-loading period. Considering the extraordinary advances since the end of the smooth-bore era in everything tending to promote celerity and decisiveness in the result of campaigns—the revolution in swiftness of shooting and length of range of firearms, the development in the science of gunnery, the increased devotion to military study, the vast additions to the military strength of the nations, looking to the facilities for rapid conveyance of troops and transportation of supplies afforded by railways and steam water-carriage, to the intensified artillery fire that can now be brought to bear on fortresses, to the manifold advantages afforded by the electric telegraph, and to the crushing cost of warfare, urging vigorous exertions toward the speedy decision of campaigns—reviewing, I say, the thousand and one circumstances encouraging to short, sharp, and decisive action in contemporary warfare, it is a strange and bewildering fact that the wars of the smooth-bore era were for the most part, shorter, sharper, and more decisive. Spite of inferiority of weapons the battles of that period were bloodier than those of the present, and it is a mathematically demonstrable proposition that the heavier the slaughter of combatants the nearer must be the end of a war. There is no pursuit now after victory won and the vanquished draws off shaken but not broken; in the smooth-bore era a vigorous pursuit scattered him to the four winds. When Wellington in the Peninsula wanted a fortress and being in a hurry could not wait the result of a formal siege or a starvation blockade, he carried it by storm. No fortress is ever stormed now, no matter how urgent the need for its reduction, no matter how obsolete its defences. The Germans in 1871 did attempt to carry by assault an outwork of Belfort, but failed utterly. It would almost seem that in the matter of forlorn hopes the Caucasian is played out.

Assertions are easy, but they go for little unless they can be proved; some examples, therefore, may be cited in support of the contentions advanced above. The Prussians are proud and with justice, of what is known as the "Seven Weeks' War of 1866" although as a matter of fact the contest with Austria did not last so long, for Prince Frederick Charles crossed the Bohemian frontier on the 23rd of June and the armistice which ended hostilities was signed at Nikolsburg on the 26th of July. The Prussian armies were stronger than their opponents by more than one-fourth and they were armed with the needle-gun against the Austrian muzzle-loading rifle. When the armistice was signed the Prussians lay on the Marchfeld within dim sight of the Stephanien-Thurm, it is true; but with the strong and strongly armed and held lines of Florisdorf, the Danube, and the army of the Archduke Albrecht between them and the Austrian capital. On the 9th of October 1806 Napoleon crossed the Saale. On the 14th at Jena he smashed Hohenlohe's Prussian army, the contending hosts being about equal strength; on the same day Davoust at Auerstadt with 27,000 men routed Brunswick's command over 50,000 strong. On the 25th of October Napoleon entered Berlin, the war virtually over and all Prussia at his feet with the exception of a few fortresses, the last of which fell on the 8th of November. Which was the swifter, the more brilliant, and the more decisive—the campaign of 1866, or the campaign of 1806?

The Franco-German war is generally regarded as an exceptionally effective performance on the part of the Germans. The first German force entered France on the 4th of August 1870. Paris was invested on the 21st of September, the German armies having fought four great battles and several serious actions between the frontier and the French capital. An armistice, which was not conclusive since it allowed the siege of Belfort to proceed and Bourbaki's army to be free to attempt raising it, was signed at Versailles on the 28th of January 1871, but the actual conclusion of hostilities dates from the 16th of February, the day on which Belfort surrendered. The Franco-German war, therefore, lasted six and a half months. The Germans were in full preparedness except that their rifle was inferior to the French *chassepot;* they were in overwhelmingly superior numerical strength in every encounter save two with French regular troops, and they had on their banners the prestige of Sadowa. Their adversaries were utterly unready for a great struggle; the French army was in a wretched state in every sense of the word; indeed, after Sedan there remained hardly any regulars able to take the field. In August 1805 Napoleon's Grande Armée was at Boulogne looking across to the British shores. Those inaccessible, he promptly altered his plans and went against Austria. Mack with 84,000 Austrian soldiers was at Ulm, waiting for the expected Russian army of co-operation and meantime covering the valley of the Danube. Napoleon crossed the Rhine on the 26th of September. Just as in 1870 the Germans on the plain of Mars-la-Tour thrust themselves between Bazaine and the rest of France, so Napoleon turned Mack and from Aalen to the Tyrol stood between him and Austria. Mack capitulated Ulm and his army on the 19th of October and Napoleon was in Vienna on the 13th of November. Although he possessed the Austrian capital, he was not, however, master of the Austrian empire. The latter result did not fall to him until the 2nd of December, when under "the sun of Austerlitz" he with 73,000 men defeated the Austro-Russian army 85,000 strong, inflicting on it a loss of 30,000 men at the cost of 12,000 of his own soldiers *hors de combat*. It took the Germans in 1870 a month and a half to get from the frontier to *outside* Paris; just in the same time, although certainly not with so severe fighting by the way but nearly twice as long a march, Napoleon moved from the Rhine to *inside* Vienna. From the active commencement to the cessation of hostilities the Franco-German war lasted six and a half months; reckoning from the crossing of the Rhine to the evening of Austerlitz Napoleon subjugated Austria in two and a quarter months. Perhaps, however, his campaign of 1809 against Austria furnishes a more exact parallel with the campaign of the Germans in 1870-71. He assumed command on the 17th of April, having hurried from Spain. He defeated the Austrians five times in as many days, at Thann, Abensberg, Landshut, Eckmuhl, and Ratisbon; and he was in Vienna on the 13th of May. Balked at Aspern and Essling, he gained his point at Wagram on the 5th of July, and hostilities ceased with the armistice of Znaim on the 11th after having lasted for a period short of three months by a week.

The Russians have a reputation for good marching, and certainly Suvaroff made good time in his long march from Russia to Northern Italy in 1799; almost as good, indeed, as Bagration, Barclay de

Tolly, and Kutusoff made in falling back before Napoleon when he invaded Russia in 1812. But they have not improved either in marching or in fighting at all commensurately with the improved appliances. In 1877, after dawdling two months they crossed the Danube on the 21st to the 27th of June. Osman Pasha at Plevna gave them pause until the 10th of December, at which date they were not so far into Bulgaria as they had been five months previously. After the fall of Plevna the Russian armies would have gone into winter quarters but for a private quasi-ultimatum communicated to the Tzar from a high source in England, to the effect that unpleasant consequences could not be guaranteed against if the war was not finished in one campaign. Alexander, who was quite an astute man in his way, was temporarily enraged by this restriction, but recovering his calmness, realised that nowhere in war books is any particular time specified for the termination or duration of a campaign. It appeared that so long as an army keeps the field uninterruptedly a campaign may continue until the Greek kalends. In less time than that Gourko and Skobeleff undertook to finish the business; by the vigour with which they forced their way across the Balkans in the heart of the bitter winter Sophia, Philippopolis, and Adrianople fell into Russian hands; and the Russian troops had been halted some time almost in face of Constantinople when the treaty of San Stephano was signed on the 3rd of March 1878. It had taken the Russians of 1877-78 eight weary months to cover the distance between the Danube and the Marmora. But fifty years earlier a Russian general had marched from the Danube to the Ægean in three and a half months, nor was his journey by any means a smooth and bloodless one. Diebitch crossed the Danube in May 1828 and besieged Silistria from the 17th of May until the 1st of July. Silistria has undergone three resolute sieges during the century; it succumbed but once, and then to Diebitch. Pressing south immediately, he worsted the Turkish Grand Vizier in the fierce battle of Kuleutscha and then by diverse routes hurried down into the great Roumelian valley. Adrianople made no resistance and although his force was attenuated by hardship and disease, when the Turkish diplomatists procrastinated the audacious and gallant Diebitch marched his thin regiments forward toward Constantinople. They had traversed on a wide front half the distance between Adrianople and the capital when the dilatory Turkish negotiators saw fit to imitate the coon and come down. Whether they would have done so had they known the weakness of Diebitch may be questioned; but again it may be questioned whether, that weakness unknown, he could not have occupied Constantinople on the swagger. His master was prepared promptly to reinforce him; Constantinople was perhaps nearer its fall in 1828 than in 1878, and certainly Diebitch was much smarter than were the Grand Duke Nicholas, his fossil Nepokoitschitsky, and his pure theorist Levitsky.

The contrast between the character of our own contemporary military operations and that of those of the smooth-bore era is very strongly marked. In 1838-39 Keane marched an Anglo-Indian army from our frontier at Ferozepore over Candahar to Cabul without experiencing any serious check, and with the single important incident of taking Ghuzni by storm on the way. Our positions at and about Cabul were not seriously molested until late in 1841, when the paralysis of demoralisation struck our soldiers because of the crass follies of a wrong-headed civilian chief and the feebleness of a decrepit general. Nott throughout held Candahar firmly; the Khyber Pass remained open until faith was broken with the hillmen; Jellalabad held out until the "Retribution Column" camped under its walls. But for the awful catastrophe which befell in the passes the hapless brigade which under the influence of deplorable pusillanimity and gross mismanagement had evacuated Cabul, no serious military calamity marked our occupation of Afghanistan and certainly stubborn resistance had not confronted our arms. From 1878 to 1880 we were in Afghanistan again, this time with breech-loading far-ranging rifles, copious artillery of the newest types, and commanders physically and mentally efficient. All those advantages availed us not one whit. The Afghans took more liberties with us than they had done forty years previously. They stood up to us in fair fight over and over again: at Ali Musjid, at the Pewar Kotul, at Charasiab, on the Takt-i-Shah and the Asmai heights, at Candahar. They took the dashing offensive at Ahmed Kheyl and at the Shuturgurdan; they drove Dunham Massy's cavalry and took British guns; they reoccupied Cabul in the face of our arms, they besieged Candahar, they hemmed Roberts within the Sherpoor cantonments and assailed him there. They destroyed a British brigade at Maiwand and blocked Gough in the Jugdulluck Pass. Finally our evacuating army had to macadamise its unmolested route down the passes by bribes to the hillmen, and the result of the second Afghan war was about as barren as that of the first.

It was in the year 1886 that, the resolution having been taken to dethrone Thebau and annex Upper Burmah, Prendergast began his all but bloodless movement on Mandalay. The Burmans of to-day have never adventured a battle, yet after years of desultory bushwhacking the pacification of Upper Burmah has still to be fully accomplished. On the 10th of April 1852 an Anglo-Indian expedition commanded by General Godwin landed at Rangoon. During the next fifteen months it did a good deal of hard fighting, for the Burmans of that period made a stout resistance. At midsummer of 1853 Lord Dalhousie proclaimed the war finished, announced the annexation and pacification of Lower Burmah, and broke up the army. The cost of the war of which the result was this fine addition to our Indian Empire, was two millions sterling; almost from the first the province was self-supporting and uninterrupted peace has reigned within its borders. We did not dally in those primitive smooth-bore days. Sir Charles Napier took the field against the Scinde Ameers on the 16th of February 1843. Next day he fought the battle of Meanee, entered Hyderabad on the 20th, and on the 24th of March won the decisive victory of Dubba which placed Scinde at his mercy, although

R

not until June did the old "Lion of Meerpore" succumb to Jacob. But before then Napier was well forward with his admirable measures for the peaceful administration of the great province he had added to British India.

The expedition for the rescue of General Gordon was tediously boated up the Nile, with the result that the "desert column" which Sir Herbert Stewart led so valiantly across the Bayuda reached Gubat just in time to be too late, and was itself extricated from imminent disaster by the masterful promptitude of Sir Redvers Buller. Notwithstanding a general consensus of professional and expert opinion in favour of the alternative route from Souakin to Berber, 240 miles long and far from waterless, the adoption of it was condemned as impossible. In June 1801, away back in the primitive days, an Anglo-Indian brigade 5000 strong ordered from Bombay, reached Kosseir on the Red Sea bound for the Upper Nile at Kenéh thence to join Abercromby's force operating in Lower Egypt. The distance from Kosseir to Kenéh is 120 miles across a barren desert with scanty and unfrequent springs. The march was by regiments, of which the first quitted Kosseir on the 1st of July. The record of the desert-march of the 10th Foot is now before me. It left Kosseir on the 20th of July and reached Kenéh on the 29th, marching at the rate of twelve miles per day. Its loss on the march was one drummer. The whole brigade was at Kenéh in the early days of August, the period between its debarkation and its concentration on the Nile being about five weeks. The march was effected at the very worst season of the year. It was half the distance of a march from Souakin to Berber; the latter march by a force of the same strength could well have been accomplished in three months. The opposition on the march could not have been so severe as that which Stewart's desert column encountered. Nevertheless, as I have said, the Souakin-Berber route was pronounced impossible by the deciding authority.

The comparative feebleness of contemporary warfare is perhaps exceptionally manifest in relation to the reduction of fortresses. During the Franco-German War the frequency of announcements of the fall of French fortresses used to be the subject of casual jeers. The jeers were misplaced. The French fortresses, labouring under every conceivable disadvantage, did not do themselves discredit. All of them were more or less obsolete. Excluding Metz and Paris, neither fortified to date, their average age was about a century and a half and few had been amended since their first construction. They were mostly garrisoned by inferior troops, often almost entirely by Mobiles. Only in one instance was there an effective director of the defence. That they uniformly enclosed towns whose civilian population had to endure bombardment, was an obvious hindrance to desperate resistance. Yet, setting aside Bitsch which was never taken, the average duration of the defence of the seventeen fortresses which made other than nominal resistance was forty-one days. Excluding Paris and Metz which virtually were intrenched camps, the average period of resistance was thirty-three days. The Germans used siege artillery in fourteen cases; although only on two instances, Belfort and Strasburg, were formal sieges undertaken. "It appears," writes Major Sydenham Clarke in his recent remarkable work on Fortification[1] which ought to revolutionise that art, "that the average period of resistance of the (nominally obsolete) French fortresses was the same as that of besieged fortresses of the Marlborough and Peninsular periods. Including Paris and Metz, the era of rifled weapons actually shows an increase of 20 per cent in the time-endurance of permanent fortifications. Granted that a mere measurement in days affords no absolute standard of comparison, the striking fact remains that in spite of every sort of disability the French fortresses, pitted against guns that were not dreamed of when they were built, acquitted themselves quite as well as the *chefs-d'œuvre* of the Vauban school in the days of their glory." Even in the cases of fortresses whose reduction was urgently needed since they interfered with the German communications—such as Strasburg, Toul, and Soissons—the quick *ultima ratio* of assault was not resorted to by the Germans. And yet the Germans could not have failed to recognise that but for the fortresses they would have swept France clear of all organised bodies of troops within two months of the frontier battles. During the Peninsular War Wellington made twelve assaults on breached fortresses of which five were successful; of his twelve attempts to escalade six succeeded. The Germans in 1870-71 never attempted a breach and

[1] *Fortification.* By Major G. Sydenham Clarke, C.M.G. (London: John Murray).

their solitary effort at escalade, on the Basse Perche of Belfort, utterly failed.

The Russians in 1877 were even less enterprising than had been the Germans in 1870. They went against three permanently fortified places, the antediluvian little Matchin which if I remember right blew itself up; the crumbling Nicopolis which surrendered after one day's fighting; and Rustchuk which held out till the end of the war. They would not look at Silistria, ruined, but strong in heroic memories; they avoided Rasgrad, Schumla, and the Black Sea fortresses; Sophia, Philippopolis, and Adrianople made no resistance. The earthworks of Plevna, vicious as they were in many characteristics, they found impregnable. I think Suvaroff would have carried them; I am sure Skobeleff would if he had got his way.

The vastly expensive armaments of the present —the rifled breech-loader, the magazine rifle, the machine guns, the long-range field-guns, and so forth, are all accepted and paid for by the respective nations in the frank and naked expectation that these weapons will perform increased execution on the enemy in war time. This granted, nor can it be denied, it logically follows that if this increased execution is not performed nations are entitled to regard it as a grievance that they do not get blood for their money, and this they certainly do not have; so that even in this sanguinary particular the warfare of to-day is a comparative failure. The topic, however, is rather a ghastly one and I refrain from citing evidence; which, however, is easily accessible to any one who cares to seek it.

The anticipation is confidently adventured that a great revolution will be made in warfare by the magazine rifle with its increased range, the machine gun, and the quick-firing field artillery which will speedily be introduced into every service. It does not seem likely that smokeless powder will create any very important change, except in siege operations. On the battlefield neither artillery nor infantry come into action out of sight of the enemy. When either arm opens fire within sight of the enemy its position can be almost invariably detected by the field-glass, irrespective of the smokelessness or non-smokelessness of its ammunition. Indeed, the use of smokeless powder would seem inevitably to damage the fortunes of the attack. Under cover of a bank of smoke the soldiers hurrying on to feed the fighting line are fairly hidden from aimed hostile fire. It may be argued that their aim is thus reciprocally hindered; but the reply is that their anxiety is not so much to be shooting during their reinforcing advance as to get forward into the fighting line, where the atmosphere is not so greatly obscured. Smokeless powder will no doubt advantage the defence.

It need not be remarked that a battle is a physical impossibility while both sides adhere to the passive defensive; and experience proves that battles are rare in which both sides are committed to the active offensive, whether by preference or necessity. Mars-la-Tour (16th August 1870) was the only contest of this nature in the Franco-German War. Bazaine had to be on the offensive because he was ordered to get away towards Verdun; Alvensleben took it because it was the only means whereby he could hinder Bazaine from accomplishing his purpose. But for the most part one side in battle is on the offensive; the other on the defensive. The invader is habitually the offensive person, just for the reason that the native force commonly acts on the defensive; the latter is anxious to hinder further penetration into the bowels of its land; the former's desire is to effect that penetration. The defensive of the native army need not, however, be the passive defensive; indeed, unless the position be exceptionally strong that is according to present tenets to be avoided. When, always with an underlying purpose of defence, its chief resorts to the offensive for reasons that he regards as good, his strategy or his tactics as the case may be, are expressed by the term "defensive-offensive."

It says a good deal for the peaceful predilections of the nations, that there has been no fairly balanced experience affording the material for decision as to the relative advantage of the offensive and the defensive under modern conditions. In 1866 the Prussians, opposing the needle-gun to the Austrian muzzle-loader, naturally utilised this pre-eminence by adopting uniformly the offensive and traditions of the Great Frederick doubtless seconded the needle-gun. After Sadowa controversy ran high as to the proper system of tactics when breech-loader should oppose breech-loader. A strong party maintained that "the defensive had now become so strong that true science lay in forcing the adversary to attack. Let him come on, and then one might fairly rely on victory." As Boguslawski observes—" This conception of tactics would paralyse the offensive, for how can an army advance if it has always to wait till an enemy attacks?" After much exercitation the Germans determined to adhere to the offensive. In the recent modest language of Baron von der Goltz:[1] "Our modern German mode of battle aims at being entirely a final struggle, which we conceive of as being inseparable from an unsparing offensive. Temporising, waiting, and a calm defensive are very unsympathetic to our nature. Everything with us is action. Our strength lies in great decisions on the battlefield." Perhaps also the guileless Germans were quite alert to the fact that Marshal Niel had shattered the French army's tradition of the offensive, and gone counter to the French soldier's nature by enjoining the defensive in the latest official instructions. Had the Teutons suborned him the Marshal could not have done them a better turn.

Their offensive tactics against an enemy unnaturally lashed to the stake of the defensive stood the Germans in excellent stead in 1870. On every occasion they resorted to the offensive against an enemy in the field; strictly refraining, however, from that expedient when it was a fortress and not soldiers *en vive force* that stood in the way. At St. Privat their offensive would probably have been worsted if Canrobert had been reinforced or even if a supply of ammunition had reached him; and a loss there of one-third of the combatants of the Guard Corps without result caused them to change for the better the method of their attack. But in every battle from Weissenburg to Sedan with the exception of the

[1] *The Nation in Arms*, by Lieutenant-Colonel Baron von der Goltz. (Allen.)

confused *mêlée* of Mars-la-Tour, the French, besides being bewildered and discouraged, were in inferior strength; after Sedan the French levies in the field were scarcely soldiers. There was no fair testing of the relative advantages of defence and offence in the Russo-Turkish War of 1877-78; and so it remains that in an actual and practical sense no firm decision has yet been established. All civilised nations are, however, assiduously practising the methods of the offensive.

It may nevertheless be anticipated that in future warfare between evenly matched combatants the offensive will get the worst of it at the hands of the defensive. The word "anticipate" is used in preference to "apprehend," because one's sympathy is naturally for the invaded state unless it has been wantonly aggressive and insolent. The invaded army, if the term may be used, having familiar knowledge of the terrain will take up a position in the fair-way of the invader; affording strong flank *appui* and a far-stretching clear range in front and on flanks. It will throw up several lines, or still better, tiers of shallow trenches along its front and flanks, with emplacements for artillery and machine guns. The invader must attack; he cannot turn the enemy's position and expose his communications to that enemy. He takes the offensive, doing so, as is the received practice, in front and on a flank. From the outset he will find the offensive a sterner ordeal than in the Franco-German War days. He will have to break into loose order at a greater distance, because of the longer range of small arms, and the further scope, the greater accuracy, and the quicker fire of the new artillery. He too possesses those weapons, but he cannot use them with so great effect. His field batteries suffer from the hostile cannon fire as they move forward to take up a position. His infantry cannot fire on the run; when they drop after a rush the aim of panting and breathless men cannot be of the best. And their target is fairly protected and at least partially hidden. The defenders behind their low épaulement do not pant; their marksmen only at first are allowed to fire; these make things unpleasant for the massed gunners out yonder, who share their attentions with the spraying-out infantrymen. The quick-firing cannon of the defence are getting in their work methodically. Neither its gunners nor its infantry need be nervous as to expending ammunition freely since plenteous supplies are promptly available, a convenience which does not infallibly come to either guns or rifles of the attack. The Germans report as their experience in the capacity of assailants that the rapidity and excitement of the advance, the stir of strife, the turmoil, exhilarate the soldiers, and that patriotism and fire-discipline in combination enforce a cool steady maintenance of fire; that in view of the ominous spectacle of the swift and confident advance, under torture of the storm of shell-fire and the hail of bullets which they have to endure in immobility, the defenders, previously shaken by the assailants' artillery preparation, become nervous, waver, and finally break when the cheers of the final concentrated rush strike on their ears. That this was scarcely true as regarded French regulars the annals of every battle of the Franco-German War up to and including Sedan conclusively show. It is true, however, that the French nature is intolerant of inactivity and in 1870 suffered under the deprivation of its *métier;* but how often the Germans recoiled from the shelter trenches of the Spicheren and gave ground all along the line from St. Privat to the Bois de Vaux, men who witnessed those desperate struggles cannot forget while they live. Warriors of greater equanimity than the French soldier possesses might perhaps stand on the defensive in calm self-confidence with simple breech-loaders as their weapons, if simple breech-loaders were also weapons of the assailants. But in his magazine rifle the soldier of the future can keep the defensive not only with self-confidence, but with high elation, for in it he will possess a weapon against which it seems improbable that the attack (although armed too with a magazine or repeating rifle) can prevail.

The assailants fall fast as their advance pushes forward, thinned down by the rifle fire, the mitraille, and the shrapnel of the defence. But they are gallant men and while life lasts they will not be denied. The long bloody advance is all but over; the survivors of it who have attained thus far are lying down getting their wind for the final concentration and rush. Meanwhile, since after they once again stand up they will use no more rifle fire till they have conquered or are beaten, they are pouring forth against the defence their reserve of bullets in or attached to their rifle-butts. The defenders take this punishment, like Colonel Quagg, lying down, courting the protection of their earth-bank. The hail of the assailants' bullets ceases; already the artillery of the attack has desisted lest it should injure friend as well as foe. The word runs along the line and the clumps of men lying prostrate there out in the open. The officers spring to their feet, wave their swords, and cheer loudly. The men are up in an instant, and the swift rush focussing toward a point begins. The distance to be traversed before the attackers are *aux prises* with the defenders is about one hundred and fifty yards.

It is no mere storm of missiles which meets fair in the face those charging heroes; no, it is a moving wall of metal against which they rush to their ruin. For the infantry of the defence are emptying their magazines now at point-blank range. Emptied magazine yields to full one; the Maxims are pumping, not bullets, but veritable streams of death, with calm, devilish swiftness. The quick-firing guns are spouting radiating torrents of case. The attackers are mown down as corn falls, not before the sickle but the scythe. Not a man has reached, or can reach, the little earth-bank behind which the defenders keep their ground. The attack has failed; and failed from no lack of valour, of methodised effort, of punctilious compliance with every instruction; but simply because the defence—the defence of the future in warfare—has been too strong for the attack. One will not occupy space by recounting how in the very nick of time the staunch defence flashes out into the counter-offensive; nor need one enlarge on the sure results to the invader as the unassailed flank of the defence throws forward the shoulder and takes in flank the dislocated masses of aggressors.

One or two such experiences will definitively settle the point as to the relative advantage of the offensive and the defensive. Soldiers will not submit themselves to re-trial on re-trial of a *res judicata*. Grant, dogged though he was, had to accept that lesson in the shambles of Cold Harbour. For the bravest sane man will rather live than die. No man burns to become cannon-fodder. The Turk, who is supposed to court death in battle for religious reasons of a somewhat material kind, can run away even when the alternative is immediate removal to a Paradise of unlimited houris and copious sherbet. There are no braver men than Russian soldiers; but going into action against the Turks tried their nerves, not because they feared the Turks as antagonists, but because they knew too well that a petty wound disabling from retreat meant not alone death but unspeakable mutilation before that release.

It is obvious that if, as is here anticipated, the offensive proves impossible in the battle of the future, an exaggerated phase of the stalemate which Boguslawski so pathetically deprecates will occur. The world need not greatly concern itself regarding this issue; the situation will almost invariably be in favour of the invaded and will probably present itself near his frontier line. He can afford to wait until the invader tires of inaction and goes home.

Magazine and machine guns would seem to sound the knell of possible employment of cavalry in battle. No matter how dislocated are the infantry ridden at so long as they are not quite demoralised, however *rusé* the cavalry leader—however favourable to sudden unexpected onslaught is the ground, the quick-firing arms of the future must apparently stall off the most enterprising horsemen. Probably if the writer were arguing the point with a German, the famous experiences of von Bredow might be adduced in bar of this contention. In the combat of Tobitschau in 1866 Bredow led his cuirassier regiment straight at three Austrian batteries in action, captured the eighteen guns and everybody and everything belonging to them, with the loss to himself of but ten men and eight horses. It is true, says the honest official account, that the ground favoured the charge and that the shells fired by the usually skilled Austrian gunners flew high. But during the last 100 yards grape was substituted for shell, and Bredow deserved all the credit he got. Still stronger against my argument was Bredow's memorable work at Mars-la-Tour, when at the head of six squadrons he charged across 1000 yards of open plain, rode over and through two separate lines of French infantry, carried a line of cannon numbering nine batteries, rode 1000 yards farther into the very heart of the French army, and came back with a loss of not quite one half of his strength. The *Todtenritt*, as the Germans call it, was a wonderful exploit, a second Balaclava charge and a bloodier one; and there was this distinction that it had a purpose and that that purpose was achieved. For Bredow's charge in effect wrecked France. It arrested the French advance which would else have swept Alvensleben aside; and to its timely effect is traceable the sequence of events that ended in the capitulation of Metz. The fact that although from the beginning of his charge until he struck the front of the first French infantry line Bredow took the rifle-fire of a whole French division yet did not lose above fifty men, has been a notable weapon in the hands of those who argue that good cavalry can charge home on unshaken infantry. But never more will French infantry shoot from the hip as Lafont's conscripts at Mars-la-Tour shot in the vague direction of Bredow's squadrons. French cavalry never got within yards of German infantry even in loose order ; and the magazine or repeating rifle held reasonably straight will stop the most thrusting cavalry that ever heard the " charge " sound.

Fortifications of the future will differ curiously from those of the present. The latter, with their towering scarps, their massive *enceintes*, their " portentous ditches," will remain as monuments of a vicious system, except where, as in the cases of Vienna, Cologne, Sedan, etc., the dwellers in the cities they encircle shall procure their demolition for the sake of elbow-room, or until modern howitzer shells or missiles charged with high explosives shall pulverise their naked expanses of masonry. In the fortification of the future the defender will no longer be "enclosed in the toils imposed by the engineer" with the inevitable disabilities they entail, while the besieger enjoys the advantage of free mobility. Plevna has killed the castellated fortress. With free communications the full results attainable by fortress artillery intelligently used, will at length come to be realised. Unless in rare cases and for exceptional reasons towns will gradually cease to be fortified even by an encirclement of detached forts. Where the latter are availed of, practical experience will infallibly condemn the expensive and complex cupola-surmounted construction of which General Brialmont is the champion. "A work," trenchantly argues Major Sydenham Clarke, "designed on the principles of the Roman catacombs is suited only for the dead, in a literal or in a military sense. The vast system of subterranean chambers and passages is capable of entombing a brigade, but denies all necessary tactical freedom of action to a battalion."

The fortress of the future will probably be in the nature of an intrenched camp. The interior of the position will provide casemate accommodation for an army of considerable strength. Its defences will consist of a circle at intervals of about 2500 yards, of permanent redoubts which shall be invisible at moderate ranges for infantry and machine guns, the garrison of each redoubt to consist of a half battalion. Such a work was in 1886 constructed at Chatham in thirty-one working days, to hold a garrison of 200 men housed in casemates built in concrete, for less than £3000, and experiments proved that it would require a "prohibitory expenditure" of ammunition to cause it serious damage by artillery fire. The supporting defensive armament will consist of a powerful artillery rendered mobile by means of tramroads, this defence supplemented by a field force carrying on outpost duties and manning field works guarding the intervals between the redoubts. Advanced defences and exterior obstacles of as formidable a character as possible will be the complement of what in effect will be an immensely elaborated Plevna, which, properly armed and fully organised, will "fulfil all the requirements of defence" while possessing important potentialities of offence.

An illustration is pertinent of the pre-eminent utility of such fortified and strongly held positions, of whose characteristics the above is the merest outline. In the event of a future Franco-German War, the immensely expensive cordon of fortresses with which the French have lined their frontier, efficiently equipped, duly garrisoned and well commanded, will unquestionably present a serious obstacle to the invading armies. The Germans talk of *vive force*— shell heavily and then storm; the latter resort one for which they have in the past displayed no predilection. Whether by storm or interpenetration, they will probably break the cordon, but they cannot advance without masking all the principal fortresses. This will employ a considerable portion of their strength, and the invasion will proceed in less force, which will be an advantage to the defenders. But if instead of those multitudinous fortresses the French had constructed, say, three such intrenched-camp fortresses as have been sketched, each quartering 50,000 men, it would appear that they would have done better for themselves at far less cost. Each intrenched position containing a field army 50,000 strong would engross a beleaguering host of 100,000 men. The positions of the type outlined are claimed to be impregnable; they could contain supplies and munitions for at least a year, detaining around them for that period 300,000 of the enemy. No European power except Russia has soldiers enough to spare so long such a mass of troops standing fast, and simultaneously to prosecute the invasion of a first-rate power with approximately equal numbers. France at the cost of 150,000 men would be holding supine on her frontier double the number of Germans—surely no disadvantageous transaction.

In conclusion, it may be worth while to point out that the current impression that the maintenance by states of "bloated armaments" is a keen incentive to war, is fallacious. How often do we hear, "There must be a big war soon; the powers cannot long stand the cost of standing looking at each other, all armed to the teeth!" War is infinitely more costly than the costliest preparedness. But this is not all. The country gentleman for once in a way brings his family to town for the season, pledging himself privily to strict economy when the term of dissipation ends, in order to restore the balance. But for a State, as the sequel to a season of war there is no such potentiality of economy. Rather there is the grim certainty of heavier and yet heavier expenditure after the war, in the still obligatory character of the armed man keeping his house. Therefore it is that potentates are reluctant to draw the sword, and rather bear the ills they have than fly to other evils inevitably worse still. Whether the final outcome will be universal national bankruptcy or the millennium, is a problem as yet insoluble.

GEORGE MARTELL'S BANDOBAST[1]

GEORGE MARTELL was an indigo-planter in Western Tirhoot, a fine tract of Bengal stretching from the Ganges to the Nepaul Terai, and roughly bounded on the west by the Gunduck, on the east by the Kussi. Planter-life in Tirhoot is very pleasant to a man in robust health, who possesses some resources within himself. In many respects it more resembles active rural life at home than does any other life led by Anglo-Indians. The joys of a planter's life have been enthusiastically sung by a planter-poet; and the frank genial hospitality of the planter's bungalow stands out pre-eminent, even amidst the universal hospitality of India. The planter's bungalow is open to all comers. The established formula for the arriving stranger is first to call for brandy-and-soda, then to order a bath, and finally to inquire the name of the occupant his host. The laws of hospitality are as the laws of the Medes and Persians. Once in the famine time a stranger in a palki reached a planter's bungalow in an outlying district, and

[1] *Bandobast* is an Indian word, which, like many others, has been all but formally incorporated into Anglo-Indian English. The meaning is, plan, scheme, organised arrangement.

sent in his card. The planter sent him out a drink but did not bid him enter. The stranger remained in the veranda till sundown, had another drink, and then went on his way. This breach of statute law became known. There was much excuse for the planter, for the traveller was a missionary and in other respects was a *persona ingrata*. But the credit of planterhood was at stake; and so strong was the force of public opinion that the planter who had been a defaulter in hospitality had to abandon the profession and quit the district. It was on this occasion laid down as a guiding illustration, that if Judas Iscariot, when travelling around looking for an eligible tree on which to hang himself, had claimed the hospitality of a planter's bungalow, the dweller therein would have been bound to accord him that hospitality. Not even newspaper correspondents were to be sent empty away.

The indigo-planter is "up in the morning early" and away at a swinging canter on his "waler" nag, out into the *dahaut* to visit the *zillahs* on which his crop is growing. He returns when the sun is getting high with a famous appetite for a breakfast which is more than half luncheon. After his siesta he may look in upon a neighbour—all Tirhoot are neighbours and within a radius of thirty miles is considered next door. He would ride that distance any day to spend an hour or two in a house brightened by the presence of womanhood. His anxious period is *mahaye* time, when the indigo is in the vats and the quantity and quality of the yield depend so much on care and skill. But except at *mahaye* time he is always ready for relaxation, whether it takes the form of a polo match, a pig-sticking expedition, or a race-meeting at Sonepoor, Muzzufferpore, or Chumparun. These race-meetings last for several days on end, there being racing and hunting on alternate days with a ball every second night. It used to be worth a journey to India to see Jimmy Macleod cram a cross-grained "waler" over an awkward fence, and squeeze the last ounce out of the brute in the run home on the flat. The Tirhoot ladies are in all respects charming; and it must remain a moot point with the discriminating observer whether they are more delightful in the genial home-circles of which they are the centres and ornaments, or in the more exciting stir and whirl of the ballroom. After every gathering hecatombs of slain male victims mournfully cumber the ground; and one all-conquering fair one, now herself conquered by matrimony and motherhood, wrung from those her charms had blighted the title of "the destroying angel."

George Martell was an honest sort of a clod. He stood well with the ryots, and the mark of his factory always brought out keen bidding at Thomas's auction-mart in Mission Row and was held in respect in the Commission Sale Rooms in Mincing Lane. He was a good shikaree and could hold his own either at polo or at billiards; but being somewhat shy and not a little clumsy he did not frequent race-balls nor throw himself in the way of "destroying angels." He had been over a dozen years in the district and had not been known to propose once, so that he had come to be set down as a misogynist.

Among his chief allies was a neighbouring planter called Mactavish. Mactavish in some incomprehensible way—he being a gaunt, uncouth, bristly Scot, whose Highland accent was as strong as the whisky with which he had coloured his nose—had contrived to woo and win a bonny, baby-faced girl, the ripple of whose laughter and the dancing sheen of whose auburn curls filled the Mactavish bungalow with glad bright sunshine. When Mac first brought home this winsome fairy Martell had sheepishly shunned the residence of his friend, till one fine morning when he came in from the *dahaut* he found Minnie Mactavish quite at home among the pipes, empty soda-water bottles, and broken chairs that constituted the principal articles of furniture in his bachelor sitting-room. Minnie had come to fetch her husband's friend and in her dainty imperious way would take no denial. So George had his bath, got a fresh horse saddled, nearly chucked Minnie over the other side as he clumsily helped her to mount her pony, and rode away with her a willing if somewhat clownish captive. Arriving at the bungalow Mactavish, honest George was bewildered by the transformation it had undergone. Flowers were where the spirit-case used to stand. There was a drawing-room with actually a piano in it; the *World* lay on the table instead of the *Sporting Times*, and the servants wore a quiet, tasteful livery. Mac himself had been trimmed and titivated almost out of recognition. He who had been wont to lounge half the day in his *pyjamas* was now almost smartly dressed; his beard was cropped, and his bristly poll brushed and oiled. If George had a weak spot in him it was for a simple song well sung. Mrs. Mac, accompanying herself on the piano, sang to him "The Land o' the Leal" and brewed him a mild peg with her own fair hands. George by bedtime did not know whether he was on his head or his heels.

He lay awake all night thinking over all he had seen. Mactavish now was clearly a better man than ever he had been before. He had told George he was living more cheaply as a married man than ever he had done as a bachelor; and in the matter of happiness there was no comparison. George rose early to go home; but early as it was Mrs. Mac was up too, and arrayed in a killing morning *négligé* that fairly made poor George stammer, gave him his *chota hazri* and stroked his horse's head as he mounted. About half-way home George suddenly shouted, "D—d if I don't do it too!" and brought his hand down on his thigh with a smack that set his horse buck-jumping.

In effect, George Martell had determined to get married. But where to find a Mrs. Martell? Mrs. Mactavish had told him she had no sisters and that her only relative was a maiden grand-aunt, whom George thought must be a little too old to marry unless in the last resort. If he took the field at the next race-meeting the fellows would chaff the life out of him; and besides, he scarcely felt himself man enough to face a "destroying angel." As he pondered, riding slowly homeward, a thought occurred to him. When he had been at home a dozen years ago his two girl-sisters had been at school, and their great playmate had been a girl of eleven, by name Laura Davidson. Laura was a pretty child. He had taken occasional notice of her; had once kissed her after having been severely scratched in the struggle; and had taken her and his sisters to the local theatre. What if Laura Davidson—now some three-and-twenty—were still single? What if she were pretty and nice? He remembered that the colour of her hair was not unlike Mrs. Mac's, and was in ringlets too. And what if she were willing to come out and make lonely George Martell as happy a man as was that lucky old Mac?

It was mail-day, and George, taking time by the forelock, sat down and wrote to his sister what had come into his head. By the return mail he had her reply: Laura Davidson was single; she was nice; she was pretty; she had fair ringlets; she had a hazy memory of George and the kissing episode, and was willing to come out and marry him and try to make him happy. But she could not well come alone; could George suggest any method of *chaperonage* on the voyage?

In the district of Champarun, which in essentials is part of Tirhoot, lies the quaint little cavalry cantonment of Segowlie. It is the last relic of the old Nepaul war, which caused the erection of a chain of cantonments along the frontier all of which save Segowlie, are now abandoned. There is just room for one native cavalry regiment at Segowlie, and the soldiers like the station because of excellent sport and the good comradeship of the planters. At Segowlie at the time I am writing of there happened to be quartered a certain Major Freeze, whose wife, after a couple of years at home, was about returning to India. George had some acquaintance with the Major and a far-off profound respect for his wife, who was an admirable and stately lady. It occurred to him to try whether it could not be managed that she should bring out the future Mrs. Martell. He saw the Major, who was only too delighted at the prospect of a new lady in the district, and the affair was soon arranged. Mrs. Freeze wrote that she and Miss Davidson were leaving by such-and-such a mail; and knowing that Martell was rather lumpy when a lady was in the case, she thoughtfully suggested that he should go down to Bombay and meet them so as to get over the initial awkwardness by making himself useful and gain his intended's respect by swearing at the niggers.

All went well. But George Martell was not quite his own master, he was only part of a "concern" and was bound to do his best for his partners. It happened, just about the time the P. and O. steamer was due at Bombay, that the most ticklish period of the indigo-planters' year was upon Martell. The juice had begun to flow from the vats. He had no assistant and he did not dare to leave the work, so he telegraphed to Bombay to explain this to Mrs. Freeze, and added that he would meet her and her companion at Bankipore where their long railway journey would end. Miss Davidson did not understand much about the absorbing crisis of indigo production, and she had a spice of romance in her composition; so that poor Martell did not rise in her estimation by his default at Bombay. When the ladies reached Bankipore there was still no Martell, but only a *chuprassee* with a note to say that the juice was still running, and that Martell sahib could not leave the factory but would be waiting for them at Segowlie. At this even Mrs. Freeze almost lost her temper.

They have a "State Railway" now in Tirhoot, but at the time I am writing of there was only one *pukha* road in all the district. The ladies travelled in palanquins, or palkis, as they are more familiarly called. It is a long journey from Bankipore to Segowlie, and three nights were spent in travelling. Bluff old Minden Wilson stood on the bank above the ghât to welcome Mrs. Freeze across the Ganges. One day was spent at young Spudd's factory, the second at the residence of a genial planter rejoicing in the quaint name of Hong Kong Scribbens; on the third morning they reached Segowlie. But still no Martell; only a *chit* to say that that plaguy juice was still running but that he hoped to be able to drive over to dinner. Miss Davidson went to bed in a huff; and Major Freeze was temporarily inclined to think that her home-trip had impaired his good lady's amiability of character.

Martell did turn up at dinner-time. But he was hardly a man at any time to create much of an impression, and on this occasion he appeared to exceptional disadvantage. He was stutteringly nervous; and there were some evidences that he had been ineffectually striving to mitigate his nervousness by the consumption of his namesake. He wore a new dress-coat which had not the remotest pretensions to fit him, and the bear's-grease which he had freely used gave unpleasant token of rancidity. The dinner was an unsatisfactory performance. Miss Davidson was extremely *distraite*, while Martell became more and more nervous as the meal progressed and was manifestly relieved when the ladies retired. Soon after they had done so the Major was sent for from the drawing-room. He found Miss Davidson sobbing on his wife's bosom. He asked what was the matter. The girl, with many sobbing interruptions, gasped out—

"He's the wrong man! O Heavens, I never saw *him* before! The man I remember who gave me sweets when I was a child had black hair; *he* has red! Oh, what shall I do? Oh, please send that man away and let me go home!"

And then Miss Davidson went off into hysterics.

Here was a pretty state of matters! The Major and his wife could not see their way clear at all. Consultation followed consultation, with visits on the Major's part to poor Martell in the dining-room irregularly interspersed. It was almost morning before affairs arranged themselves after a fashion. The new basis agreed upon was that the previously existing arrangement should be regarded as dead, and that a courtship between Martell and Miss Davidson should be commenced *de novo*—he to do his best to recommend himself to the lady's affections, she to learn to love him if she could, red hair and all. And so George went home, and the Segowlie household went to bed.

Poor George at the best had a very poor idea of courting acceptably; and surely no man was more heavily handicapped in the enterprise prescribed him. He had to court to order, and to combat, besides, both the bad impression made at starting and the misfortune of his red hair. The poor fellow did his best. He used to come and sit in Mrs. Freeze's drawing-room hours on end, glowering at Miss Davidson in a silence broken by spasmodic efforts at forced talk. He brought the girl presents, gave her a horse, and begged of her to ride with him. But the great stupid fellow had not thought of a habit and the girl felt a delicacy in telling him that she had not one. So the horse ate his head off in idleness, and George's heart went farther and farther down in the direction of his boots. He had so bothered Mrs. Freeze that she had washed her hands of him, and had bidden him worry it out on his own line.

In less than a month the crisis came. Miss Davidson could not bring herself to think of poor George as affording the makings of a husband. She told Mrs. Freeze so, and begged, for kindness sake, that the Major would break this her determination to Mr. Martell and desire him to give the thing up as hopeless. The Major thought the best course to pursue was to write to George to this effect. Next morning in the small hours the poor fellow turned up in the Segowlie veranda in a terribly bad way. He would not accept his fate at second-hand in this fashion; he must see Miss Davidson and try to move her to be kind to him. In the end there was an interview between them, from which George emerged quiet but very pale. His notable matrimonial bandobast had proved the deadest of failures;

and the poor fellow's lip trembled as he thought of Mactavish's happy home and his own forlorn bungalow.

But although he had red hair and did not know in the least what to do with his feet, George Martell was a gentleman. The lady continuing anxious to go home, he insisted on his right to pay her return passage as he had done her passage outward, urging rather ruefully that, having taken a shot at happiness and having missed fire, he must be the sole sufferer. It is a little surprising that this uncouth chivalry did not melt the lady, but she was obdurate, although she let him have his way about the passage money. So in the company of an officer's wife going home Miss Davidson quitted Segowlie and journeyed to Bombay. Poor old George, with a very sore heart, was bent on seeing the last of her before settling down again to the old dull bachelor life. He dodged down to Bombay in the same train, travelling second class that he might not annoy the girl by a chance meeting; and stood with a sad face leaning on the rail of the Apollo Bunder, as he watched the ship containing his miscarried venture steam out of Bombay harbour on its voyage to England.

The same night he set out on his return to his plantation. At near midnight the mail-train from Bombay reaches Eginpoora, at the head of the famous Bhore ghât. Some refreshment is ordinarily procurable there, but it is not much of a place. George Martell had had a drink, and was sauntering moodily up and down the platform waiting for the whistle to sound. As he passed the second class compartment reserved for ladies he heard a low, tremulous voice exclaim, " Oh, if I could only make them understand that I'd give the world for a cup of tea!" George, if uncouth, was a practical man. His prompt voice rang out, "*Qui hye, ek pyala chah lao!*" Promptly came the refreshment-room *khitmutghar*, hurrying with the tea; and George, taking off his hat, begged to know whether he could be of any further service.

It was a very pleasant face that looked out on him in the moonlight, and there was more than mere conventionality in the accents in which the pleasant voice acknowledged his opportune courtesy. Insensibly George and the lady drifted into conversation. She was very lonely, poor thing; a friendless girl coming out to be governess in the family of a *burra sahib* at Chupra. Now Chupra is only across the Gunduck from Tirhoot, so George told his new acquaintance they were both going to nearly the same place, and professed his cordial willingness to assist her on the journey. He did so, escorting her right into Chupra before he set his face homeward; and he thenceforth got into a habit of visiting Chupra very frequently. Need I prolong the story? I happened to be in Bankipore when the Prince of Wales visited that centre of famine-wallahs. It fell to my pleasant lot to take Mrs. Martell in to dinner at the Commissioner's hospitable table. Mrs. Mactavish was sitting opposite; and I went back to my bedroom-tent in the compound without having made up my mind whether she or Mrs. Martell was the prettier and the nicer. So you see George Martell did not make quite so bad a *bandobast* after all.

THE LUCKNOW OF TO-DAY—1879

IT was in Cawnpore on my way up country, during the Prince of Wales's tour through India, that there were shown to me some curious and interesting mementoes of the siege of Lucknow. The friend in whose possession they were was near Havelock as he sat before his tent in the short Indian twilight, a short time before the advance on Lucknow made by him and Outram in September 1857. Through the gloom of the falling twilight there came marching towards the General a file of Highlanders escorting a tall, gaunt Oude man, on whose swarthy face the lamplight struck as he salaamed before the General Lord Sahib. Then he extracted from his ear a minute section of quill sealed at both ends. The General's son opened the strange envelope forwarded by a postal service so hazardous, and unrolled a morsel of paper which seemed to be covered with cabalistic signs. The missive had been sent out from Lucknow by Brigadier Inglis, the commander of the beleaguered garrison of the Lucknow Residency, and its bearer was the stanch and daring scout, Ungud. As I write the originals of this communication and of others which came in the same way lie before me; and two of those missives in their curious mixture of characters may be found of interest to readers of to-day.

LUKHNOW, *Septr.* 16*th.* (Recd. 19th.)

MY DEAR GENERAL—The last letter I recd. from you was dated 24th ult°, since when I have rec^d νο νεϖς whatever from y^r καμπ or of y^r μονεμεντς but am now δαιλη εξπεκτινγ to receive ιντελιγενσε of y^r αδυανσε in this διρεκτιον. Since the date of my last letter the enemy have continued to persevere unceasingly in their efforts against this position & the firing has never ceased day or night; they have about σιξτην guns in position round us—many of them 18 p^{rs}. On 5th inst. they made a very determined attack after exploding 2 mines and συκσηδεδ for a μομεντ in αλμοστ γετινγ into one of our βατεριες, but were eventually repulsed on all sides with heavy loss. Since the above date they have kept up a cannonade & musketry fire, occasionally throwing in a shell or two. My ωηκλη λοσες continue very ενη both in οφισερς & μεν. I shall be quite out of ρυμ for the μεν in ειτ δαις, but we have been λινινγ on ρεδυσεδ ρατιονς & I hope to be αβλε to γετ on τιλ about φιρστ προξ. If you have not ρελιευεδ us by θεν we shall have νο μεατ λεφτ, as I must κηπ some few βυλοκς to μουε my γυνς about the ποσιτιονς. As it is I have had to κιλ almost all the γυν βυλοκς, for my men c^d not περφορμ the αρδ ωορκ ωιθουτ ανιμαλ φοοδ. There is a report, tho' from a source on which I cannot implicitly rely, that μανσινγ has just αρινεδ in λυκνοω havg. λεφτ παρτ of his φορς ουτσιδε the σιτη. It is said that ἡ is in ουρ ιντερεστ and that ἡ has τακεν the αβουε στεπ at the ινστιγατιον of Βριτιsh αθοριτη. But I cannot say whether συch βη θη κασε, as all I have to go upon is βαζαρ ρυμουρ. I am μοστ ανξιους to ἑαρ of yr. αδυανσε to εναβλε μη to ρη-ασυρε ουρ νατιυε σολδιερς.[1]—Yours truly,
J. INGLIS, *Brigadier*,
H.M. 32^d Reg^t.

To Brig^r Havelock, Commg. Relieving Force.

---

[1] The reader will observe that the words are English, though the characters are Greek.

The other missive is of an earlier date, and was brought out in the same manner as the first.

August 16. (Recd. 23rd August.)

My dear General—A note from Colonel Tytler to Mr. Gubbins reached last night, dated "Mungalwar, 4th instant," the latter part of which is as follows:—"You must αιδ us in ενερη way even to cutting yʳ way out if we καντ φορϲε ουρ way in. We have ονλη α ϲμαλλ φορϲε." This has καυϲεδ μη much υνεαϲινεϲϛ, as it is quite ιμποϲιβλε with my ωεακ & ϲhατερεδ φορϲε that I can λεαυε my δεφενϲεϛ. You must bear in mind how I am ἀμπερεδ, that I have upwards of ονε υνδρεδ & τωεντη-ϲικ ωουνδεδ, and at the least τωο υνδρεδ & τωεντη ωομεν, & about τωο υνδρεδ & θιρτη chιλδρεν, & no καριαγε of any δεϲκριπτιον, besides ϲακριφιϲινγ τωεντη-θρη λακϛ of τρεαϲυρε & about θιρτη γυνϛ of ϲορτϛ. In consequence of the news recᵈ I shall soon put the φορϲε on αλφ ρατιονϛ, unless I ἑαρ φρομ you. Ουρ προυιϲιονϛ will λαϲτ us θεν till αβουτ the τενθ ϲεπτεμβερ. If you ὁπε to ϲανε θιϛ φορϲε νο τιμε μυϲτ be λοϲτ in pushing forward. We are δαιλη being ατακεδ by the ενεμη, who are within a few yards of our δεφενϲεϛ. Their μινεϛ have αλρεαδη ωεακενεδ ουρ ποϲτ, & I have ευερη ρεαϲον to βελιευε that are carrying on οθερϛ. Their ητεεν πουνδερϛ are within 150 yards of ϲομε οφ ουρ βατεριεϛ, & φρομ their ποϲιτιονϛ & ουρ ιναβιλιτη to φορμ ωορκινγ παρτιεϛ, we κανοτ ρεπλι to θεμ. θη δαμαγε δονε ουρλη is very γρεατ. My ϲτρενγθ now in ευροπεανϛ is θρη υνδρεδ & φιφτη, & about θρη ὑνδρεδ νατιυεϛ, & the men δρεαδφυλη ἀραϲϲεδ, & owing to παρτ of the ρεϲιδενϲη having been βρουγhτ δοων by ρουνδ ϲhοτ are without ϲhελτερ. Our νατιυε φορϲε havᵍ been αϲυρεδ on Col. Tytler's authority of yʳ νεαρ απροach ϲομε τωεντη φιυε δαιϛ αγο αρε νατυραλλη λοϲινγ κονφιδενϲε, ανδ ιφ θη λεαυε us I do not ϲη ὁω θε δεφενϲεϛ are to be μαννεδ. Did you ρεϲειυε α λεττερ & πλαν φρομ the μαν Υνγυδ?—Kindly answer this question.—Yours truly,

J. Inglis, *Brigadier*.

Cawnpore is an engrossing theme, and Bithoor

T

alone would furnish material for an article; but my present subject is Lucknow, and I must get to it. There is a railway now to Lucknow from Cawnpore, but the railway bridge across the Ganges is not yet finished and passengers must cross by the bridge of boats to the Oude side. Behind me, as the gharry jingles over the wooden platform, is the fort which Havelock began, which Neill completed, and in which Windham found the shelter which alone saved him from utter defeat. Before me is the low Gangetic shore, with the dumpy sand-hills gradually rising from the water's edge. A few years ago there used to ride at the head of that noble regiment the 78th Highlanders, a smooth-faced, gaunt, long-legged, stooping officer on an old white horse. The Colonel had a voice like a girl and his men irreverently called him the "old squeaker"; but although you never heard him talk of his deeds he had a habit of going quietly and steadily to the front, taking fighting and hardship philosophically as part of the day's work. Those sand-banks were once the scene of some quiet, unsensational heroism of his. He commanded the two companies of Highlanders whom Havelock threw on the unknown shore as the vanguard of his advance into Oude. No prior reconnaissance was possible. Oude swarmed with an armed and hostile population. The chances were that an army was hovering but a little way inland, waiting to attack the head of the column on landing. But it was necessary to risk all contingencies, and Mackenzie accepted the service as he might have done an invitation to a glass of grog. In the dead of the night the boats stood across with the little forlorn hope with which Havelock essayed to grapple on to Oude. Landing in the rain and darkness, it was Mackenzie's task to grope for an enemy if there should be one in his vicinity. There was not; but for four-and-twenty hours his little band hung on to the Oude bank as it were by their eyelids, detached, unsupported, and wholly charged with the taking care of themselves until it was possible to send a reinforcement. The charge of this vague, uncertain, tentative enterprise, fraught with risks so imminent and so vast, required a cool, steady-balanced courage of no common order.

"Onao!" shouts the conductor of the train at the first station from Cawnpore, and we look out on a few railway bungalows and a large native village apparently in a ruinous state. All this journey is studded with battlefields, and this is one of them. If I had time I should like to make a pilgrimage to the street mouth into which dashed frantically Private Patrick Cavanagh of the 64th, who, stung to madness by the hesitation of his fellows, was cut to pieces by the tulwars of the mutineers. We jog on very slowly; the Oude and Rohilcund Railway is to India in point of slowness what the Great Eastern used to be to us at home; but every yard of the ground is interesting. Along that high road passed in long, strangely diversified procession the people whom Clyde brought away from Lucknow—the civilians, the women, the children, and the wounded of the immortal garrison. That swell beyond the mango trees under which the *nhil gau* are feeding, is Mungalwar, Havelock's menacing position. No wonder though the outskirts of this town on the high road present a ruined appearance. It is Busseerutgunge, the scene of three of Havelock's battles and victories, fought and won in a single fortnight. We pass Bunnee, where Havelock and Outram tramping on to the relief, fired a royal salute in the hope that the sound of it might reach to the Residency and cheer the hearts of its garrison. And now we are on the platform of the Lucknow station which has more of an English look about it than have most Indian stations. There is a bookstall, although it is not one of Smith's; and there are lots of English faces in the crowd waiting the arrival of the train. The natives, one sees at a glance, are of very different physique from the people of Bengal. The Oude man is tall, square-shouldered, and upright; he has more hair on his face than has the Bengali, and his carriage is that of a free man. The railway station of Lucknow is flanked by two earthwork fortifications of considerable pretensions.

Lucknow is so full of interest and the objects of interest are so widely spread that one is in doubt where to begin the pilgrimage. But the Alumbagh is on the railway side of the canal and therefore nearest; and I drive directly to it before going into the town. From the station the road to the Alumbagh turns sharp to the left and the two miles' drive is through beautiful groves and gardens. Then the plain opens up and there is the detached temple which so long was one of Outram's outlying pickets; and to the left of it the square-walled enclosure of the Alumbagh itself with the four corners flanked by earthen bastions. The top of the wall is everywhere roughly crenelated for musketry fire, and on two of its faces there are countless tokens that it has

been the target for round shot and bullets. The
Alumbagh in the pre-Mutiny period was a pleasure-
garden of one of the princes of Oude. The enclosed
park contained a summer palace and all the surroundings were pretty and tasteful. It was for the
possession of the Alumbagh that Havelock fought his
last battle before the relief; here it was where he
left his baggage and went in ; here it was that
Clyde halted to organise the turning movement
which achieved the second relief. Hither were
brought from the Dilkoosha the women and children
of the garrison prior to starting on the march for
Cawnpore ; here Outram lay threatening Lucknow
from Clyde's relief until the latter's ultimate capture
of the city. But these occurrences contribute but
trivially to the interest of the Alumbagh in comparison with the circumstance that within its enclosure is the grave of Havelock. We enter the
great enclosure under the lofty arch of the castellated
gateway. From this a straight avenue bordered by
arbor vitæ trees, conducts to a square plot of ground
enclosed by low posts and chains. Inside this there
is a little garden the plants of which a native
gardener is watering as we open the wicket. From
the centre of the little garden there rises a shapely
obelisk on a square pedestal and on one side of the
pedestal is a long inscription. " Here lie," it begins,
" the mortal remains of Henry Havelock ; " and so,
methinks, it might have ended. There is needed no
prolix biographical inscription to tell the reverent
pilgrim of the deeds of the dead man by whose
grave he stands—so long as history lives, so long
does it suffice to know that " here lie the mortal

remains of Henry Havelock"—and the text and verse of poetry grate on one as redundancies. He sickened two days before the evacuation of the Residency and died on the morning of the 24th of November in his dooly in a tent of the camp at the Dilkoosha. The life went out of him just as the march began, and his soldiers conveyed with them, on the litter on which he had expired, the mortal remains of the chief who had so often led them on to victory.

On the following morning they buried him here in the Alumbagh, under the tree which still spreads its branches over the little garden in which he lies. There stood around the grave-mouth Colin Campbell and the chivalrous Outram, and stanch old Walter Hamilton, and the ever-ready Fraser Tytler; and the "boy Harry" to whom the campaign had brought the gain of fame and the loss of a father; and the devoted Harwood with "his heart in the coffin there with Cæsar;" and the heroic William Peel; and that "colossal red Celt," the noble, ill-fated Adrian Hope, sacrificed afterwards to incompetent obstinacy. Behind stood in a wide circle the soldiers of the Ross-shire Buffs and the "Blue Caps" who had served the dead chief so stanchly, and had gathered here now, with many a memory of his ready praise of valour and his indefatigable regard for the comfort of his men, stirring in their war-worn hearts—

> Guarded to a soldier's grave
> By the bravest of the brave,
> He hath gained a nobler tomb
> Than in old cathedral gloom.

Nobler mourners paid the rite,
Than the crowd that craves a sight;
England's banners o'er him waved,
Dead he keeps the name he saved.

The burial-place was being temporarily abandoned, and as the rebels desecrated all the graves they could discover it was necessary to obliterate as much as possible the tokens of the interment. A big "H" was carved into the bark of the tree and a small tin plate fastened to its trunk, to guide to the subsequent investigation of the spot. Dr. Russell tells us that when he visited the Alumbagh before his return home after the mutiny in Oude was stamped out, he found the hero's grave a muddy trench near the foot of a tree which bore the mark of a round shot and had carved into its bark the letter "H." The tree is here still and the dent of the round shot, and faintly too is to be discerned the carved letter but the bark around it seems to have been whittled away, perhaps by the sacrilegious knives of relic-seeking visitors. There is the grave of a young lieutenant in a corner of the little garden and a few private soldiers lie hard by.

I turn my face now toward the Charbagh bridge, following the route taken by Havelock's force on the 25th of September—the memorable day of the relief. There is the field where, as at a table in the open air Havelock and Outram were studying a map, a round shot from the Sepoy battery by the Yellow House ricochetted between them. There is the spot where stood the Yellow House itself, whence after a desperate struggle Maude's artillerymen drove the Sepoy garrison and its guns. Presently with a sweep the road comes into a direct line with the Charbagh bridge over the canal. Now there is not a house in the vicinity; the Charbagh garden has been thrown into the plain and the steep banks of the canal are perfectly naked. But then the scene was very different. On the Lucknow side the native city came close up to the bridge and lined the canal. The tall houses to right and left of the bridge on the Lucknow side were full of men with firearms. At that end of the bridge there was a regular overlapping breastwork, and behind it rose an earthwork battery solidly constructed and armed with five guns, one a 42-pounder, all crammed to the muzzle with grape. Let us sit down on the parapet and try to realise the scene. Outram with the 78th has made a detour to the right through the Charbagh garden to clear it of the enemy, and, gaining the canal bank, to bring a flanking fire to bear on its defenders. There is only room for two of Maude's guns; and there they stand out in the open on the road trying to answer the fire of the rebel battery. Thrown forward along the bank to the left of the bridge is a company of the Madras Fusiliers under Arnold, lying down and returning the musketry fire from the houses on the other side. Maude's guns are forward in the straight throat of the road where it leads on to the bridge close by, but round the bend under cover of the wall the Madras Fusiliers are lying down. In a bay of the wall of the Charbagh enclosure General Neill is standing waiting for the effect of Outram's flank movement to develop, and young Havelock, mounted, is on the other side of the road somewhat forward. Matters are at a deadlock. It seems as if Outram had lost his way. Maude's gunners are all down; he has repeatedly called for volunteers from the infantry behind, and now his gallant subaltern, Maitland, is doing bombardier's work. Maude calls to young Havelock that he shall be forced to retire his guns if something is not done at once; and Havelock rides across through the fire and in his capacity as assistant adjutant-general urges on Neill the need for an immediate assault. Neill " is not in command; he cannot take the responsibility; and General Outram must turn up soon." Havelock turns and rides away down the road towards the rear. As he passes he speaks encouragingly to the recumbent Fusiliers, who are getting fidgety at the long detention under fire. "Come out of that, sir," cried one soldier, "a chap's just had his head taken off there!" It is a grim joke that reply which tickles the Fusiliers into laughter: "And what the devil are we here for but to get our heads taken off?" Young Havelock is bent on the perpetration of what, under the circumstances, may be called a pious fraud. His father, who commands the operations, is behind with the Reserve, and he disappears round the bend on the make-belief of getting instructions from the chief. The General is far in the rear but his son comes back at the gallop, rides up to Neill, and saluting with his sword, says, "You are to carry the bridge at once, sir." Neill, acquiescing in the superior order, replies, "Get the regiment together then, and see it formed up." At the word and without waiting for the regiment to rise and form the gallant and eager Arnold springs up from his advanced position and dashes on to the bridge, followed by about a dozen of his nearest skirmishers. Tytler and Havelock, as eager as Arnold, set spurs to their horses and are by his side in a moment. The brave and ardent 84th, commanded by Willis, dashes to the front. Then the hurricane opens. The big gun crammed to the muzzle with grape, sweeps its iron sleet across the bridge in the face of the gallant band, and the Sepoy sharpshooters converge their fire on it. Arnold drops shot through both thighs, Tytler's horse goes down with a crash, the bridge is swept clear save for young Havelock erect and unwounded, waving his sword and shouting for the Fusiliers to come on, and a Fusilier corporal, Jakes by name, who, as he rams a bullet home into his Enfield, says cheerily to Havelock, " We'll soon have the —— out of that, sir!" And corporal Jakes is a true prophet. Before the big gun can be loaded again the stormers are on the bridge in a rushing mass. They are across it, they clear the barricade, they storm the battery, they are bayoneting the Sepoy gunners as they stand. The Charbagh bridge is won, but with severe loss which continues more or less all the way to the Residency; and when one comes to know the ground it becomes more and more obvious that the strategy of Havelock, overruled by Outram, was wise and prescient, when he counselled a wide turning movement by the Dilkoosha, over the Goomtee near the Martinière, and so along its northern bank to the Badshah-bagh, almost opposite to the Residency and commanding the iron bridge.

I recross the Charbagh bridge and bend away to the left by the byroad along the canal side by which the 78th Highlanders penetrated to the front of the Kaiser-bagh. Most of the native houses are now destroyed, whence was poured so deadly a fire on the advancing Ross-shire men that three colour-bearers fell in succession, and the colour fell to the grasp of the gallant Valentine M'Master, the assistant-surgeon of the regiment. And now I stand in front of the main entrance to the Kaiser-bagh, hard by the spot where stood the Sepoy battery which the Highlanders so opportunely took in reverse. Before me on the *maidan* is the plain monument to Sir Mountstuart Jackson, Captain Orr, and a sergeant, who were murdered in the Kaiser-bagh when the success of Campbell's final operations became certain. I enter the great square enclosure of the Kaiser-bagh and stand in the desolation of what was once a gay garden where the King of Oude and his women were wont to disport themselves. The place stands much as Campbell's men left it after looting its multifarious rich treasures. The dainty little pavilions are empty and dilapidated, the statues are broken and tottering. Quitting the Kaiser-bagh, I try to realise the scene of that informal council of war in one of the outlying courtyards of the numerous palaces. I want to fix the spot where on his big waler sat Outram, a splash of blood across his face, and his arm in a sling; where Havelock, dismounted, walked up and down by Outram's side with short, nervous strides, halting now and then to give emphasis to the argument, while all around them were officers, soldiers, guns, natives, wounded men, bullocks, and a surging tide of disorganisation momentarily pouring into the square. But the attempt is fruitless. The whole area has been cleared of buildings right up to the gate of the Residency, only that hard by the Goomtee there still stands the river wing of the Chutter Munzil Palace with its fantastic architecture, and that the palace of the King of Oude is now the station library and assembly rooms. The Hureen Khana, the Lalbagh, the courts of the Furrut Bux Palace, the Khas Bazaar, and the Clock Tower have alike been swept away, and in their place there opens up before the eye trim ornamental grounds with neat plantations which extend up to the Baileyguard itself. One archway alone stands—a gaunt commemorative skeleton—a pedestal for the statue of a noble soldier. It was from a chamber above the crown of this arch that the sepoy shot Neill as he sat on his horse urging the confused press of guns and men through the archway. The spot is memorable for other causes. This archway led into that court which is world-famous under the name of Dhooly Square. Here it was that the native bearers abandoned the wounded in the doolies which poor Bensley Thornhill was trying to guide into the Residency; here it was where they were butchered and burned as they lay, and here it was where Dr. Home and a handful of men of the escort did what in them lay to cover the wounded and defended themselves for a day and a night against continuous attacks of countless enemies.

The *via dolorosa*, the road of death up which Outram and Havelock fought their way with Brazier's Sikhs and the Ross-shire Buffs, is now a pleasant open drive amid clumps of trees, leading on to the Residency. A strange thrill runs through one's frame as there opens up before one that reddish-gray crumbling archway spanning the roadway into the Residency grounds. Its face is dented and splintered with cannon-shot and pitted all over by musket-bullets. This is none other than that historic Baileyguard gate which burly Jock Aitken and his faithful Sepoys kept so stanchly. You may see the marks still of the earth banked up against it on the interior during the siege. To the right and left runs the low wall which was the curtain of the defence, now crumbled so as to be almost indistinguishable. But there still stands, retired somewhat from the right of the archway, Aitken's post—the guard-house and treasury, its pillars and façade cut and dented all over with the marks of bullets fired by "Bob the Nailer" and his comrades from the Clock Tower which stood over against it. And in the curtain wall between the archway and the building is still to be traced the faint outline of the embrasure through which Outram and Havelock entered on the memorable evening. The turmoil and din and conflicting emotions of that terrible, glorious day have merged into a strange serenity of quietude. The scene is solitary, save for a native woman who is playing with her baby on a spot where once dead bodies lay in heaps. But the other older scene rises up vividly before the mind's eye out of the present calm. Havelock and Outram and the staff have passed through the embrasure here, and now there are rushing in the men of the ranks, powder-grimed, dusty, bloody; but a minute before raging with the stern passion of the battle, now full of a woman-like tenderness. And all around them as they swarm in there crowd a mass of folk eager to give welcome. There are officers and men of the garrison, civilians whom the siege has made into soldiers; women, too, weeping tears of joy down on the faces of the children for whom they had not dared to hope for aught but death. There are gaunt men, pallid with loss of blood, whose great eyes shine weirdly amid the torchlight and whose thin hands tremble with weakness as they grip the sinewy, grimy hands of the Highlanders. These are the wounded of the long siege who have crawled out from the hospital up yonder, as many of them as could compass the exertion, with a welcome to their deliverers. The hearts of the impulsive Highlanders wax very warm. As they grasp the hands held out to them they exclaim, " God bless you!" "Why, we expected to have found only your bones!" "And the children are living too!" and many other fervid and incoherent ejaculations. The ladies of the garrison come among the Highlanders, shaking them enthusiastically by the hand; and the children clasp the shaggy men round the neck, and to say truth, so do some of the mothers. But Jessie Dunbar and her " Dinna ye hear it?" in reference to the bagpipe music, are in the category of melodramatic fictions.

The position which bears and will bear to all time the title of the Residency of Lucknow, is an elevated plateau of land, irregular in surface, of which the highest point is occupied by the Residency building, while the area around was studded irregularly with buildings, chiefly the houses of the principal civilian officials of the station. When Campbell brought away the garrison in November 1857 it lapsed into the hands of the mutineers, who held it till his final occupation of the city and its surroundings in March of the following year. They pulled down not a few of the already shattered buildings, and left their fell imprint on the spot in an atrociously ghastly way by desecrating the graves in which brave hands had laid our dead country-people and flinging the exhumed corpses into the Goomtee. When India once more became settled the Residency, its commemorative features uninterfered with, was laid out as a garden and flowers and shrubs now grow on soil once wet with the blood of heroes. The *débris* has been removed or dispersed; the shattered buildings are prevented from crumbling farther; tablets bearing the names of the different positions and places of interest are let into the walls; and it is possible, by exploring the place map in hand, to identify all the features of the defence. The avenue from the Baileyguard gate rises with a steep slope to the Residency building. On either side of the approach and hard by the gate, are the blistered and shattered remnants of two large houses; that on the right is the banqueting house which was used as the hospital during the siege; that on the left was Dr. Fayrer's house. The banqueting house is a mere shell, riven everywhere with shot and pitted over by musket-bullets as if it had suffered from smallpox. The ground-floor has escaped with less damage but the banqueting hall itself has been wholly wrecked by the persistent fire which the rebels showered upon it, and to which, notwithstanding the mattresses and sandbags with which the windows were blocked, several poor fellows fell victims as they lay wounded on their cots. Dr. Fayrer's house is equally a battered ruin. In its first floor, roofless and forlorn, its front torn open by shot and the pillars of its windows jagged into fantastic fragments, is the veranda in which Sir Henry Lawrence, 4th July 1857, died, exposed to fire to the very last. At the top of the slope of the avenue and on the left front of the Residency building as we approach it—on what, indeed, was once the lawn—has been raised an artificial mound, its slopes covered with flowering shrubs, its summit bearing the monumental obelisk on the pedestal of which is the terse, appropriate inscription: "In memory of Major-General Sir Henry Lawrence and the brave men who fell in defence of the Residency. *Si monumentum quæris Circumspice!*" Beyond this lies the scathed and blighted ruin of the Residency House, once a large and imposing structure, now so utterly wrecked and shivered that one wonders how the crumbling reddish-gray walls are kept erect. The veranda was battered down and much of the front of the building lies bodily open, the structure being supported on the battered and distorted pillars assisted by great balks of wood. Entering by the left wing I pass down a winding stair into the bowels of the earth till I reach the spacious and lofty vaults or *tykhana* under the building. Here, the place affording comparative safety, lived immured the women of the garrison, the soldiers' wives, half-caste females, the wives of the meaner civilians and their children. The poor creatures were seldom allowed to come up to the surface, lest they should come in the way of the shot which constantly lacerated the whole area, and few visitors were allowed access to them. Veritably they were in a dungeon. Provisions were lowered down to them from the window orifices near the roof of the vaulting, and there were days when the firing was so heavy that orders were given to them not even to rise from their beds on the floor. For shot occasionally found a way even into the *tykhana;* you may see the holes it made in penetrating. The miserables were billeted off ten in a room, and there they lived, without sweepers, baths, dhobies, or any of the comforts which the climate makes necessities. Here in these dungeons children were born, only for the most part to die. Ascending another staircase I pass through some rooms in which lived (and died) some of the ladies of the garrison, and passing from the left wing by a shattered corridor am able to look up into the room in which Sir Henry Lawrence received his death-wound. Access to it is impossible by reason of the tottering condition of the structure; and turning away I clamber up the worn staircase in the shot-riven tower on the summit of which still stands the flagstaff on which were hoisted the signals with which the garrison were wont to communicate with the Alumbagh. The walls of the staircase and the flat roof of the tower are scratched and written all over with the names of visitors; many of the names are those of natives, but more are those of British soldiers, who have occasionally added a piece of their mind in characteristically strong language.

I set out on a pilgrimage under the still easily

traceable contour of the intrenchment. Passing "Sam Lawrence's Battery" above what was the water-gate, I traverse the projecting tongue at the end of which stood the "Redan Battery" whose fire swept the river face up to the iron bridge. Returning, and passing the spot where "Evans's Battery" stood, I find myself in the churchyard in a slight depression of the ground. Of the church, which was itself a defensive post, not one stone remains on another and the mutineers hacked to pieces the ground of the churchyard. The ground is now neatly enclosed and ornamentally planted and is studded with many monuments, few of which speak the truth when they profess to cover the dust of those whom they commemorate. There are the regimental monuments of the 5th Madras Fusiliers, the 84th (360 men besides officers), the Royal Artillery, the 90th (a long list of officers and 271 men). The monument of the 1st Madras Fusiliers bears the names of Neill, Stephenson, Renaud, and Arnold, and commemorates a loss of 352 men. There is a monument to Mr. Polehampton the exemplary chaplain, and hard by a plain slab bears the inscription, "Here lies Henry Lawrence, who tried to do his duty; may the Lord have mercy on his soul!" words dictated by himself on his deathbed. Other monuments commemorate Captain Graham of the Bengal Cavalry and two children; Mr. Fairhurst the Roman Catholic chaplain; Major Banks; Captain Fulton of the 32nd who earned the title of "Defender of Lucknow;" Lucas, the travelling Irish gentleman who served as a volunteer and fell in the last sortie; Captain Becher; Captain Moorsom; poor Bensley

Thornhill and his young daughter; "Mrs. Elizabeth Arne, burnt with a shell-ball during the siege;" Lieutenant Cunliffe; Mr. Ommaney the Judicial Commissioner; and others. The nameless hillocks of poor Jack Private are plentiful, for here were buried many of those who fell in the final capture; and there are children's graves. Interments take place still. I saw a freshly-made grave; but only those are entitled to a last resting-place here who were among the beleaguered during the long defence. I have seen the medal for the defence of Lucknow on the breast of a man who was a child in arms at the time of the siege, and such an one would have the right to claim interment in this doubly hallowed ground. From the churchyard I pass out along the narrow neck to that forlorn-hope post, "Innes's Garrison," and along the western face of the intrenchment by the sides of the sheep-house and the slaughter-house, to Gubbins's post. The mere foundations of the house are visible which the stout civilian so gallantly defended, and the famous tree, gradually pruned to a mere stump by the enemy's fire, is no longer extant. Along the southern face of the position there are no buildings which are not ruined. Sikh Square, the Brigade Mess House, and the Martinière boys' post, are alike represented by fragmentary gray walls shivered with shot and shored up here and there by beams. The rooms of the Begum Kothi near the centre of the position, are still laterally entire but roofless. The walls of this structure are exceptionally thick and here many of the ladies of the garrison were quartered. All around the Residency position the native houses which at the time of the siege crowded close up on the intrenchment, are now destroyed; and indeed the native town has been curtailed into comparatively small dimensions and is entirely separated from the area in which the houses of the station are built.

Quitting the Residency I drive westward by the river side, over the site of the Captan Bazaar, past also that huge fortified heap the Muchee Bawn, till I reach the beautiful enclosure in which the great Imambara stands. This majestic structure—part temple, part convent, part palace, and now part fortress—dominates the whole *terrain*, and from its lofty flat roof one looks down on the plain where the weekly *hât* or market is being held, on the gardens and mansions across the river, and southward upon the dense mass of houses which constitute the native city. Sentries promenade the battlements of the Muchee Bawn, and the Imambara—an apartment to which for space and height I know none in Europe comparable—is now used as an arsenal, where are stored the great siege guns which William Peel plied with so great skill and gallantry. Just outside the Imambara, on the edge of the *maidan* between it and the Moosabagh, I come on a little railed churchyard where rest a few British soldiers who fell during Lord Clyde's final operations in this direction. Then, with a sweep across the plain to the south and by a slight ascent, I reach the gate of the city which opens into the Chowk or principal street—the street traversed in disguise by the dauntless Kavanagh when he went out from the garrison to convey information and afford guidance to Sir Colin Campbell on his first advance. The gatehouse is held by a strong force of native policemen, armed as if they were soldiers; and as I pass the guard I stand in the Chowk itself, in the midst of a throng of gaily clad male pedestrians, women in chintz trousers, laden donkeys, multitudinous children, and still more multitudinous stinks. All down both sides the fronts of the lower stories are open, and in the recesses sit merchants displaying paltry jewelry, slippers, pipes, turban cloths, and Manchester stuffs of the gaudiest patterns. The main street of Lucknow has been called "The Street of Silver," but I could find little among its jewelry either of silver or of gold. The first floors all have balconies, and on these sit draped, barefooted women of Rahab's profession. The women of Lucknow are fairer and handsomer, and the men bolder and more stalwart, than those in Bengal, and it takes no great penetration to discern that Lucknow is still ruled by fear and not by love.

It remained for me still to investigate the scenes of the route by which Lord Clyde came in on both his advances; but to do justice to these would demand separate articles. Let me begin the hasty sketch at the Dilkoosha Palace, two miles and more away to the east of the Residency; for on both occasions the Dilkoosha was Clyde's base. Wajid Ali's twenty-foot wall has now given place to an earthen embankment surrounding a beautiful pleasure park, and there are now smooth green slopes instead of the dense forest through which Clyde's soldiers marched on their turning movement. On a swell in the midst of the park, commanding a view of the fantastic architecture of the Martinière down by the tank, stands the gaunt ruin of the once trim and dainty Dilkoosha Palace or rather garden-house. From one of the pepper-box turrets up there Lord Clyde directed the attack on the Martinière on his ultimate operation ; and here it was that, as Dr. Russell tells us, a round shot dispersed his staff on the adjacent leads. After quietude was restored the Dilkoosha was the headquarters for a time of Sir Hope Grant, but now it has been allowed to fall into decay although the garden in the rear of it is prettily kept up. On the reverse slope behind the Dilkoosha was the camp in one of the tents of which Havelock died. We drive down the gentle slope once traversed at a rushing double by the Black Watch on their way to carry the Martinière, past the great tank out of the centre of which rises the tall column to the memory of Claude Martine, and reach the entrance of the fantastic building which he built, in which he was buried, and which bears his name. We see at the angle of the northern wing the slope up which the gun was run which played so heavily on the Dilkoosha up on the wooded knoll there. The Martinière is now, as it was before the Mutiny, a college for European boys, and the young fellows are playing on the terraces. Grotesque stone statues are in niches and along the tops of the balconies ; you may see on them the marks of the bullets which the honest fellows of the Black Watch fired at them, taking them for Pandies. I go down into a vault and see the tomb of Claude Martine ; but it is empty, for the mutineers desecrated his grave and scattered his bones to the winds of heaven.

Then I make for the roof, through the dormitories of the boys and past fantastic stone griffins and lions and Gorgons, till I reach the top of the tower and touch the flagstaff from which, during the relief time, was given the answering signal to that hoisted on the tower of the Residency. I stand in the niches where the mutineer marksmen used to sit with their hookahs and take pot shots at the Dilkoosha. I look down to the eastward on the Goomtee, and note the spot where Outram crossed on that flank movement which would have been very much more successful than it was had he been permitted to drive it home. To the north-east beyond the topes is the battle-ground of Chinhut, where Lawrence received so terrible a reverse at the beginning of the siege. Due north is the Kookrail viaduct which Outram cleared with the Rifles and the 79th, and in whose vicinity Jung Bahadour, the crafty and bloodthirsty generalissimo of Nepaul, "co-operated" by a demonstration which never became anything more. And to the west there lie stretched out before me the domes, minarets, and spires of Lucknow, rising above the foliage in which their bases are hidden, and the routes of Clyde in the relief and capture. The rays of the afternoon sun are stirring into colour the dusky gray of the Secunderbagh and of the Nuddun Rusool, or "Grave of the Prophet," used as a powder magazine by the rebels. Below me, on the lawn of the Martinière, is the big gun—one of Claude Martine's casting—which did the rebels so much service at the other angle of the Martinière and which was spiked at last by two men of Peel's naval brigade, who swam the Goomtee for the purpose. That little enclosure slightly to the left surrounds "all that can die" of that strange mixture of high spirit, cool daring, and weak principle, the famous chief of Hodson's Horse. By Hodson's side lies Captain da Costa of the 56th N.I., attached to Brazier's Sikhs. Of this officer is told that, having lost many relatives in the butchery of Cawnpore, he joined the regiment likeliest to be in the front of the Lucknow fighting, and fell by one of the first shots fired in the assault on the Kaiser-bagh.

Descending from the Martinière tower I traverse the park to the westward passing the grave of Captain Otway Mayne, cross the dry canal along which are still visible the heaps of earth which mark the stupendous first line of the rebels' defences, and bending to the left reach the Secunderbagh. This famous place was a pleasure garden surrounded with a lofty wall with turrets at the angles and a castellated gateway. The interior garden is now waste and forlorn, the rank grass growing breast-high in the corners where the slaughter was heaviest. Here in this little enclosure, not half the size of the garden of Bedford Square, 2000 Sepoys died the death at the hands of the 93rd, the 53rd, and the 4th Punjaubees. Their common grave is under the low mound on the other side of the road. The loopholes stand as they were left by the mutineers when our fellows came bursting in through the ragged breach made in the reverse side from the main entrance by Peel's guns. Farther on — that is, nearer to the Residency — I come to the Shah

Nujeef, with its strong exterior wall enclosing the domed temple in its centre. It is still easy to trace the marks of the breach made in the angle in the wall by Peel's battering guns, and the tree is still standing up which Salmon, Southwell, and Harrison climbed in response to his proffer of the Victoria Cross. Opposite the Shah Nujeef white girls are playing on the lawn of that castellated building, for the Koorsheyd Munzil, on the top of which there was hoisted the British flag in the face of a *feu d'enfer*, is now a seminary for the daughters of Europeans. A little beyond, on the plain in front of the Motee Mahal, is the spot where Campbell met Outram and Havelock—a spot which, methinks, might well be marked by a monument; and after this I lose my reckoning by reason of the extent of the demolition, and am forced to resort to guesswork as to the precise localities.

THE MILITARY COURAGE OF ROYALTY

WRITING of the late Alexander III. of Russia, a foreign author has recently permitted himself to observe: "Marvellous personal courage is not a striking characteristic of the dynasty of the Romanoffs as it was of the English Tudors." It will be conceded that periods materially govern the conditions under which sovereigns and their royal relatives have found opportunities for proving their personal courage. The Tudor dynasty had ended before the Romanoff dynasty began. It is true, indeed, that the ending of the former with the death of Elizabeth in 1603 occurred only a few years before the foundation of the latter by the election to the Tzarship of Michael Feodorovitz Romanoff in 1612. But of the five sovereigns of the Tudor dynasty it happened that only one, Henry VII., the first monarch of that dynasty, found or made an opportunity for the display of marked—scarcely perhaps of "marvellous"—personal courage; and thus the selection of the Tudor dynasty by the writer referred to as furnishing a contrasting illustration in the matter of personal courage to that of the Romanoffs was not particularly fortunate. Henry VIII. was only once in action; he shared in the skirmish known as the

"Battle of the Spurs," because of the precipitate flight of the French horse. Edward VI. died at the age of sixteen, and the two remaining sovereigns of the dynasty were women, of whom it is true that Elizabeth was a strong and vigorous ruler, but in the nature of things had no opportunity for showing "marvellous personal courage." Henry VII. literally found his crown in the heart of the *mêlée* on Bosworth field, it matters not which of the alternative stories is correct, that he himself killed Richard, or that Richard was killed in the act of striking him a desperate blow. But Henry at Bosworth in 1485 still belonged to the days of chivalry—to an era in which monarchs were also armour-clad knights, who headed charges in person and gave and took with spear, sword, and battle-axe. Long before Peter the Great, more than two centuries after Bosworth, foamed at the mouth with rage and hacked with his sword at his panicstricken troops fleeing from the field of Narva on that winter day of 1700, the face of warfare had altered and the *métier* of the commander, were he sovereign or were he subject, had undergone a radical change.

Of a family of the human race it is not rationally possible to predicate a typical generic characteristic of mind. A physical trait will endure down the generations, as witness the Hapsburg lip and the swarthy complexion of the Finch-Hattons, in the face of alliances from outside the races; but, save as regards one exception, there is no assurance of a continuous inheritance of mental attributes. What a contrast is there between Frederick the Great and his father; between George III. and his successor;

between the present Emperor of Austria and his hapless son; between the genial, wistful, and well-intentioned Alexander II. of Russia and the not less well-intentioned but narrow-minded and despotic sovereign who succeeded him! But there may be reserved one exception to the absence of assurance of inherited mental attributes—one mental feature in which identity takes the place of dissimilarity, and even of actual contrast. And that feature—that inherited characteristic of a race whose progenitors happily possessed it—is personal courage.

Take, for example, the Hohenzollerns. One need not hark back to Carlyle's original Conrad, the seeker of his fortune who tramped down from the ancestral cliff-castle on his way to take service under Barbarossa. Before and since the "Grosse Kurfurst" there has been no Hohenzollern who has not been a brave man. He himself was the hero of Fehrbellin. His son, the first king of the line, Carlyle's "Expensive Herr," was "valiant in action" during the third war of Louis XIV. The rugged Frederick William, father of Frederick the Great, had his own tough piece of war against the volcanic Charles XII. of Sweden and did a stout stroke of hard fighting at Malplaquet. Of Fritz himself the world has full note. Bad, sensual, debauched Hohenzollern as was his successor, Frederick the Fat, he had fought stoutly in his youth-time under his illustrious uncle. His son, Frederick William III., overthrown by Napoleon who called him a "corporal," did good soldierly work in the "War of Liberation" and fought his way to Paris in 1814. His eldest son, Frederick

William IV., the vague, benevolent dreamer whom *Punch* used to call "King Clicquot" and who died of softening of the brain, even he, too, as a lad had distinguished himself in the "War of Liberation" and in the fighting during the subsequent advance on Paris. As for grand old William I., the real maker of the German Empire on the *quid facit per alium facit per se* axiom, he died a veteran of many wars. He was not seventeen when he won the Iron Cross by a service of conspicuous gallantry under heavy fire. He took his chances in the bullet and shell fire at Königgrätz, and again on the afternoon of Gravelotte. Not a Hohenzollern of them all but shared as became their race in the dangers of the great war of 1870-71; even Prince George, the music composer, the only non-soldier of the family, took the field. William's noble son, whose premature death neither Germany nor England has yet ceased to deplore, took the lead of one army; his nephew Prince Frederick Charles, a great commander and a brilliant soldier, was the leader of another. One of his brothers, Prince Albert the elder, made the campaign as cavalry chief; whose son, Prince Albert junior, now a veteran Field-Marshal, commanded a brigade of guard-cavalry with a skill and daring not wholly devoid of recklessness. Another brother, Prince Charles, the father of the "Red Prince," made the campaign with the royal headquarters; Prince Adalbert, a cousin of the sovereign and head of the Prussian Navy, had his horse shot under him on the battlefield of Gravelotte.

The trait of personal courage has markedly

characterised the House of Hanover. As King of England George I. did no fighting, but before he reached that position he had distinguished himself in war not a little; against the Danes and Swedes in 1700 and in high command in the war of the Spanish succession from 1701 to 1709. His successor, while yet young, had displayed conspicuous valour in the battle of Oudenarde, and later in life at Dettingen; and he was the last British monarch who took part in actual warfare. Cumberland had no meritorious attribute save that of personal courage, but that virtue in him was undeniable. At Dettingen he was wounded in the forefront of the battle; at Fontenoy the "martial boy" was ever in the heart of the fiercest fire, fighting at "a spiritual white heat." His grand-nephew the Duke of York was an unfortunate soldier, but his personal courage was unquestioned. In the present reign a cousin and a son of the sovereign have done good service in the field; and that venerable lady herself in situations of personal danger has consistently maintained the calm courage of her race.

The foreign author has written that "marvellous personal courage is not the striking characteristic of the dynasty of the Romanoffs." He makes an exception to this quasi-indictment in favour of the Emperor Nicholas, who, he admits, "was absolutely ignorant of fear, and could face a band of insurgents with the calm self-possession of a shepherd surveying his bleating sheep." The monarch who at the moment of his accession illustrated the dominant force of his character by confronting amid the bullet fire the ferocious mutiny of half an army corps, and who crushed the bloodthirsty *émeute* with dauntless resolution and iron hand; the man who, facing the populace of St. Petersburg crazed with terror of the cholera and red with the blood of slaughtered physicians, quelled its panic-fury by commanding the people in the sternest tones of his sonorous voice to kneel in the dust and propitiate by prayers the wrath of the Almighty—such a man is scarcely, perhaps, adequately characterised by the expressions which have been quoted. But setting aside this instance of the fearlessness of Nicholas, facts appear to refute pretty conclusively reflections on the personal courage of the Romanoffs. No purpose can be served by cumbering the record by going back into the period of Russia's semi-civilisation; illustrations from three generations may reasonably suffice. At Austerlitz Alexander I. was close up to the fighting line in the Pratzen section of that great battle, and so recklessly did he expose himself that the report spread rearward that he had fallen. He was riding with Moreau in the heart of the bloody turmoil before Dresden when a French cannon-ball mortally wounded the renegade French general, and he was splashed by the latter's blood. Moreau had insisted on riding on the outside, else the ball which caused his death would certainly have struck Alexander. That monarch participated actively and forwardly in most of the battles of the campaign of 1814 which culminated in the allied occupation of Paris. Marmont's bullets were still flying when he rode on to the hill of Belleville and looked down through the smoke of battle on the French capital. The captious foreign writer has admitted that Nicholas, the successor of Alexander, was "absolutely ignorant of fear," and I have cited a convincing instance of his "marvellous personal courage." Two of his sons—the Grand Dukes Nicholas and Michael—were under fire in the battle of Inkerman and shared for some time the perils of the siege of Sevastopol. Alexander II. was certainly a man of real, although quiet and undemonstrative, personal courage. But for his disregard of the precautions by which the police sought to surround him he probably would have been alive to-day. The Third Section was wholly unrepresented in Bulgaria and His Majesty's protection on campaign consisted merely of a handful of Cossacks. No cordon of sentries surrounded his simple camp; his tent at Pavlo and the dilapidated Turkish house which for weeks was his residence at Gorni Studen were alike destitute of any guards. The imperial Court of Russia is said to be the most punctiliously ceremonious of all courts; in the field the Tzar absolutely dispensed with any sort of ceremony. He dined with his suite and staff at a frugal table in a spare hospital marquee; his guests, the foreign attachés and any passing officers or strangers who happened to be in camp. When he drove out his escort consisted of a couple of Cossacks. In the woods about Biela at the beginning of the war there still remained some forlorn bivouacs of Turkish families; he would alight and visit those, his sole companion the aide-de-camp on duty; and would fearlessly venture among the sullen Turks all of whom were armed with deadly weapons, try to persuade them to return to their homes, and, unmoved by their refusal, promise to send them food and medicine. Dispensing with all etiquette he would see without delay any one coming in with tidings from fighting points, were he officer, civilian, or war correspondent. During the September attack on Plevna he was continually in the field while daylight lasted, looking out on the slaughter from an eminence within range of the Turkish cannon-fire, and manifestly enduring keen anguish at the spectacle of the losses sustained by his brave, patient troops. Later, during the investment of Plevna, his point of observation was a redoubt on the Radischevo ridge still closer to the Turkish front of fire, and it was thence he witnessed the surrender of Osman's army on the memorable 10th December 1877. If Alexander was fearless alike in camp and in the field on campaign, he was certainly not less so in St. Petersburg, when he returned thither after the fall of Plevna.

Alexander II. literally sacrificed his life to his self-regardless concern for the suffering. After the first bomb had burst on the Alexandra Canal Road, striking down civilians and Cossacks of the following escort but leaving the Emperor unhurt, his coachman begged to be allowed to dash forward and get clear of danger. But Alexander forbade him with the words, "No, no! I must alight and see to the wounded;" and as he was carrying out his heroic and benign intention, the second bomb exploded and wrought his death.

As did the men of the Hohenzollern house in 1870, so in 1877 the adult male Romanoffs went to the war with scarce an exception. The Grand Duke Nicholas, brother of the Emperor and Com-

X

mander-in-Chief of the Russian armies in Europe, was neither a great general nor an honest man; but there could be no question as to his personal courage. That attribute he evinced with utter recklessness when arriving, as was his wont, too late for a deliberate and careful survey, he galloped round the Turkish positions on the morning on which began the September bombardment of Plevna, in proximity to Turkish cannon-fire so dangerous that his staff remonstrated, and that even the sedate American historian of the war speaks of him as having "exposed himself imprudently to the Turkish pickets." His son, the Grand Duke Nicholas, jun., in 1877 scarcely of age, was nevertheless a keen practical soldier, imbued with the wisdom of getting to close quarters and staying there. He was among the first to cross the Danube at Sistova under the Turkish fire, and he fought with great gallantry under Mirsky in the Schipka Pass. The brothers, Prince Nicholas and Prince Eugene of Leuchtenberg, members of the imperial house, commanded each a cavalry brigade in Gourko's dashing raid across the Balkans at the beginning of the campaign, and both were conspicuous for soldierly skill and personal gallantry in the desperate fighting in the Tundja Valley. The Grand Duke Vladimir, the second brother of Alexander III., headed the infantry advance in the direction of Rustchuk, and served with marked distinction in command of one of the corps in the army of the Lom. A younger brother, the Grand Duke Alexis, the nautical member of the imperial family, had charge of the torpedo and subaqueous mining operations on the Danube, and was held to have shown practical skill, assiduity, and vigour. Prince Serge of Leuchtenberg, younger brother of the Leuchtenbergs previously mentioned, was shot dead by a bullet through the head in the course of his duty as a staff officer at the front of a reconnaissance in force made against the Turkish force in Jovan-Tchiflik in October of the war. He was a soldier of great promise and had frequently distinguished himself. No unworthy record, it is submitted, earned in war by the members of a family of which, according to the foreign author, "personal courage is not the striking characteristic."

That writer may be warranted in stating that the late Tzar had been frequently accused of cowardice —an indictment to which, it must be admitted, many undeniable facts lent a strong colouring of probability; and he further tells of "the Emperor's aversion to ride on horseback, and of his dread of a horse even when the animal was harnessed to a vehicle." There is something, however, of inconsistency in his observation that Alexander III. might well have been a contrast to his grandfather without deserving the epithet craven-hearted. The melancholy explanation of the strange apparent change between the Tzarewitch of 1877 and the Tzar of 1894 may lie in the statement that "Alexander's nerves had been undoubtedly shaken by the terrible events in which he had been a spectator or actor." In 1877, when in campaign in Bulgaria, Alexander did not know what "nerves" meant. He was then a man of strong, if slow, mental force, stolid, peremptory, reactionary; the possessor of dull but firm resolution. He had a strong though clumsy seat on horseback and was no infrequent rider. He had two ruling dislikes: one was war, the other was officers of German extraction. The latter he got rid of; the former he regarded as a necessary evil of the hour; he longed for its ending, but while it lasted he did his sturdy and loyal best to wage it to the advantage of the Russian arms. And in this he succeeded, stanchly fulfilling the particular duty which was laid upon him, that of protecting the Russian left flank from the Danube to the foothills of the Balkans. He had good troops, the subordinate commands were fairly well filled, and his headquarter staff was efficient—General Dochtouroff, its *sous-chef*, was certainly the ablest staff-officer in the Russian army. But Alexander was no puppet of his staff; he understood his business as the commander of the army of the Lom, performed his functions in a firm, quiet fashion, and withal was the trusty and successful warden of the eastern marches. His force never amounted to 50,000 men, and his enemy was in considerably greater strength. He had successes and he sustained reverses, but he was equal to either fortune; always resolute in his steadfast, dogged manner, and never whining for reinforcements when things went against him, but doing his best with the means to his hand. They used to speak of him in the principal headquarter as the only commander who never gave them any bother. So highly was he thought of there that when, after the unsuccessful attempt on Plevna in the September of the war, the Guard Corps was arriving from Russia and there was the temporary intention to use it with other troops in an immediate offensive movement across the Balkans, he was named to take the command of the enterprise. But this intention having been presently departed from, and the reinforcements being ordered instead to the Plevna section of the theatre of war, the Tzarewitch retained his command on the left flank, and thus in mid-December had the opportunity of inflicting a severe defeat on Suleiman Pasha, just as in September he had worsted Mehemet Ali in the battle of Carkova. It is sad to be told that a man once so resolute and masterful should later have been the victim of shattered nerves; it is sadder still to learn that he was a mark for accusations of cowardice. He never was a gracious, far less a lovable man; but, as I can testify from personal knowledge, he was a cool and brave soldier in the Russo-Turkish War of 1877.

PARADE OF THE COMMISSIONAIRES

1875

ON a Sunday morning in early June, just before the church bells begin to ring, there is wont to be held the annual general parade and inspection of the Corps of Commissionaires, on the enclosed grass plot by the margin of the ornamental water in St. James's Park. On the ground, and accompanying the inspecting officer on his tour through the opened ranks, there are always not a few veteran officers, glad by their presence on such an occasion to countenance and recognise their humbler comrades in arms in bygone war-dramas enacted elsewhere than within hearing of London Sunday bells. No scene could be imagined presenting a more practical confutation of the ignorant calumny that the British army is composed of the froth and the dregs of the British nation, and that there exists no cordial feeling between British soldiers and British officers. It is good to see how the face kindles of the veteran guardsman at the sight and the kindly greeting of Sir Charles Russell. Doubtless the honest private's thoughts go back to that misty morning on the slopes of Inkerman, when officer and private stood shoulder to shoulder in the fierce press, and there rang again in his ears the cheer with which the Guards greeted the act of valour by the performance of which the baronet won the Victoria Cross. There is a feeling deeper than a mere formality in the half-dozen words that pass between Sir William Codrington and the old soldier of the 7th Royal Fusiliers, to whom the gallant general showed the way up to the Russian front, through the shot-torn vineyards on the slopes of the Alma. When one feeble old ex-warrior is smitten suddenly on parade with a palsied faintness, it is on the yet stalwart arm of his old chief that he totters out of the ranks, and the twain do not part till the superior has exacted a pledge that his humble ex-subordinate shall call upon him on the morrow, with a view to medical advice and strengthening comforts.

Notwithstanding that in the true old martial spirit it shows what in the Service is known as a good front, it is not a very athletic or puissant cohort this, that stands on parade here on the grass within hearing of the church bells. The grizzled old soldiers, sooth to say, look rather the worse for wear. There is a decided shortcoming among them of the proper complement of limbs, and one at least, in speaking of the battlefields he had seen, might with truth echo the old soldier in Burns's *Jolly Beggars*—

And there I left for witness a leg and an arm.

They carry no weapons; to some may belong the knowledge only of the obsolete "Brown Bess" manual exercise; and not many have been so recently on active service as to have learnt the handling of the modern breech-loader. On the whole, a battered, fossil, maimed army of superannuated fighting men, scarcely fitted to shine in the new tactics of the "swarm-attack" by which the battles of the future are to be won or lost. But you cannot jibe at the worn old soldiers as "lean and slippered pantaloons." Look how truly, with what instinctive intuition, the dressing is taken up at the word of command; note how the old martial carriage comes back to the most dilapidated when the adjutant calls his command to "attention." Age and wounds have not quenched the fighting spirit of the old soldiers; there is not a man of them but would, did the need arise, "clatter on his stumps to the sound of the drum." There are few breasts in those ranks that are not decorated with medals. In very truth the parade is a record of British campaigns for the last thirty years. Among the thicket of medals on the bosom of this broken old light dragoon note the one bearing the legend, "Cabul 1842" within the laurel wreath. Its wearer was a trooper in the famous "rescue" column. The skeletons of Elphinstone's hapless force littered the slopes of the Tezeen Valley, up which the squadron in which he rode charged straight for the tent of the splendid demon Akbar Khan. He rode behind Campbell at the battle of Punniar, and won there that star of silver and bronze which hangs from the famous "rainbow" ribbon. "Sutlej" is the legend on another of his medals, and he could recount to you the memorable story of Thackwell's cavalry operations against the Sikh field works, and how that division of seasoned horsemen reduced outpost duty to a methodical science.

"Punjab" medals for Gough's campaign of 1848-49 are scattered up and down in the ranks. The sword-cut athwart this wiry old trooper's cheek he got in the hot *mêlée* of Ramhuggur, where a certain Brigadier Colin Campbell whom men knew afterwards as Lord Clyde, found it hard work to hold his own, and where gallant Cureton and the veteran William Havelock fell at the head of their light horsemen as they crashed into the heart of 4000 Sikhs. His neighbour took part in the storm of Mooltan, and saw stout, calm-pulsed Sergeant John Bennet of the 1st Bombay Fusiliers plant the British ensign on the crest of the breach and quietly stand by it there, supporting it in the tempest of shot and shell till the storming party had made the breach their own. This old soldier of the 24th can tell you of the butchery of his regiment at Chillianwallah; how Brooks went down between the Sikh guns, how Brigadier Pennycuick was killed out to the front, and how his son, a beardless ensign, maddened at the sight of the mangling of his father's body, rushed out and fought against all comers over the corpse till the lad fell dead on his dead father; how on that terrible day the loss of the 24th was 13 officers killed, 10 wounded, and 497 men killed and wounded; and how the issue of the bloody combat might have been very different but for the display, on the part of Colin Campbell, of "that steady coolness and military decision for which he was so remarkable." Scarcely a great show on a troop-horse would this bent and gnarled old 12th Lancer make to-day, but he and his fellows rode right well on the day for which he wears this "Cape" medal, with the blue and orange ribbon and the lion and mimosa bush on the reverse. Because of its prickles the Boers call the mimosa the "wait-a-bit" thorn, but there was no thought of waiting a bit among the 12th Lancers at the Berea, when they charged the savage Basutos and captured their chief Moshesh. This one-armed veteran of the Royal Fusiliers was left lying wounded in the Great Redoubt on the Russian slope of the Alma, when the terrible fire of grape and musketry forced Codrington's brigade of the Light Division temporarily to give ground after it had struggled so valiantly up the rugged broken banks, and through the hailstorm of fire that swept through the vineyards. This still stalwart man was one of the nineteen sergeants of the 33rd—the Duke of Wellington's Own—who were either killed or wounded in defence of the colours on the same bloody but glorious day. A few files farther down the line stands an old 93rd man. The veteran Sutherland Highlander was one of that "thin red line" which disdained to form square when the Russian squadrons rode with seeming heart at the kilted men on Balaclava day. He heard Colin Campbell's stern repressive rebuke— "Ninety-third, ninety-third, damn all that eagerness!" when the hotter spirits of the regiment would fain have broken ranks and met the Russians half-way with the cold steel; he saw the Scotch wife chastise the fugitive Turks with her tongue and her frying-pan. Speak to his tall, shaggy neighbour of the "bonny Jocks," and you will call up a flush of pleasure on the harsh-featured Scottish face; for he was a trooper in the Greys on that self-same Balaclava day when the avalanche of Russian horsemen thundered down upon the heavy brigade. He was among those who heard, and with sternly rapturous anticipation obeyed Scarlet's calm-pitched, far-sounding order, "Left wheel into line!" He was among those who, when the trumpets had sounded the charge, strove in vain by dint of spur to overtake the gallant old chief with the long white moustache, as he rode foremost on the foe with the dashing Elliot and the burly Shegog on either flank of him; he was among those who, as they hewed and hacked their way through the press, heard already from the far side of the *mêlée* the stentorian adjuration of big Adjutant Miller, as standing up in his stirrups the burly Scot shouted, "Rally, rally on me, ye muckle ———!" Mightily knocked about has been this man with the empty sleeve, but he does not belie the familiar sobriquet of his old regiment; he was one of the "Diehards," a title well earned by the 57th on the bloody height of Albuera, and it was under their colours that he lost his arm on Inkerman morning. There is quite a little regiment of men who were wounded in the "trenches" or about the Redan. There is no "19" now on the buttons of this scarred veteran, but the number was there when he followed Massy and Molesworth over the parapet of the Redan on the day when so much good English blood was wasted. Shoulder to shoulder now, as oft of yore, stand two old soldiers of the Buffs both of whom went down in the same assault; and an umwhile bugler of the Perthshire Grey-breeks "minds the day" well also by reason of the wound that has crippled him for life. As he stands on parade this calm Sabbath morning, that maimed man of the

60th Rifles can remember another and a very different Sabbath—the 10th of May 1857 in Meerut—day and place of the first outburst of the Mutiny; a fell Sabbath of burning, slaughter, and dismay, of disregard of sex, age, and rank, of fierce brutality and of nameless agony. He was one of the rifles whose fire in the assault of Delhi covered the desperate duty of blowing open the Cashmere Gate, performed with so methodical calmness by Home, Salkeld, and Burgess; and his comrade hero with the maimed limb, when the hour had come for a rush to close quarters, followed Reid and Muter over the breastwork at the end of the serai of Kissengunge. Proud, yet their pride dashed by sadness, must be the soldiering memories of this stout northman, erstwhile a front rank man in the old Ross-shire Buffs, a regiment ever true to its noble Celtic motto of *Cuidichn Rhi.* At Kooshab, in the short, but brilliant Persian War, he fought in the same field where Malcolmson earned the Victoria Cross by one of the most gallant acts for which that guerdon of valour ever has been accorded. He was in Mackenzie's company at Cawnpore when the Highlanders, stirred by the wild strains of the war-pibroch, rushed upon the Nana's battery at the angle of the mango tope with the irresistible fury of one of their own mountain torrents in spate. And next day he was among those who, with drawn ghastly faces and scared eyes, looked into that fearful well, filled to the lip with the mangled corpses of British women and children. He was one of those who, standing by that well, pledged the oath administered by the bareheaded Ross-shire sergeant over the long, heavy tress of auburn hair which a demon's tulwar had severed from the head of an Englishwoman, that while strong arm and trusty steel lasted to no living thing of the accursed race should quarter be accorded. And he was one of those who, having battled their way over the Charbagh Bridge, having threaded the bullet-torn path to the Kaiser-bagh, and having forced for themselves a passage up to the embrasures by the Baileyguard Gate, melted from the stern fierceness of the fray when the siege-worn women and children in the residency of Lucknow sobbed out upon their necks blessings for the deliverance. His rear-rank man is an ex-Bengal Fusilier, wounded once at Sabraon, again at Pegu, and a third time at Delhi. He will not be offended if you hail him as one of the "old Dirty-shirts;" for it was in honourable disregard of appearances as they toiled night and day in the trenches of Delhi that the regiment, which now in the Queen's service is numbered 101, gained the nickname. Time and space fail one to tell a tithe of the stories of valour and hardship linked in the medals and wounds borne by men on this unostentatious parade—a parade the members of which have shed their blood on the soil of every quarter of the globe. The minutest military annals scarcely name some of the obscure combats in which men here to-day have fought and bled. This man desperately wounded at Najou, near Shanghai; that one wounded in two places at Owna, in Persia; this one with a sleeve emptied at Aroga, in Abyssinia—who among us remember aught, if, indeed, we have ever heard, of Najou, Owna, or Aroga? On the breast of this bent, hoary old man, note these strange emblems, the Cross of San Fernando and the Order of the Tower and Sword. Their wearer is a relic of the British Legion in the Carlist War of 1837, and they were won under brave old De Lacy Evans at the siege of Bilbao.

Over the modest portals of the Commissionaire Barracks in the Strand might well be inscribed the legend, " To all the military glories of Britain." But just as we have not long ago seen the pride of a palace in another land on whose façade is a kindred inscription, abased by the occupation of a foreign conqueror, so there was a time when the living emblems of Britain's military glory were wont to undergo much humiliation and adversity when their career of soldiering had come to an end. Germany recompenses her veterans by according them, as a right, reputable civil employ when they have served their time as soldiers; the custom of Britain, on the contrary, has been too commonly to leave her scarred and war-worn soldiers to their own resources, or to a pension on which to live is impossible. We were always ready enough to feel a glow at the achievements of our arms; but till lately we were prone to reckon the individual soldier as a social pariah, and to regard the fact of a man's having served in the ranks as a brand of discredit. To this estimate, it must be allowed, the ex-soldier himself very often contributed not a little. Destitute of a future, and often debarred by wounds or by broken health from any laborious industrial employment, he made the most of the present; and his idea of making the most of the future not unfrequently took the form of beer and shiftlessness. Recognising the disadvantages that bore so hard on the deserving old soldier, recognising too, in the words of the late Sir John Burgoyne, that "there are many qualities peculiar to the soldier and sailor, and imbibed by him in the ordinary course of his service, which, added to good character and conduct, may render such men more eligible than others for various services in civil life," Captain Edward Walter founded the Corps of Commissionaires. That organisation, beginning with seven men, has now a strength of several hundreds, and its ranks are still open to all the eligible recruits who choose to come forward. The Commissionaire is no recipient of charity; what Captain Walter has done is simply to show him how he may earn an honest and comfortable livelihood, and to provide him, if he desires it, with a home of a kind which the ex-militaire naturally most appreciates. The advantages are open to him of a savings-bank and of a sick and burial fund, and when the evil days come when he can no longer earn his own bread, the "Retiring Fund" guarantees the thrifty and steady Commissionaire against the prospect of ending his days in the workhouse. Among the fruits of Captain Walter's devoted and gratuitous services in this cause has been a wholesome change in the bias of popular opinion as to the worth of old soldiers. No longer are they regarded as the mere chaff and *débris* of the cannon fodder—"no account men," as Bret Harte has it; he has furnished them with opportunity to prove, and they have proved, that they can so live and so work as to win the respect and trust of their brethren of the civilian world. The man who has done this thing deserves well, not alone of the British army, but of the British nation. He has brought it about that the time has come when most men think with Sir Roger de Coverley. "You must know," says Sir Roger, "I never make use of anybody to row me that has not lost either a leg or an arm. I would rather bate him a few strokes of his oar than not employ an honest man that has been wounded in the Queen's service. If I was a lord or a bishop . . . I would not put a fellow in my livery that had not a wooden leg."

THE INNER HISTORY OF THE WATERLOO CAMPAIGN

THE actual fighting phase of this memorable campaign was confined to the four days from the 15th to the 18th of June, both days inclusive. The literature concerning itself with that period would make a library of itself. Scarcely a military writer of any European nation but has delivered himself on the subject, from Clausewitz to General Maurice, from Berton to Brialmont. Thiers, Alison, and Hooper may be cited of the host of civilian writers whom the theme has enticed to description and criticism. There is scarcely a point in the brief vivid drama that has not furnished a topic for warm and sustained controversy; and the cult of the Waterloo campaign is more assiduous to-day than when the participators in the great strife were testifying to their own experiences.

Quite recently an important work dealing chiefly with the inner history of the campaign has come to us from the other side of the Atlantic.[1] Its author, Mr. John Ropes, is a civilian gentleman of

[1] *The Campaign of Waterloo: a Military History.* By John Codman Ropes. New York: Charles Scribner's Sons. February 1893.

Boston, who has devoted his life to military study. He has given years to the elucidation of the problems of the Waterloo campaign, has trodden every foot of its ground, and has burrowed for recondite matter in the military archives of divers nations. A citizen of the American Republic, he is free alike from national prejudices and national prepossessions; if he is perhaps not uniformly correct in his inferences, his rigorous impartiality is always conspicuous. By his research and acute perception he has let light in upon not a few obscurities; and it may be pertinent briefly to summarise the inner history of the campaign, giving what may seem their due weight to the arguments and representations of the American writer.

The following were the respective positions on the 14th of June:—Wellington's heterogeneous army, about 94,000 strong with 196 guns, lay widely dispersed in cantonments from the Scheldt to the Charleroi-Brussels chaussée, its front extending from Tournay through Mons and Binche to Nivelles and Quatre Bras. Of the Prussian army under Blücher, about 121,000 strong with 312 guns, one corps was at Liège, another near the Meuse above Namur, a third at Namur, and Ziethen's in advance holding the line of the Sambre. The mass of Blücher's command had already seen service and, with the exception of the Saxons, was full of zeal; the corps were well commanded, and their chief, although he had his limits, was a thorough soldier. The French army, consisting of five corps d'armée, the Guard, four cavalry corps and 344 guns— total fighting strength 124,500—Napoleon had succeeded in assembling with wonderful celerity and secrecy south of the Sambre within an easy march of Charleroi. Its officers and soldiers were alike veterans but its organisation was somewhat defective. Napoleon scarcely preserved the phenomenal force of earlier years; but, in Mr. Ropes's words, he disclosed "no conspicuous lack of energy and activity." Soult was far from being an ideal chief of staff. Ney, to whom was assigned the command of the left wing, only reached the army on the 15th, and without a staff; Grouchy, to whom on the 16th was suddenly given the command of the right wing, was not a man of high military capacity.

Napoleon's plan of campaign was founded on the circumstance that the bases of the allied armies lay in opposite directions—the English base on the German Ocean, the Prussian through Liège and Maestricht to the Rhine. The military probability was that if either army was forced to retreat, it would retreat towards its base; and to do this would be to march away from its ally. Napoleon was in no situation to manœuvre leisurely, with all Europe on the march against him. His engrossing aim was to gain immediate victory over his adversaries in Belgium before the Russians and Austrians should close in around him. His expectation was that Blücher would offer battle about Fleurus and be overwhelmed before the Anglo-Dutch army could come to the support of its Prussian ally. To make sure of preventing that junction the Emperor's intention was to detail Ney with the left wing to reach and hold Quatre Bras. The Prussians thoroughly beaten, drifting rearward toward their base, and reduced to a condition of comparative inoffensiveness, he would then turn on Wellington and force him to give battle.

Mr. Ropes refutes the contention maintained by a great array of authorities, that Napoleon's design was to "wedge himself into the interval between the allied armies" by seizing simultaneously Sombreffe and Quatre Bras, in order to cut the communication between the two armies and then defeat them in succession. Against this view he successfully marshals Napoleon himself, Wellington by the mouth of Lord Ellesmere, and the great German strategist Clausewitz. It will suffice to quote Napoleon:—

The Emperor's intention was that his advance should occupy Fleurus, the mass concealed behind this town; he took good care . . . above all things not to occupy Sombreffe. To have done so would have caused the failure of all his dispositions, for then the battle of Ligny would not have been fought, and Blücher would have had to make Wavre the concentration-point for his army.

Wellington alludes pointedly to the obvious danger to the French army of the suggested wedge position in what the Germans call *die taktische Mitte*, where, instead of being able to defeat the allies in succession, it would itself be liable to be crushed between the upper and the nether millstone.

At daybreak of the 15th Napoleon took the offensive, driving in Ziethen on and through Charleroi although not without sharp fighting. On that evening three French corps, the Guard, and most of the cavalry, were concentrated about

Charleroi and forward toward Fleurus, ready to attack Blücher next day. Controversy has been very keen on the question whether or not on the afternoon of the 15th Napoleon gave Ney verbal orders to occupy Quatre Bras the same evening. Mr. Ropes holds it "almost certain" that the order was given. From Napoleon's bulletin despatched on the evening of the 15th, which is the only piece of strictly contemporary evidence, he quotes: "Le Prince de la Moskowa (Ney) a eu le soir son quartier général aux Quatres-Chemins;" and he remarks that this must have been the belief in the headquarter "unless we gratuitously invent an intention to deceive the public." There is no need for Mr. Ropes to put that strain on himself, since the main purport of Napoleon's bulletins notoriously was to deceive the public. But if Napoleon had not intended that Ney should occupy Quatre Bras on the night of the 15th, the statement that this had been done would have been a purposeless futility; and if he had intended that Ney should do so it is unlikely that he should have omitted to give him instructions to that effect. Grouchy claims to have heard Napoleon censure Ney for his omission to occupy Quatre Bras; an omission which had its importance, for the reason, among others, that it was ominous of the Marshal's infinitely more harmful disobedience of orders next day.

All writers agree that Blücher ordered the concentration of his army in the fighting position previously chosen in the event of the French advancing by Charleroi, "without," in Mr. Ropes's words, "any definite agreement or undertaking with Wellington that he was to have English aid in the impending battle." He was content to take his risk of the English general's possible inability for sundry obvious reasons, to come to his support. And while the Prussian army with the unfortunate exception of Bülow's corps, was on the 15th moving toward the chosen position of Ligny, where its right was to be on St. Amand, its centre on and behind Ligny, and its left about Balâtre, what was happening in the Anglo-Dutch army lying spread out westward of the Charleroi-Brussels chaussée?

Wellington was at Brussels expecting the French invasion by or west of the Mons-Brussels road, to meet which he considered his army very well placed, but could expect no Prussian cooperation. His courier service, with his forces so dispersed, should have been well organised and alert, but it was neither; and Napoleon's secrecy and suddenness in taking the offensive were worthy of his best days. It has been freely imputed to Wellington that he was thereby in a measure surprised. There is the strange and probably mythical story in the work professing to be Fouché's *Memoirs* to the effect that Wellington was relying on him for information of Napoleon's plans, and that he—Fouché—played the English commander false. "On the very day of Napoleon's departure from Paris," say the *Memoirs*, "I despatched Madame D——, furnished with notes in cipher, narrating the whole plan of the campaign. But at the same time I privately sent orders for such obstacles at the frontier, where she was to pass, that she could not reach Wellington's headquarters till after the event. This was the real explanation of the inactivity of the British generalissimo which excited such universal astonishment." Readers of the *Letters of the First Earl of Malmesbury* will remember the apparently authentic statement of Captain Bowles, that Wellington, rising from the supper-table at the famous ball,

whispered to ask the Duke of Richmond if he had a good map. The Duke of Richmond said he had, and took Wellington into his dressing-room. Wellington shut the door and said, "Napoleon has humbugged me, by God; he has gained twenty-four hours' march on me. . . . I have ordered the army to concentrate at Quatre Bras; but we shall not stop him there, and if so I must fight him *there*" (passing his thumb-nail over the position of Waterloo). The conversation was repeated to me by the Duke of Richmond two minutes after it occurred.

Facts, however, are stronger evidence than words; and this confession on Wellington's part is inconsistent with the circumstance that he had not hurried to retrieve the time he is represented as having owned that Napoleon had gained on him—that he had, on the contrary, allowed his adversary to gain several hours more. Wellington's combination of caution and decision throughout this momentous period is a very interesting study. It was not until 3 P.M. (of the 15th) that there reached him tidings almost simultaneously of firing between the outposts about Thuin and that Ziethen had been attacked before Charleroi, the two places ten miles apart and both occurrences in the early morning. Those affairs might have been casual outpost skirmishes; and the Duke, in anticipation of further information, took no measures for some hours. At length, in default of later tidings he determined on the precautionary step of assembling his divisions at their respective rendezvous points in readiness to march; further specifically directing a concentration of 25,000 men at Nivelles on his then left flank, when it should have been ascertained for certain that the enemy's line of attack was by Charleroi. These orders were sent out early in the evening—" between 5 and 7." Later in the evening came a letter from Blücher announcing the concentration of the Prussian army to occupy the Ligny fighting position, in which disposition Wellington acquiesced; but, still uncertain of Napoleon's true line of attack—his conviction being, as is well known, that Napoleon should have moved on the British right—he would not definitely fix the point of ultimate concentration of his army until he should receive intelligence from Mons. But Blücher's tidings caused him to issue about 10 P.M. a second set of orders, commanding a general movement of the army, not as yet to any specific point of concentration but in prescribed directions towards its left (eastward). At length, when the news came from Mons that he need have no further serious solicitude about his right since the whole French army was advancing by Charleroi, he saw his way clear. Towards midnight, writes Müffling the Prussian Commissioner at his headquarters, Wellington informed him of the tidings from Mons, and added: "The orders for the concentration of my army at Nivelles and Quatre Bras are already despatched. Let us, therefore, go to the ball."

There are three definite evidences that before midnight of the 15th Wellington had resolved to concentrate about Quatre Bras, and had issued final orders accordingly—his statement to the Duke of Richmond, his statement to Müffling, and his statement in his official report to Lord Bathurst. Yet Mr. Ropes believes that his decision to that effect "could not have been arrived at very long before he left Brussels" on the morning of the 16th, which he did "probably about half-past seven." He founds this belief on two orders dated "16th June" sent to Lord Hill in the early morning of that day, in which there is no allusion to a concentration at Quatre Bras. But those were merely supplementary instructions as to points of detail; for example, one of them enjoined that a division ordered earlier to Enghien should move instead by way of Braine le Comte, that being a nearer route toward the final general destination of Quatre Bras specified in the earlier (the "towards midnight") orders. The latter orders are not extant, having been lost according to Gurwood, with De Lancey's papers when he fell at Waterloo; but that they must have been issued is proved by the fact that they were acted upon by the troops; and that they were issued before midnight of the 15th is made clear by Wellington's three specific statements to that effect.

When the Duke left Brussels for the front on the morning of the 16th he took with him a singularly optimistic paper styled "Disposition of the British Army at 7 A.M., 16th June," which was "written out for the information of the Commander of the Forces by Colonel Sir W. de Lancey," his Quartermaster-General. In the nature of things for the most part guess-work, the wish as regarded almost every particular set out in this document was father to the thought. Wellington was no doubt reasonably justified in accepting and relying on this flattering " Disposition ;" but its terms, as Mr. Ropes conclusively shows, simply misled him and caused him also unconsciously to mislead Blücher, both by the expressions of the letter written by him to that chief on his arrival at Quatre Bras and later when he met the Prussian commander at the mill of Brye. Wellington was indeed trebly fortunate in finding the Quatre Bras position still available to him— fortunate that Ney on the previous evening had defaulted from his orders in refraining from occupying it; fortunate that Ney still on this morning was remaining passive; and more fortunate still that it had been occupied, defended, and reinforced by Dutch-Belgian troops not only without orders from him but in bold and happy violation of his orders. Perponcher's division was scarcely a potent representative of the Anglo-Dutch army, but there was nothing more at hand ; and pending the coming up of reinforcements Wellington, with rather a sanguine reliance on Ney's maintenance of inactivity, rode over to Brye and had a conversation with Blücher. There are contradictory accounts of its tenor, and Gneisenau certainly seems to have formed the impression that the Duke gave a positive pledge of support. Mr. Ropes considers that, misled by the erroneous " Disposition," Wellington honestly believed he would be able to co-operate with Blücher, and that he "certainly did give that commander some assurance of support by the Anglo-Dutch army in the impending battle." Müffling, who was present, states that the Duke's last words were: "Well, I will come, provided I am not attacked myself;" and this probably was the final undertaking. Wellington's words were in accordance with the caution of his character; and it is certain that Blücher had decided to fight at Ligny whether assured or not of his brother-commander's support. That Wellington regarded Blücher's dispositions for battle as objectionable is proved by his blunt comment to Hardinge—"If they fight here they will be damnably licked!"

It would have been possible for Napoleon to have crushed the Prussian army in the early hours of the 16th when it was in the throes of formation for battle; and this he would probably have done if Ney had occupied Quatre Bras on the previous evening. But in Ney's default of accomplishing this Napoleon, in his solicitude that Wellington should be hindered from supporting Blücher, determined to delay his own stroke against the latter until Ney should be in possession of Quatre Bras with the left wing, where, in Soult's words, "he ought to be able to destroy any force of the enemy that might present itself," and then come to the support of the Emperor by getting on the Prussian rear behind St. Amand. Napoleon's instructions were explicit that Ney was to march on Quatre Bras, take position there, and then send an infantry division and Kellerman's cavalry to points eastward, whence the Emperor might summon them to participate in his own operations. If Ney had fulfilled his orders by utilising the whole force at his disposal, in all human probability he would have defeated Wellington at Quatre Bras, whose troops, arriving in detail, would have been crushed by greatly superior numbers as they came up. As it was, although at the beginning of the battle he was in superior strength, Ney never utilised more than 22,000 men; whereas by its close Wellington had 31,000, and, thanks to the stanchness of the British infantry, was the victor in a very hard-fought contest. But Mr. Ropes has reason in holding it humanly certain that he would have been beaten — in which case the battle of Waterloo would never have been fought—had not D'Erlon's corps of Ney's command while marching towards Quatre Bras, been turned aside in the direction of the Prussian right.

In the justifiable belief that Ney was duly carrying out his orders Napoleon at half-past one opened the battle of Ligny. He had expected to have to deal with but a single Prussian corps, but the actual fact was that, while he had 74,000 men on the field, Blücher had 87,000 with a superior strength of artillery. The fighting was long and severe. From the first, recognising the defects of his adversary's position, Napoleon was satisfied that he could defeat the Prussian army. But he needed to do more—to crush, to rout it, so that he need give himself no further concern regarding it. This he saw his way to accomplish if Ney were to strike in presently on the Prussian right; and so, with intent to stir that chief to vigorous enterprise, the message was sent him that "the fate of France was in his hands." The battle proceeded, Blücher throwing in his reserves freely, Napoleon chary of his and playing the waiting game pending Ney's expected co-operation. About half-past five he was preparing to put in the Guard and strike the decisive blow, when information reached him from his right that a column, presumably hostile, was visible some two miles distant marching toward Fleurus. Napoleon sent an aide to ascertain the facts and until his return postponed the decisive moment. Two hours later the information was brought back that the approaching column was D'Erlon's from Ney's wing. This intelligence dispelled all anxiety. Strangely enough, no instructions were sent to the approaching reinforcement, and the suspended stroke was promptly dealt. The Prussians, after desperate fighting, were everywhere driven back. Napoleon with part of the Imperial Guard broke Blücher's centre, and the French army deployed on the heights beyond the stream. In a word, Napoleon had defeated the Prussians, but had neither crushed nor routed them. There was no pursuit.

D'Erlon's corps on this afternoon had achieved the doubly sinister distinction of having prevented Ney from gaining a probable victory at Quatre Bras, and of detracting from the thoroughness of Napoleon's actual victory at Ligny. While it was leisurely marching towards Frasnes in support of Ney, it was diverted eastward towards the Prussian right flank in consequence of an order given (whether authorised or not is uncertain) by an aide-de-camp of the Emperor. It was about to deploy for action, when, on receiving from Ney a peremptory order to rejoin his command; and in absence of a command from Napoleon to strike the Prussian flank, it went about and tramped back towards Frasnes. D'Erlon's promenade was as futile as the famous march of the King of France up the hill and then down again.

Mr. Ropes considers that on the morning of the 17th Napoleon had thus far in the main fulfilled his programme. This view may be questioned. He had merely defeated two of the four Prussian corps; he had not wrecked Blücher. He had failed to occupy Quatre Bras; the Anglo-Dutch army had succeeded in effecting a partial concentration and in repulsing his left wing there. Still it must be admitted that with two corps absolutely intact and with no serious losses in the Guard and cavalry, Napoleon was in good shape for carrying out his plan. If Ney had sent him word overnight that Wellington's army was bivouacking about Quatre Bras in ignorance, as it turned out, of the result of Ligny, he might have attacked it to good purpose in conjunction with Ney in the early morning of the 17th. But Ney was silent and sulky; Napoleon himself was greatly fatigued, and Soult was of no service to him.

During the night the Prussians "had folded their tents like the Arabs, and as silently stolen away." They had neither been watched nor followed up, all touch of them had been lost, and there was nothing to indicate their line of retreat. This slovenliness on the part of the French would not have occurred in Napoleon's earlier days; nor in those days of greater vigour would he have delayed until after midday of the 17th to follow up an army which he had defeated on the previous evening, and which had disappeared from before him in the course of the night. The reports which had been sent in from a cavalry reconnaissance despatched in the morning indicated that the Prussians were retiring on Namur. No reconnaissance had been made in the direction of Tilly and Wavre. This was a strange error, since Blücher had two corps still untouched, and as above everything a fighting man, was not likely to throw up his hands and forsake his ally after one partial discomfiture. Napoleon tardily determined to despatch Grouchy on the errand of following up the Prussians with a force consisting of about 33,000 men with ninety-six guns. Thus far all authorities are agreed; but as regards the character of the orders given to Grouchy for his guidance in an obviously somewhat complicated enterprise, there is an extraordinary contrariety of evidence. It is stated in the *St. Helena Memoirs* that Grouchy received positive orders to keep himself always between the main French army and Blücher; to maintain constant communication with the former and in a position easily to rejoin it; that since it was possible that Blücher might retreat on Wavre, he (Grouchy) was to be there simultaneously; if the Prussians should continue their march on Brussels and should pass the night in the forest of Soignies, he was to follow to the edge of the forest; should they retire on the Meuse, he was to watch them with part of his cavalry and himself occupy Wavre with the mass of his force, where he should be in position for easy communication with Napoleon's headquarters. Those orders are certainly specific enough, but there is no record of them; and they may be assumed to represent rather what Napoleon at St. Helena considered Grouchy should have done, than what he was actually ordered to do.

Grouchy's version, again—and it is adequately corroborated—is to the effect that about midday of the 17th on the field of Ligny, the Emperor gave him the verbal order to take the 3rd and 4th Corps and certain cavalry and "go in pursuit of the Prussians." Grouchy raised sundry objections which the Emperor overruled and repeated his commands, adding that "it was for me (Grouchy) to discover the route taken by Blücher; that he himself was going to fight the English, and that it was for me to complete the defeat of the Prussians by attacking them as soon as I should have caught up with them." So much for Grouchy for the moment.

Soon after the Emperor had given Grouchy this verbal order, tidings came in from a scouting party that a body of Prussian troops had been seen about 9 A.M. at Gembloux, considerably northward of the Namur road. The abstract probability no doubt was that the Prussians would retire towards their base. But that Napoleon kept an open mind on the subject is evidenced by his instruction to Grouchy to "go and discover the route taken by Blücher," and this later intelligence, it may be assumed, opened his mind yet further. He thought it well, then, to send to Grouchy a supplementary written order which in the temporary absence of Marshal Soult he dictated to General Bertrand. This order enjoined on Grouchy to proceed with his force to Gembloux;

to explore in the directions of Namur and Maestricht; to pursue the enemy; explore his march; and report upon his manœuvres, so that "I (Napoleon) may be able to penetrate what the enemy is intending to do; whether he is separating himself from the English, or whether they are intending still to unite in trying the fate of another battle to cover Brussels or Liège." To me I confess—and the view is also that of Chesney and Maurice—this written order is simply an amplification in detail of the previous verbal order, which by instructing Grouchy "to discover the route taken by Blücher" clearly evinced doubt in Napoleon's mind as to the Prussian line of retreat. Mr. Ropes, on the other hand, bases an indictment on Grouchy's conduct on the argument that not only was the tone of the written order altogether different from that of the verbal order, but that the duty assigned to Grouchy by the former was wholly different from that specified in the latter.

He adds that Grouchy constantly and persistently denied having received any other than the verbal order, that in this denial Grouchy lied, and that "the mischievous influence of this deliberate concealment of his orders by Grouchy caused for nearly thirty years after the battle of Waterloo to be prevalent a wholly false notion as to the task assigned by Napoleon to the Marshal." Certainly Grouchy's conduct is inexplicable to any one holding the belief, as I do, that there is nothing in the written order to account for Grouchy's denial of having received it. It is more inexplicable than Mr. Ropes appears to be aware of. It is true, as Mr. Ropes proves, that Grouchy vehemently denied receiving the written order in all his works printed from 1818 to 1829. But he had actually acknowledged its receipt almost immediately after Waterloo. In his son's little book, *Le Maréchal de Grouchy du 16me au 19me Juin,* 1815, is printed among the *Documents Historiques Inédits* a paper styled "Allocution du Maréchal Grouchy à quelques-uns des officiers généraux sous les ordres, lorsqu'il eût appris les désastres de Waterloo." From this document I make the following extract: "A few hours later the Emperor modified his first order, and caused to be written to me by the Grand Marshal Bertrand the order to betake myself to Gembloux, and to send reconnaissances towards Namur. 'It is important,' continued the order, 'to discover the intentions of the Prussians— whether they are separating from the English, or have the design to take the chance of a new battle.'" It is strange that this acknowledgment should never have been cited against Grouchy; stranger still that in the face of it he should have maintained his denials; yet more strange that those denials were never exposed; and most strange of all, that finally the "written order" should have appeared for the first time in a casual article published in 1842, without evoking any explanation from Grouchy, or any strictures on his persistent mendacity.

It may be questioned whether the force of 33,000 men entrusted to Grouchy was not either too large or too small. The main French army, in the possible contingencies before it, could not safely spare so large a detachment, as events showed. Grouchy's command was not sufficiently strong to oppose the whole Prussian army; two corps of which could certainly have "held" it, while the other two were free to support Wellington. Mr. Ropes thinks it might have been diminished by one-half, but then a single Prussian corps could have dealt with it. It is difficult to discern in what respect the 6000 cavalry assigned to Grouchy should have been inadequate to such service as could reasonably have been expected of his whole command.

The British force about Quatre Bras on the morning of the 17th amounted to about 45,000 men. Early on that morning Wellington was in conversation with the Captain Bowles previously mentioned, when an officer galloped up and, to quote Captain Bowles,

whispered to the Duke, who then turned to me and said, "Old Blücher has had a d—d good licking and has gone back to Wavre. As he has gone back, we must go too. I suppose in England they will say we have been licked—I can't help that."

He quietly withdrew his troops from their positions, an operation which Ney, with 40,000 men at his disposal, did not attempt to molest, notwithstanding repeated orders from Napoleon to move on Quatre Bras. Early in the afternoon Napoleon reached that vicinity with the Guard, 6th Corps, and Milhaud's Cuirassiers, picked up Ney's command, and mounting his horse led the French army, following up Wellington's retreat. His energy and activity throughout the march is described as intense. Those characteristics he continued to evince during the following night and in the morning of the eventful 18th. In the dead of night he spent two hours on the picquet line, and about seven he was out again on the foreposts in the mud and rain. His anxiety was not as to the issue of a battle with Wellington, but lest Wellington should not stand and fight. That apprehension was dispelled when, as he rode along his front about 8 A.M., he saw the Anglo-Dutch army taking up its ground. He was aware that at least one "pretty strong Prussian column"—which actually consisted of the two corps beaten at Ligny—had retired on Wavre. But notwithstanding the disquieting vagueness and ineptitude of Grouchy's letter of 10 P.M. of the 17th from Gembloux, and that up to the morning of the battle he had sent no suggestions or instructions to that officer, he yet trusted implicitly to him to fend off the Prussians; and it did not seem to occur to him that Wellington's calm expectant attitude indicated his assurance of Blücher's co-operation.

In one of the cavalry charges toward the close of the battle of Ligny, Blücher had been overthrown, ridden over, almost taken prisoner, and severely bruised; but the gallant old hussar was almost himself again next morning, thanks to copious doses of gin and rhubarb, for the effluvium of which restorative he apologised to Hardinge as he embraced that wounded officer, in the extremely plain expression, "*Ich stinke etwas.*" Gneisenau, his Chief of Staff, rather distrusted Wellington's good faith, and doubted whether it was not the safer policy for the Prussian army to fall back toward Liège. But Blücher prevailed over his lieutenants; and on the evening of the 17th all four Prussian corps in a strength of about 90,000 men, were concentrated about Wavre, some nine miles east of the Waterloo position, full of ardour and confident of success. That same night Müffling informed Blücher by letter that the Anglo-Dutch army had occupied the position named, wherein to fight next day; and Blücher's loyal answer was that Bülow's corps at daybreak should march by way of St. Lambert to strike the French right; that Pirch's would follow in support; and that the other two would stand in readiness. This communication, which reached Wellington at headquarters at 2 A.M. of the 18th, has been held to have been the first actually definite assurance of Prussian support. The story to the effect that on the evening of the 17th the Duke rode over to Wavre to make sure from Blücher's own mouth that he could rely on Prussian support next day, to the truth of which not a little of vague testimony has been adduced, may be now definitely disregarded. The evidence against the legend is conclusive. An authoritative contradiction was given to it in an article in the *Quarterly Review* of 1842, from the pen of Lord Francis Egerton, afterwards Lord Ellesmere, who confessedly wrote under the inspiration of the Duke, and in this instance directly from a memorandum drawn up by his Grace. Quite recently there have been found and are now in the possession of the Rev. Frederick Gurney, the grandson of the late Sir John Gurney, the notes of a "conversation with the Duke of Wellington and Baron Gurney and Mr. Justice Williams, Judges on Circuit, at Strathfieldsaye House, on 24th February 1837." The annotator was Baron Gurney, to the following effect:—"The conversation had been commenced by my inquiring of him (the Duke) whether a story which I had heard was true of his having ridden over to Blücher on the night before the battle of Waterloo, and returned on the same horse. He said—'No, that was not so. I did not see Blücher on the day before Waterloo. I saw him the day before, on the day of Quatre Bras. I saw him after Waterloo, and he kissed me. He embraced me on horseback. I had communicated with him the day before Waterloo.'" The rest of the conversation made no further reference to the topic of the ride to Wavre.

It is not proposed to give here any account of the memorable battle, the main incidents of which are familiar to all. It was of course Wellington's policy to take up a defensive attitude; both because of the incapacity of his raw soldiers for manœuvring, and since every minute before Napoleon should begin the offensive was of value to the English commander, as it diminished the length of punishment he would have to endure single-handed. Further, he was numerically weaker than his adversary, while his troops were at once of divers nationalities and divers character; his main reliance was on his British troops and those of the King's German Legion. Napoleon for his part deliberately delayed to attack when celerity of action was all-important to him, disregarding the obvious probability of Prussian assistance to Wellington, and sanguinely expecting that Grouchy would either avert that support or reach him in time to neutralise it. Mr. Ropes has written an admirable criticism of the errors of the French in their contest with the Anglo-Dutch army, for which Ney was for the most part responsible, since from before 3 P.M.

Napoleon was engrossed in preparing his right flank for defence against the Prussians. The issue of the great battle all men know. The badness of the roads retarded the Prussians greatly, and, save in Bülow's corps, there was no doubt considerable delay in starting; but the proverb that "All's well that ends well" might have been coined with special application to the battle of Waterloo.

It only remains briefly to refer to Mr. Ropes's elaborate *résumé* of the melancholy adventures of Grouchy, on whom he may be regarded as too severe. Sent out too late on a species of roving commission, more was expected from him by Napoleon than could have been accomplished by any but a leader of the highest order, whereas Grouchy had never given evidence of being more than respectable. He received from his master neither instructions nor information from the time he left the field of Ligny until 4 P.M. of the 18th, nor until at Walhain he heard the cannonade of Waterloo had he any knowledge of the whereabouts of the French main army. On the morning of the 18th he was late in leaving Gembloux, on not the most direct route towards Wavre; instead of moving on which, when he heard the noise of the battle, he should no doubt have marched straight for the Dyle bridges at Ottignies and Moustier. Had he done so, spite of all delays he could have been across the Dyle by 4 P.M. But when Mr. Ropes claims that thus Grouchy would have been able to arrest the march toward the battlefield of the two leading Prussian corps, one of which was four miles distant from him and the other still farther away, he is too exacting. Had Grouchy made the vain attempt, the two nearer Prussian corps would have taken him in flank and headed him off, while Bülow and Ziethen pressed on to the battlefield. If he had marched straight and swiftly on the cannon-thunder of Waterloo, he might perhaps have been in time to effect something in the nature of a diversion, although it is extremely improbable that he could have materially changed the fortune of the day; but instead, acting on the letter of Napoleon's instructions despatched to him on the morning of the battle, he moved on Wavre and engaged in a futile action with the Prussian 3rd Corps there. A shrewd and enterprising man would have at least seen into the spirit of his orders; Grouchy could not do this, and he is to be pitied rather than blamed.

THE END

Printed by R. & R. CLARK, LIMITED, *Edinburgh*.

www.ingramcontent.com/pod-product-compliance
Lightning Source LLC
Chambersburg PA
CBHW032355230426
43672CB00007B/713